Extras of Early Hollywood

TWENTY-FIRST CENTURY WORKS
BY KERRY SEGRAVE AND FROM MCFARLAND

Extras of Early Hollywood: A History of the Crowd, 1913–1945 (2013)

Policewomen: A History, 2d ed. (2013)

Parking Cars in America, 1910–1945: A History (2012)

Begging in America, 1850–1940: The Needy, the Frauds, the Charities and the Law (2011)

Vision Aids in America: A Social History of Eyewear and Sight Correction Since 1900 (2011)

Lynchings of Women in the United States: The Recorded Cases, 1851–1946 (2010)

America Brushes Up: The Use and Marketing of Toothpaste and Toothbrushes in the Twentieth Century (2010)

Film Actors Organize: Union Formation Efforts in America, 1912–1937 (2009)

Parricide in the United States, 1840–1899 (2009)

Actors Organize: A History of Union Formation Efforts in America, 1880–1919 (2008)

Obesity in America, 1850–1939: A History of Social Attitudes and Treatment (2008)

Women and Capital Punishment in America, 1840–1899: Death Sentences and Executions in the United States and Canada (2008)

Women Swindlers in America, 1860–1920 (2007)

Ticket Scalping: An American History, 1850–2005 (2007)

America on Foot: Walking and Pedestrianism in the 20th Century (2006)

Suntanning in 20th Century America (2005)

Endorsements in Advertising: A Social History (2005)

Women and Smoking in America, 1880 to 1950 (2005)

Foreign Films in America: A History (2004)

Lie Detectors: A Social History (2004)

Product Placement in Hollywood Films: A History (2004)

Piracy in the Motion Picture Industry (2003)

Jukeboxes: An American Social History (2002)

Vending Machines: An American Social History (2002)

Age Discrimination by Employers (2001)

Shoplifting: A Social History (2001)

Movies at Home: How Hollywood Came to Television (1999; paperback 2009)

American Television Abroad: Hollywood's Attempt to Dominate World Television (1998; paperback 2013)

Tipping: An American Social History of Gratuities (1998; paperback 2009)

Baldness: A Social History (1996; paperback 2009)

Payola in the Music Industry: A History, 1880–1991 (1994; paperback 2013)

The Sexual Harassment of Women in the Workplace, 1600 to 1993 (1994; paperback 2013)

Women Serial and Mass Murderers: A Worldwide Reference, 1580 through 1990 (1992; paperback 2013)

Drive-in Theaters: A History from Their Inception in 1933 (1992; paperback 2006)

Extras of Early Hollywood

A History of the Crowd, 1913–1945

KERRY SEGRAVE

McFarland & Company, Inc., Publishers
Jefferson, North Carolina, and London

LIBRARY OF CONGRESS CATALOGUING-IN-PUBLICATION DATA

Kerry Segrave, 1944–
 Extras of early Hollywood : a history of the crowd, 1913–1945 / Kerry Seagrave.
   p.   cm.
 Includes bibliographical references and index.

   ISBN 978-0-7864-7330-4 ∞
   softcover : acid free paper

  1. Extras (Actors)—United States. 2. Motion picture industry—United States—History—20th century. I. Title.
PN1995.9.E97S43 2013
384'.8097309041—dc23   2013011161

BRITISH LIBRARY CATALOGUING DATA ARE AVAILABLE

© 2013 Kerry Segrave. All rights reserved

No part of this book may be reproduced or transmitted in any form or by any means, electronic or mechanical, including photocopying or recording, or by any information storage and retrieval system, without permission in writing from the publisher.

Front cover image: Crowd/Brand X Pictures/Thinkstock

Manufactured in the United States of America

McFarland & Company, Inc., Publishers
 Box 611, Jefferson, North Carolina 28640
  www.mcfarlandpub.com

Table of Contents

Preface — 1
Introduction — 3

1. Conditions, Agents and Governments — 5
2. Central Casting Bureau — 31
3. Morals and Corruption — 44
4. A Surplus of Extras — 64
5. Unions — 84
6. Rags to Riches — 114
7. Wages and Statistics — 137
8. Conclusion — 149

Statistical Appendix — 155
Chapter Notes — 165
Bibliography — 175
Index — 185

Preface

This book looks at the subject of the film extra during Hollywood's golden era ending, for the purposes of this book, in 1945. While the atmosphere players far outnumber the stars, the supporting cast, the character actors, and so forth, they never got much attention.

Of course, they were and are important in motion pictures. A few weeks before I wrote this preface I watched a showing of the 1942 cult movie *Cat People*. The guest host on Turner Classic Movies introducing the movie mentioned it had been made on a very small budget. Specifically he pointed out the lack of extras in some of the street scenes (set in New York). Despite the fact some of those scenes were set in Manhattan in the daytime there were hardly any people on the streets, outside of the principals, signifying the budget for the film was so small as to preclude the hiring of even a sufficient number of atmosphere people. Extras, like music, can influence the perception of a film and its enjoyment. Too much of the latter can undermine, overwhelm, and weaken a film, as can too little of the former. Like a Rodney Dangerfield character, extras get no respect.

Research for this book was mostly done online at the University of British Columbia in Vancouver and at the Vancouver Public Library in Vancouver, British Columbia. Most useful were the online databases covering the newspapers of the first half of the 20th century, mostly accessed through Proquest. Also useful was the online database newspaperarchive.com. As well, the show business trade publications provided the greatest amount of material, *Variety* much more so than *Billboard*.

Introduction

For the purposes of this book, the term "film extras" refers to persons who were used by the major film studios, also known as the film cartel, the "majors," or the Motion Picture Producers and Distributors Association of America. Over time that cartel, which formed in 1922 (earlier film cartels existed), has undergone a number of name changes and exists to this day. Today it is the Motion Picture Association of America. For the purposes of the book and more in keeping with its earlier name, it will be referred to herein as the MPAA. The MPAA functioned as the Hollywood film industry lobby group and was often referred to as the Hays group or Hays organization, in honor of its first head Will Hays, the so-called "czar" of the motion picture industry. The film cartel consisted of eight to ten member firms over the years covered by this book, and included all of the best known and most highly visible of the film producers: Warner Brothers, Columbia, Universal, Paramount, RKO, MGM, United Artists, and 20th Century–Fox. Something on the order of 85 percent of all the extras used in motion pictures in Hollywood were employed by the majors. For extras and would-be extras there was, effectively, no other game in town.

Chapter 1 looks at the general conditions in the industry, including some glimpses into the lives of extras. Private employment agencies were involved in the early years of the industry and extracted large commissions from the extras as well as imposing other abuses on them. These led to increasing complaints from the atmosphere players and generated governmental investigations into the situation. Those went far enough to lead to government regulations regarding the use of females and minors as film extras.

Chapter 2 explores the Central Casting Bureau, its origins and formation. Those governmental probes mentioned in chapter 1, and the fear of further regulatory intrusion into the industry, were the main reason for the film cartel to organize Central Casting. Also explored herein are the struggles Central had with the registration of extras as well as mention of the three heads of Central through 1945 — Dave Allen, Campbell Mac-Culloch, and Howard Philbrick, with each of the first two men leaving the post under a cloud.

Chapter 3 deals with morals and corruption in the extra field, mainly the sexual harassment of the female atmosphere players. The practice was likely much more pervasive than could be found reflected in the media accounts. The period covered by this book was a time before the phrase was used and at a time when women were supposed to bear such assaults in silence. However, several allusions in some articles indicated a likely widespread problem.

In chapter 4 the problem of a surplus of extras is the topic. Everyone involved in the industry from the studios to Central to the several unions involved all tried to find solutions to the problem of far too many extras chasing far too few jobs. All failed. As well, the federal government through the NRA (National Recovery Administration) tried to solve the problem. It also failed.

Chapter 5 is devoted to the problems involved for the extras in getting unionized. First there was a problem in getting a union at all. And then, after SAG was certified, there was a problem for the extras is getting a proper voice and vote within that union. That led to struggles for union autonomy for the extras.

In chapter 6 several different topics are discussed. One is the rags-to-riches stories often published and which helped to draw in to Hollywood that surplus of extras. Other items discussed include the wardrobe responsibilities of the extras, the elite "dress extras" and the Hollywood cattle call in the form of the "dress parade."

Chapter 7 details wages and statistics for extras and illustrates the difficulties they had in making a living wage.

1

Conditions, Agents and Governments

From the earliest days of the Hollywood film industry the conditions under which motion picture extras labored gave rise to complaint after complaint as the extras struggled to better their conditions. Agents were a particular bone of contention, with governments at both the state and federal level entering, or threatening to enter, into the fray.

During the filming of *Polly at the Circus* in the spring of 1917, which was produced in Fort Lee, New Jersey, at the Goldwyn studios, about 800 men, women, and children were inspected for extra roles by Charles Gill of the New York City–based Globe Agency. Those people assembled at the Fort Lee ferry one Sunday at 5:00 P.M. and waited for about two hours, at which point they were told the mayor of Fort Lee would not permit the film producers to shoot on a Sunday. When the assembly was dismissed each person was given 10 cents for carfare. One day later the groups assembled again, at 5:00 P.M. on the Monday. This time the hopefuls proceeded by ferry to Fort Lee where the principal scenes shot involved a fire that moved through the circus tents, causing the extras to panic and stampede from their seats to the exits, and so forth. At about midnight what one report described as a "meager" lunch was served. Two hours later a hastily chosen committee drawn from the extras approached the producers and made a request for overtime pay, as filming was expected to continue for several more hours. Adult extras had previously been told they would receive pay of $1.70 and 15 cents carfare for the filming but upon the refusal of the producers to meet the overtime request, they all quit. According to a reporter for the show business magazine *Variety* similar incidents had occurred from time to time, and upon investigation by *Variety* the fault was said to have rested with the agencies who furnished such extra people and who, apparently, were not always honest with respect to pay and conditions. "Motion picture producers wishing supernumeries [an old term for "extras"] claim they cannot devote their time to raising an army of extras in a short space of time and say their only means of securing such help is through the medium of agencies," said a reporter.[1]

As an occupational classification, the category of "film extra" found itself at odds with the United States government when World War I broke out. On the morning of July 31, 1918, two of the largest film studios in Hollywood were the scenes of raids led by police officers Brown and Waugh of the "work or fight" squad within the Los Angeles Police Department. Some 150 men, all motion picture extras, were taken into police custody for violation of the proclamation that all able-bodied men between the ages of 21 and 31 had to have a "useful" occupation, or become part of the military. A superficial examination of the men was made on the Hollywood lots by the arresting officers, and those holding registration and classification cards were released. However, 100 of the men had none of the appropriate paperwork and were bundled into wagons and taken to police headquarters. Chairman Long, of Local Registration Board No. 17, was notified and came to the police station where he held court on the men. The majority of the men proved to the satisfaction of Long that they were not fight slackers, but he ordered them to be turned over to the respective draft boards for final disposition. Later that day Long reiterated that film companies had to recruit extras from men over the draft age and those exempt from the draft for medical reasons.[2]

Harassment of extras had reached the level of that raid after the Los Angeles Police Department formally announced that appearing in mob and crowd scenes in motion pictures was not work essential to the winning of the war and that participation in such activities for the movies was not "working" in the sense intended by Provost Marshall General Crowder in his "work or fight" order. The police order was directed at film extras that were hired by the day by one studio or another. Such warnings were issued by the police more than once and led, finally, to the raids wherein a hundred or so men were taken into custody. Final disposition of those cases was not reported in the press except to say that some of the men were taken before their draft boards, others were allowed to look for "more useful employment" while still others were held by the police.[3]

A punch to the jaw of a "Mexican agitator" effectively discouraged, on August 29, 1919, a strike of 140 film extras who were about to demand $5 instead of the specified $3 wage for their day's work as East Indian natives in the movies. Those Mexicans had been engaged from a private agency by Webster Cullison, an assistant director, with Alla Nazimova the actress, and gathered in front of the Metro studio on the morning of August 29. Cullison (who spoke Spanish) overheard one of the men urging the crowd to strike for more money "because it is too late to get others, and they must pay us," according to a reporter. At that point Cullison made his way through the crowd without a word and knocked the "agitator" down. He then informed the others that, with respect to more money, there was "nothing doing." Every man in the crowd then worked, reportedly, at the price agreed upon.[4]

A news story published at the beginning of 1921 declared that statistics compiled recently by the census bureau showed that about 10,000 men past the age of 60 were employed weekly as film extras in the studios around New York and Los Angeles. Each day there were issued from the motion picture studios work calls for "hundreds of old men" to fill the parts of war veterans, rural male gossips, jurists, courtroom spectators, and innumerable character parts of a similar nature. "The demands made upon the aged actors by studio work are light, calling for little physical or mental exertions, and not more than two or three hours of actual activity a day," said the account. "Their average income from picture work is $7.50 per day."[5]

Hollywood was often ambivalent about extras, accepting the need of such players but irritated by the sheer numbers of such hopefuls who besieged the studios. On the other hand, Hollywood regularly encouraged the arrival of such hordes of people from all over America who descended upon and besieged the studios. Fueling it all was the desire on the part of the hopefuls that one of the best ways to the glories of Hollywood stardom lay in getting one's start by appearing as an extra. In reality that almost never happened. Hollywood was not above getting what looked to be studio publicity pieces printed as apparent news stories, extolling the ease of extra work and reinforcing the idea that being an extra was a pathway to stardom in motion pictures.

One of the earliest such pieces appeared as a full-page "news" story in the *Los Angeles Times* on February 13, 1921. It was supposedly written by a Catherine Fleming and presented itself as an account of the author's experiences as an extra, which occupation she began at the age of 60. The article was a glamorous type of piece full of appeal, one that would have, undoubtedly, fueled a rush to Hollywood by would-be extras. Such articles were picked up from the wire services and printed in papers across America. Fleming's story was full of hope and optimism that extras could rise in the film world and told of a nondemanding and easily passed workday that ran from 9 to 5 and was not in the least arduous. According to the account Fleming's relative got her the job as an extra, although no details were provided. She said, "I dreaded the ordeal before me. The idea of a woman of sixty aspiring to a place in the film world was a bit appalling."

But, she added, "Who, in all the civilized world, has not felt, some time in his life, a desire to shine before the footlights or on the silver screen? If everyone were honest he would acknowledge that in the secret recesses of his brain such a wish has fluttered. And in his innermost consciousness that person is convinced that, given an opportunity, he would have become a star of the greatest magnitude."[6]

Fleming's orders for her job were to be on the lot at 9:00 A.M. and to arrive there already "made up." Somehow, although again no details were provided, she knew just what makeup she should use and did so. (Extras, apparently, did their own makeup, at least in this era. As well, they had to provide all their own clothing for their scenes — with the obvious exception for films set in a different time period.) As people arrived on the lot that day Fleming believed some of them must be principals in the film (and not fellow extras), as some came in cars, but "I concluded the principals had not arrived and that these important people were just extras like myself, with the difference that they had been in the business long enough to realize how necessary they were to the success of the pictures." She and the other extras were paid $3 a day. Continuing with her story, Fleming related that she and one other extra were picked out by the director for close-up scene with the star. And, generally, "Though the work was fast there were ample rests for everybody between scenes as all did not 'act' at the same time." She concluded there was "no better way to prepare for parts or even to rise toward stardom" than by being an extra. "Then there are the ambitious ones who believe they can advance more rapidly by beginning at the bottom," she added. "Some of them are educated, refined people whose faces and poise show culture and fine social affiliations. It seemed to me that in those older women I could see the grande dames of the screen in days to come, and in the younger ones the stars who are to draw capacity houses in the near future. Let us hope so." Most likely, this was a film cartel press release posing in the newspaper as news. It stressed the importance of extras, their excellent treatment by the studios, the number of breaks in the day, and the good chances for advancement. If Jane Doe in Peoria had been mulling over the possibility of giving up that clerical job in her hometown for the excitement and glamor of Hollywood then this piece was designed to push her further and faster in that direction. The other telltale sign that the article was studio-planted propaganda was the complete absence of detail in the story. No name of a film was given by Fleming, nor were the names of any of the principal actors, or a director's name, or a studio name. Of course that very conveniently prevented any checking of the story. Hollywood got to be so successful in drawing in hopefuls from all over America that in later years it would

1. Conditions, Agents and Governments 9

have to issue terse press releases declaring that hopefuls should not come west.[7]

Two years after Fleming's article appeared extolling the benefits and joys of working as a film extra, a quite different story began to emerge. On February 2, 1923, a complaint was filed with Thomas Barker, the California Deputy Labor Commissioner, charging that extras were being subjected to the illegal discounting of their studio paychecks by the Service Bureau, the film cartel's jointly run clearinghouse for minor players. Reportedly, that complaint marked the beginning of what the leaders in the ranks of the extras had declared would be an all out fight for independence from the Service Bureau's booking-office control. Specifically the complaint charged Harry St. Alwyns, manager of the Service Bureau at 1036 South Hill Street, Los Angeles, with the discounting of pay checks due to minor players for any and all work not obtained through the Bureau. Making the complaint was an extra that for 14 years had appeared before the Hollywood cameras. Fears that the complainant would be blacklisted by studio casting directors because he had complained to the state Labor Commissioner's office led Barker to state the complainant's name would be kept secret until after a hearing was held. In filing his complaint the extra stated he had obtained a month's work at Universal City from his own efforts and that he was not registered with the Service Bureau. (It was not necessary to be registered with the Bureau to obtain work — being the "friend of a friend" always worked, for example. However, registered or not with the Bureau and regardless of how an extra obtained work all checks in payment were cut by the Service Bureau and delivered by them.) When the man in question received his daily check from the Bureau he found an unauthorized 50 cents deduction had been made. When he complained to the Bureau he said he was told "he had better take what he could get."[8]

Barker commented that the office of the state Labor Commissioner in Los Angeles had been "deluged" with a flood of anonymous complaints charging booking offices with "gouging" extras by the discounting of pay checks in violation of the law. The signed complaint, he stated, would lead to a thorough investigation. "I suppose my filing this complaint will mean that I am 'out' so far as pictures are concerned, but I am determined to make an effort to end existing conditions," said the complainant extra. He added, "I would rather quit right now than submit to the orders that require extras to give 7 percent of their earnings, and often it is higher than that, for the privilege of working in motion pictures." A man described as "prominent" in the affairs of film actors (but also not named) accompanied the complainant to the Labor Commissioner's office and told

Barker of scores of other complaints involving other agencies furnishing film talent in Los Angeles that had been filed in his office. Barker left an impression with a newspaper reporter that as a result of this one signed complaint being filed, practically every booking office supplying minor players to Hollywood would soon be under fire, and that subpoenas would be freely used.[9]

One result of the publicity was that Barker called on W. R. Reynolds, secretary of the Motion Picture Producers' Association (MPAA — the film cartel). He said Reynolds told him the studios would welcome a system that would be as efficient as the one then in effect. The one in use, Reynolds had admitted, required that the bulk of extras needed by the studios be poured through the Service Bureau. Reynolds also told Barker the Service Bureau had been operated in the past under a special verbal agreement with a former state Labor Commissioner after it had been demonstrated to the latter that the state labor laws were impractical when applied to the film industry. That special agreement had been made some four years earlier after public hearings before the Labor Commission had resulted in the airing of hundreds of complaints by extras. However, extras in 1923 said no action had ever been taken. Barker promised he would search the files of his office to unearth the record of that earlier hearing.[10]

On February 20, 1923, more than a dozen extras were subpoenaed before California Deputy Labor Commissioner Thomas Barker at the State Labor Commission office at West Sixth and Olive Streets in downtown Los Angeles to give testimony. Specific charges were made by many that commissions had been exacted by the Service Bureau from extras who had obtained their positions through their own initiatives directly, the Bureau being in no way responsible for their employment. As well, several of the witnesses told of the existence of a blacklist maintained by the Bureau whereby certain actors who had protested against the payment of the commissions were banned from future film work. Those commissions, according to the testimony, entailed a deduction of 7 percent from the studio checks of the extras. Those minor players said they felt forced to pay the commissions for fear that any protest or complaint would land them on the blacklist and finish their careers. It was also stated by several witnesses that they had protested to the Bureau and as a result had been unable to get any more work through the Bureau. Harry St. Alwyns branded as "absolute fabrications" the testimony about commissions being deducted. He acknowledged that now and then "clerical errors" might occur but denied emphatically that it was the custom of the Bureau, which he said supplied practically all the big studios with help, to charge commissions unless it obtained the positions for the extras. That a blacklist comprised of those who protested the deductions existed was also emphatically denied by St. Alwyns. His testimony followed that of almost a dozen witnesses who all said independently that it was tacitly understood that the Service Bureau would benefit by at least 50 cents from every $7.50 check whether the extras obtained their positions with the help of the Bureau or without it. It was promised by Barker that at a future session of the hearing St. Alwyns would appear again and on that occasion open his organization's books. Charges against the Screen Talent organization, a similar company to the Bureau, managed by Dave Allen were also expected to be heard at the same upcoming session when St. Alwyns was to reappear. Nothing more was heard about Allen in connection with these complaints, but he went on to become the first manager of Central Casting.[11]

One of the extras who testified that day was William Griffin, who said he had been in motion picture work in Los Angeles for more than a year. He said that from October 26 to November 16, 1922, he had obtained a direct engagement at Universal City in *Social Buccaneers*. During that time he was paid $7.50 a day and was forced to pay the Bureau 50 cents on each day's check, although he had obtained his employment directly through Bob Webb, one of the studio's directors, and had never registered at the Bureau. Griffin said he protested to a Mr. Skiff at the Bureau offices but was told if "I desire I can get you lots less work than you are now getting." Tex Marcell testified at the hearing that at one time he had been hired directly by Eddie Sauters at Universal to play in *Merry Go Round*. Marcell said he worked 26 days in that production and each day was forced to pay the customary 7 percent from his check to the Service Bureau. Ed Stafford testified he got a job as an extra through his own efforts in *Foolish Wives*, worked 40 days on that film and paid the commissions under protest to the Bureau, when he was warned "that he would be through if he did not pay them." Ten witnesses were put forward by H. M. Gentry, attorney for the Service Bureau. All of them staunchly denied stories of business misconduct and contended that the Bureau was a necessity and a great time-saving organization for the actors. During his testimony St. Alwyns stated the MPAA supervised the running of the Service Bureau, had access to their books and employed the bookkeeper.[12]

The war between the film extras and the Service Bureau broke out anew, and violently, on March 16, 1923, when over 200 extras went to the Bureau's office at 1036 South Hill Street, to receive their pay for appearing in *The Hunchback of Notre Dame*. The men expected to be paid at a rate of $5 a day. Reportedly, a Service Bureau spokesman told the men that all were to receive the same pay, $3, stating, "The pay will be only $3 on this picture and those who aren't willing to take $3 will please go away." Angry growls from the crowd was the response, and a security guard employed by the Bureau, Bernard Lane, came forward and tried to herd the crowd out of the building. While he was arguing with the players someone from the Bureau called the police and declared there were I.W.W. (Industrial Workers of the World, a radical trade union of the time often tarred with the label of being Communists, or Reds. Their nickname was the Wobblies) agitators there making trouble. Detective Lieutenant Lane (not related to guard Lane) of the Los Angeles Police Department Wobbly squad answered the call. He mingled with the crowd for some time but was unable to detect any signs of I.W.W. agitation. Satisfied that the crowd was orderly, though angry, he went away. After the detective left Bernard Lane managed to get the crowd moving but instead of leaving the area completely they went into the rear yard of the office. Reportedly Bernard became angry at this point and drew his revolver. "Put away the gun," "Take it away from him" and similar shouts came from the crowd. Someone, it was alleged, pushed the guard and he stumbled and fell. When he regained his feet he was alleged to have begun to fire his revolver. Lane later told the police he was being attacked by the mob and exhibited a bruised nose to prove it. He added that he had been struck several times and at last fired in self-defense, aiming low so as not to kill. The extras denied that story, declaring Bernard got his bruised nose when he stumbled and fell. When the firing started the extras scattered and the noise attracted three police officers— one of whom was Detective Lane, who had not gone far. They arrested Bernard and hustled him into a room in the Bureau office to separate him from the irate crowd. Next, those three officers sent in a riot call to headquarters. Four of the five shooting victims were injured as follows: left leg, right thigh, right knee, and both left heel and left shoulder for the fourth.[13]

Prompt arrival of a squad of men from headquarters was reported to have saved Bernard from being lynched by the angry mob and saved the three officers from perhaps some rough handling from the players. It was reported that the mob with cries of "Bring him out! Lynch him!" was storming a rear room into which the officers had retreated with their captive. Forming a guard around the handcuffed prisoner Bernard, the reinforced police rushed him to a patrol wagon, while other cars were taking the wounded men to hospital. Bernard fired a total of six shots, wounding five men, hitting one with two shots. None of the injuries were life threatening. At the police station Bernard was charged with assault with a deadly weapon with intent to commit murder. Detective Lane reiterated, "There were no I.W.W.'s there. The men who refused to accept $3 were hooting and booing ... but there wasn't a Wobbly in the crowd." Most of the men who arrived at the Bureau that day believed they were to be paid $5 a day.

H. A. Boushey, production manager at Universal, stated later on the day of the incident that the extras used in the filming of *Hunchback* were being paid three rates, $3, $5, and $7 a day but that he could not state what wages had been cited to the men by the Service Bureau. The injured men were Ben Dueck, H. Perlas, Charles Hoffman, E. L. Davis, and Emery McNee. Adding insult to the situation was the fact that with the Service Bureau's commission of 20 cents taken out, the men would receive only $2.80 for their day's work. Shortly after the shooting broke out St. Alwyns left the premises, ostensibly to go to the bank, and had not returned at a much later hour of that day. Five other Service Bureau employees were in the office that day, excluding Bernard. There were M. F. Ballerino, Charles Skiff, Perry Ferguson, telephone operator Rose Lehman, and secretary Mrs. E. Herbert. All declared they were upstairs at the time of the incident and knew little of the circumstances other than that a "crowd of Bolsheviks had been inciting a riot."[14]

Bernard Lane was described in a news account as having been "hard-boiled" on previous occasions, although no details were provided. When a reporter summarized the situation, he said that for several months an undercurrent of revolt against the Service Bureau had existed among thousands of film extras who thronged the premises for small parts in studio productions. It was said to have reached its height at the hearing before Barker mentioned earlier. The complete testimony of that hearing had been forwarded to the State Labor Commission main office in Sacramento for review and final decision. When the reporter noted the chief complaint of the extras had been that of being forced to pay commissions to the Bureau on jobs not obtained through the Bureau the reporter added, "This was refuted at the recent hearing by Mr. St. Alwyns, who produced records on cases mentioned, showing that the bureau had obtained the positions for the witnesses." Extras said, in the wake of the shooting incident, that film producers had been cooperating with the Bureau in the supplying of extras and had been themselves benefiting financially through the commissions paid to the Service Bureau. A decision on the testimony taken at the Barker hearing was expected to be handed down by the California State Labor Commission before April, 1923, the date of the expiration of the license of the Service Bureau. If it was handed down it was not reported in the press.[15]

However, a bit of the fallout was reported. One week after his arrest Bernard Lane had his bail reduced from $5,000 to $1,000, which sum was furnished. At the same time four of the extras involved in the incident were placed under arrest by Justice of the Peace Scott, on charges of assault and battery, after he listened to their testimony. The men arrested and charged were four of the five shooting victims: Ben Dueck, Harry Perlas, Earl L. Davis, and Emery McNee. On April 3, 1923, Bernard Lane had all charges against him dismissed in Los Angeles Superior Court.[16]

A little later in April that year Earl Louis Davis filed a civil suit in court in the amount of $25,500 against the Service Bureau. Nothing more was reported in the press relating to the incident.[17]

One day in August 1923 the offices of *Variety* were visited by three young actors (Robert Shaw, W. J. Flynn, and Walter Lewis), all of whom had spent the summer working as film extras. They explained they represented 60 to 70 other extras who had been working for an agent named Ben Weiss, who had hired them all to be minor players on a motion picture starring William Faversham and Charlotte Walker, and directed by William Christy Cabanne. That film had been shooting all summer in New York City but the extras did not know which producer was making it. When the players approached the trade publication the filming had been completed. Although it was customary for agents to pay extras the day following work, Weiss, said the extras, was still holding out money due the men 10 days earlier. When a final demand at the Weiss office that day produced no result the trio had gone to the show business magazine. They explained they had been delegated by the other extras to come to *Variety* "because it is known as the only trade paper which reaches all branches of show business and has made several campaigns on behalf of the actor against gypping agents." According to the extras, when Weiss was asked by them for their salaries due he told the men he had not received his check from the producers of the picture and until he did he was not going to pay them. In response the extras told Weiss they were working for him, not any company he may have contracted with; that the rule was for agents to pay the extras the day following the engagement. Weiss answered, "Try and get it," and when they said they would complain to the Legal Aid Society, the New York State Labor Department, and the courts, Weiss said he did not care and "Take me to court and see what I care for them." Those players had been unable to collect what was owing to them since August 13 and made their complaint to *Variety* on August 23. Complaints had been lodged against Weiss with the Labor Department while the Legal Aid Society promised to look into the matter. As well, the New York License Bureau said it would speak to Weiss.[18]

In October 1924 it was reported there were some 30,000 motion picture extras in the Los Angeles area. And most of them were said to be not pleased with the way Julius Bernheim, general manager of Universal studio, had treated them. A scene was to be shot for a film in which a circus was used. Through the rumor mill, extras had known about it for a month or more. All of the agencies were said to have assured the extras there would be a couple of day's work for at least 1,000 of them in the film. Then came the bombshell. In a story appearing in the local daily papers the readers were invited to visit Universal City on a Sunday afternoon to see the circus. Kids were especially sought with a qualifier being that they had to be accompanied by a guardian. None of those stories implied that a film of the circus and the spectators would be taken, or that they were being called upon to replace, for free, the salaried extras. Three of the extras who saw the stories wrote a letter to the area press pointing out that those attending the free circus would be taking food from the mouths of other children, whose parents had for years depended on motion picture work for a livelihood. However, the public apparently paid no attention to such appeals from the extras as there were more citizens on hand when the scene was shot than could be accommodated. It was also reported that the extras planned to protest to Will Hays (the motion picture "czar"—head of the MPAA cartel) regarding the actions of Bernheim and request him to ensure that in the future producers only used extras that were paid, as opposed to recruiting free minor players through subterfuge.[19]

Up to this point the California Labor Department had taken no concrete action to stop the abuses atmosphere players were subjected to, except to hold once-in-a-while hearings and to receive an apparently large number of complaints from the extras. As 1925 began it looked like all that might change. Early in January a reporter speculated that extras were destined to make more money in their film work if legislation to regulate film employment agencies, which the state Department of Labor was going to ask for, was passed by the California Legislature. It had been learned from State Labor Commissioner Mathewson, who arrived in Los Angeles on January 12 for conferences with local labor officials, that his department would attempt to secure a state law that would materially aid the film extra. According to the Labor Commissioner, private employment agencies then extracted a commission of anywhere from 7 to 10 percent for securing each position for the film extra. Mathewson declared that, thus, the extras virtually were forced to pay out 10 percent of their year's earnings to secure steady work. He added that he had been advised that the payroll for movie extras was about $3 million annually, and that meant private employment agencies were collecting about $300,000 of that amount.[20]

When *Variety* reported the story later that same month they used the same figure of 10 percent of the total skimmed off by private employment agencies but put the annual total at $8 million paid by motion picture producers for extras. Mathewson felt the extras were being taken advantage of, and he planned to ask the State Legislature to enact a law prohibiting the charging of "large" fees by those employment agencies. He felt the casting directors of the studios could handle the minor player situation without a need to go to outside agencies, and that way the extra could retain the full amount of money earned. While in Los Angeles, Mathewson discussed the matter with Fred Beetson, the Los Angeles representative for Will Hays and the MPAA cartel. Mathewson promised to return to Sacramento soon to have the bills drafted and introduced.[21]

Days of work on the part of eight film extra girls in the spring of 1925 came to nothing on May 8 when the police took into custody one Al Griffith, 20. He was also a motion picture extra and was accused of having passed a worthless check for payment of his office rent in the Pantages Theater Building. Those extra women were involved in the case because Griffith had promised them all a great deal. They all wanted to shine in Hollywood but they had no work and little apparent prospect of obtaining a chance to strut their stuff. Into the situation came Griffith, who formed the Alpine Movie Club, an organization for unemployed movie extra girls. Since they had little or no money themselves he could hardly bilk much money from them, but he had an inspiration. He organized what he said would be a gala night for the extras, the night of the Movie Extras Ball (ostensibly to allow the girls to display themselves before industry executives), slated for the Biltmore ballroom in Los Angeles on May 23. Those eight girls were given the task of selling tickets to the event; priced at 50 cents each, they sold fast. However, with the tickets mostly all sold the police arrived and arrested Griffith.[22]

As 1925 unfolded there was more focus on extras and their plight in the media and more rumblings from the government that it might have to impose some regulations. None of this sat well with the Hollywood cartel, who countered by moving to "self-regulation" to ward off any threats of government intervention. Far better, thought the cartel, to pretend to impose a seeming self-regulation than to suffer perhaps a real hit from government-imposed rules. It was in 1925 that the cartel first publicly presented the idea of Central Casting (see chapter 2). Coincidentally, a couple of articles to appear at this time painted either a rosy picture of an extra's life, or held them up in a very negative light, as poor quality employees, and so forth.

One article appeared in *Variety* in August 1925 and told of scams supposedly worked by extras on the job. Some of the minor players were said to have played the old Army game of soldiering on the job by reporting on a set early in the morning, disappearing, and then reappearing again at night in time to get their pay slips signed without having done any work. At the larger studios where sets called for 150 to 1,000 extra people there had been, reportedly, from 2 to 5 percent playing the soldiering game and getting away with it. They collected from $5 to $10 for a few minutes each day. One of the largest Hollywood studios was said to have tightened up the system to the extent the game could not be played there any longer. It was also reported that "quite a number" of minor players in mob scenes would report at one studio and get a check at the casting office and an order for a wardrobe. When they had obtained the wardrobe they would hide it on some part of the lot, go out through the back gate over to another studio about a mile away and there work for the day, if they chose, otherwise go through the same game at the second studio. At the end of the day they would turn in the wardrobe, get the pay voucher at the second studio and then return to the first studio to repeat the same routine. When told of that scam studio officials reportedly tightened up the exiting and entering procedures on their lots, with much more paperwork, and so forth. At one of the largest studios, it was said that soldiering of extras had been very costly. No reader of such an article would expect to see the specific extras named but the complete lack of details could lead a cynic to see yet another cartel-placed propaganda piece, instead of a true news account. How was it determined that 2 to 5 percent soldiered successfully? Why were no films, directors, or studios named? Perhaps more importantly why was there not a single quote from anyone, or a single name used?[23]

Then, in October 1925, an article appeared in which the views of Emmet Flynn, Fox motion picture director, were aired, wherein the "poor down-trodden film extra is neither as poor nor as downtrodden as he is painted." Flynn stated his list of acquaintances and friends included several hundred professional extras and that "most of them make an average living and are as content as it is possible to be anywhere." He added, "The professional extra averages a weekly salary which would be reckoned as a large one in any place but Hollywood. The ones who make a business of working as extras get fairly steady employment; a great many of them own homes and cars." The director went on to say it was a popular sport to pity the poor extra, but "personally, I don't think the real extra needs or expects commiseration. The professional extra, who is known at studios and in casting offices, who owns his own wardrobe for picture purposes, has no such difficult time." And, "Most of the younger ones—the dress-suit brigade—are irrepressible, frolicking youths who have gathered from all over the world to take a chance in pictures." Flynn declared there were about 1,000 "regular" extras in Hollywood and they owned good wardrobes and could be depended on by casting directors. Thus, they got the first calls for work as extras. "Most of them—except during the infrequent slumps—average about five working days a week and occasionally they get steady engagements of two weeks or so. Those professionals are paid sometimes as high as $15 a day, and rarely less than $7.50." And, Flynn concluded, five days a week at $10 or $15 a day is a salary many working men with families would be glad to get. That was true. The problem was that Flynn's numbers were wrong. Of the 30,000 or so extras in Hollywood around 1,000 of them were regulars, dress extras with enormous expenses to maintain wardrobes that would allow them to appear in dinner party scenes and on swank nightclub sets, and so on, with characters and as characters all of whom were rich. And those wardrobes had to be replenished every year as styles constantly changed. Flynn implied most of those 1,000 worked five days a week. The industry itself compiled statistics—through the soon to be established Central Casting. The number of male and female extras who worked five days a week all year in 1928 was two; it was one in each of 1929, 1930, and 1931. For those four years the number of extras who worked three to five days a week all year was, respectively, 121, 105, 80, and 63 (see Appendix). This was out of the 1,000 "regular" extras and out of the 30,000 total of extras.[24]

Also in the summer of 1925, a reporter named Copeland Burg presented a piece on the life of an extra, that was a little more realistic but held out an unrealistic expectation of an extra rising to stardom, as a lottery ticket held out the unrealistic dream of a life of ease. According to Burg, Hollywood film studios spent $6 million annually employing extras who were paid from $5 to $7.50 daily, for the most part, for their services. "They work only three or four times a week ordinarily, and their life is not particularly an easy one, for their work generally calls for their appearance at night." He acknowledged the pay they received "is not enough to more than give them decent board and room, however, studios were constantly besieged by hundreds of extras, burning with a desire to act; In long lines they may be seen moving to the various studios, night after night, filled with the never-fading hope that some scene will attract a director or producer who will cast them in an important role." Waxing eloquent, Burg declared, "Scores of the leading actors and actresses have come up from the extra crowds." Examples he listed were Gloria Swanson, a former Mack Sennett bathing girl, Betty Compton, Florence Vidor, Marie Prevost, Phyllis Haver, and Bessie Love. According to Burg the then late Thomas Ince had been forever peering into the faces of extras, searching for a star. Annually Ince spent thousands of dollars in the development of extras who showed promise. It was reported that Ince discovered Charles Ray, a one-time extra and made him a star. As well, Burg continued, Lloyd Hughes and "scores of other actors" first entered films as players in mob scenes, later did bits, and finally were cast in roles of importance.[25]

1. Conditions, Agents and Governments 19

California's Labor Commission was not the only agency investigating the conditions of extras in the Hollywood studios. Due to complaints that women and children extras were being worked under unfavorable conditions in the motion picture studios, Miss Marion Mel, assistant secretary of the California Industrial Welfare Commission, initiated an investigation, starting in October 1925. Accusations had surfaced that women worked overtime hours without any more compensation and that they were not paid for the full time they were present on the lot. Mel explained that other complaints were that extras told to report to the studio at 7:00 A.M. were compelled to wait around until 10:00 A.M. and sometimes until noon before being taken to the set, and they were paid only from the time they reached the set. Many of the extras, especially women and children, were alleged to have worked ten and 12 hours a day without overtime pay. Also brought to the attention of Mel were reports that extras were sometimes called from Hollywood early in the morning to work at a Culver City studio, but upon arrival in Culver City over an hour later, the shoot had been called off with the result the extra called over got no work and was paid nothing at all.[26]

On the evening of November 18, 1925, a public hearing was held in the Chamber of Commerce office in Los Angeles by the state Industrial Welfare Commission for the purpose of completing an investigation into the working conditions of women and children extras in the Hollywood studios. Some 300 extra people attended. Favored plan then was the establishment of a specific number of hours as a standard day's work and payment of overtime for all time in excess of the standard. Under this suggested plan a standard day would include time spent in wardrobe, time spent having costumes fitted, time spent in putting on makeup, time spent in rehearsing dance numbers, and time spent going to and from work on location shoots. Payment for loss of time and for carfare on weather-permitting calls was also expected to receive some sort of attention. Other problems that had surfaced during the investigation included the methods of keeping records of the actual hours worked, provision for the comfort and transportation of extras when they were obliged to work at night, proper provisions for dressing rooms and comfort and welfare at studios and on location, and payment of wages in cash or negotiable checks at the end of each day in such a fashion as to not involve loss of time or carfare and possibly adversely affect other employment.[27]

With the reported cooperation and approval of Frederick W. Beetson and the MPAA, regulations governing the employment of females and minors as extras were drawn up by the California Industrial Welfare Commission and released in early January 1926. All work of such extras in excess of a standard day of eight hours were to be paid for at not less than one-quarter of the daily wage after eight hours and up to ten hours, and similarly for each following two-hour block of time on the job. Payment was to be made for all time spent by the extra when she first reported for work; for example, if she was to report to a Culver City studio to spend 30 minutes in wardrobe and then 30 minutes being transported to a Long Beach shoot, that hour was paid. Prior to these regulations none of such activities were compensated. The definition of a woman extra was a person employed on a daily basis and paid a wage of $15 a day or less.[28]

Before the regulations the female extra might have spent 16 hours on the job but with the studio declaring some of the work not really being work. In any event she got the standard daily rate of, say $8. The number of hours was irrelevant. With the new rules in place she was paid $1 an hour ($8 for the standard day of eight hours) and all hours spent at work were to be paid. Thus, in this example she would have received $16 for her long day. Other rules imposed were that extras required to try on and fit costumes either at the studio or on location were to be paid not less than a full day's wage if afterward they were not employed. Women called upon to work at night were to be released from work early enough to permit returning to their homes by public transportation, or else the studio had to supply transportation. Meals and hot drinks were to be provided for all extra women required to work in excess of the standard day after 11:30 P.M. Film studios were required to pay their extras in cash or negotiable paper (checks) at the end of each day's work. Carfare was to be paid on "weather-permitting" calls.[29]

Another piece extolling the "good" life of the extra appeared in the *Washington Post* in June 1927. It argued that the extra that had been pitied and commiserated with for so long was neither so downtrodden nor as pitiable as the public had been led to believe. That, at least, was the opinion formed by an unnamed reporter during the filming of the cabaret scenes for *The Tender Hour*, George Fitzmaurice's First National film then screening in Washington. Those cabaret scenes required about 75 couples in smart, informal costume, to dance in the background while the principals acted. Thus, they worked an average of four days a week and many, for weeks at a stretch, did not have an idle day. Also noted was that the extras whose wardrobe contained formal dress and smart street clothes were rarely paid less than $10 a day and sometimes received as much as $15, "far above the average salary paid to workingmen throughout the country." Then the article shifted focus to point out the potential was always there for the extra to become a star. "In addition, they have a certain amount of leisure every week, and the greatest consideration of all is the fact that they are constantly being given an opportunity to attract the eye of the producer or director," said the article, "with a possibility of their being given a chance at better roles and the attendant increased earning power." Mentioned also was that Ben Lyon, one of the leads in *The Tender Hour*, started his career as a motion picture extra.[30]

During a night in March 1928, all available Hollywood police officers were required to subdue and disperse a mob of 1,000 Russian film extras that had rioted outside the Paramount studios. The minor players claimed they had been called for work and then been refused pay and transportation expenses.[31]

As of October 1928 it was reported that film studios faced the possibility of being hauled before the California Department of Industrial Relations as a result of alleged frequent violations of regulations laid down in January 1926, affecting extras. There were two state labor regulations said to be violated most frequently. One provided that if extras were called for work and for some reason or other the company was unable to work that day (even if the reason was beyond the studio's control) a notice had to be posted at the hour designated for the call stating the set would not work and instructing the extras to collect carfare. If they were not dismissed immediately from the set they were to be paid their regular wages for a standard eight-hour day. Three large Hollywood studios were reported to be violating this regulation consistently. Alleged was that they kept the extras on the lot working them for an hour or two and then dismissed them with only a one-quarter day's pay instead of paying them for a full day.[32]

The other regulation not being observed was one providing that when extras completed eight hours of work on the set and were held for a period of time — up to an hour in some cases — to turn in their wardrobe, they were to be paid an additional one-quarter day's check for the overtime. One film studio, using several hundred specially costumed extras, dismissed them from the set at 6:00 P.M. All had to turn in their costumes before they received their daily checks. Due to the length of the wardrobe lines, it was an hour and a half before they were lined up in front of the cashier's window to receive their check, only for the standard of eight hours with nothing for the extra hour and a half. One of the extras protested vigorously and threatened action. His name and address were taken and the next day he received his extra one-quarter day's check by mail. As far as was known he was the only one out of the hundreds to collect for the overtime. Reportedly, that practice was repeated generally among the studios that frequently used big mobs, and said a journalist, "That the extras have not protested long ago is attributed to their fear of being blacklisted."[33]

Wages and work were so sparse for extras, especially in the Depression years, that many operated sidelines designed to produce a little extra income. One man, a dress extra (as a minor player was called if he or she maintained an extensive and expensive wardrobe) with just such a huge wardrobe tried to rent pieces of it out to his fellow extras at a fee of 25 cents a day and up. Another minor player always declined to take the studio bus that transported the crowd to location sites, preferring to drive there in his own car. That was because his vehicle was jammed full of bottled pop, chewing gum and even shoelaces, all of which he tried to sell at the location site. Still another extra was an agent for a makeup company, selling the cosmetics to other extras and bit players. Largest group of extras though, for a single sideline, were the ones dealing in bootleg alcohol, doing a small time bootlegging business as they made calls from studio to studio in search of the elusive $7.50 a day for extra work.[34]

One of Hollywood's leading directors (unnamed) delivered his own negative conclusions about extras in October 1931 when he stated they were lazy and indifferent. He claimed that once an extra got a job his or her interest in pictures immediately vanished until it was time to look for another engagement. "Rarely does an extra take any interest in the picture being made, or appear to want to learn anything from the acting of the principal," grumbled the anonymous director. "Yet they have the greatest opportunity offered to any one class in this direction." Extras were engaged for atmosphere, the director asserted, and that was about the only mission in life they wanted to fulfill. "As to ambition to get somewhere, it barely exists." His opinions were reportedly based on a survey he had made during films he directed. At those times he had assistants check on the activities of extras when they were held on the set between shots or when scenes were being filmed in which only the principals were used. Analysis showed that of every 100 extras only one would be found watching the scenes as if taking an interest; two would be watching casually; six would be looking anywhere but at the principals; seven would be sleeping or trying to sleep; 11 would be reading newspapers or magazines; 24 would be playing bridge while eight watched them, and the remaining 41 would be gossiping.[35]

Journalist Dan Thomas surveyed the condition of the atmosphere players in a May 9, 1932, piece, after he declared there were 17,541 of them in Hollywood. Thomas wondered, rhetorically, how they managed to live. For years he had heard that question asked but never had anyone been found who could answer it. Even the extras themselves did not know. "They just seem to struggle along somehow, existing for days at a time on nothing but toast and coffee — without cream," thought Thomas. Harking back to the "good old days" he argued there was a time when the extra ranks were open to all comers. A boy or a girl landed in Hollywood, started making the rounds of studio casting offices, and that was all there was to it. He or she got jobs—sometimes. That was the way a large percentage of filmdom's stars of the silent era broke into motion pictures, Thomas continued. He cited Clara Bow, Janet Gaynor, Charles Farrell, Gloria Swanson, Norma Shearer, Richard Arlen, George O'Brien, and a great many others as all having started out that way. But then the extra ranks soon increased to unmanageable proportions. Casting directors became so overwhelmed with jobseekers that they had time for little else. And so the Central Casting Bureau was organized. Shortly after Central was opened nearly 12,000 extras were registered, Thomas added. Each was classified as to age, height, weight, complexion and type. That simplified things greatly for casting directors. They stopped interviewing all extras. Then the talkies arrived. At first the sound film reduced the demand for extras. "So the bureau doors were closed to all new applicants—except a scattered few exceptionally talented ones who were recommended by various casting directors." Those 17,541 extras Thomas mentioned were an increase of only 200 from one year earlier. They competed for the average of 606 jobs available each day, with the result the average weekly wage earned by an extra was only about $9 a week.

While Central Casting tried to distribute the work over as many extras as possible, Thomas admitted there were limitations. "Certain directors have a few favorite extras whom they know are good. When putting calls, they request those persons." He argued that not only had the demand for extras diminished, but the hope of an individual ever rising above the extra ranks then was "infinitely less than it was during the days of silent pictures." To get an idea of how many extras could become featured players or stars, Thomas canvassed the RKO studio, which had then about 40 contract players. Of those, only three rose from the extra ranks—Joel McCrea, Betty Grable, and Lita Chevret. All of the others (from the group of 40), explained Thomas, got their contracts as featured players before even stepping in front of a camera (coming from the legitimate stage, or vaudeville, for example).[36]

During those Depression years the studios made some attempts to reduce expenses. One way was to reduce the number of days it took to shoot a film. Warner Brothers wanted to cut $250,000 off of the budget set for the last 40 motion pictures on its 1932–1933 schedule. One of the main economy moves was in the engaging of extras. Under the newly instituted efficiency scheme no mobs were engaged unless schedules allowed for the extra players to be used on at least two sets. The old plan of allowing directors to use atmosphere players whenever needed was out. Production schedules were so arranged that scenes calling for mobs in two films were shot on the same day, allowing for doubling up on a single paycheck. Warner had also been saving on extras by utilizing practices heretofore confined only to the independent studios. When he needed a big dance hall scenes, studio manager Bill Koenig vetoed the director's call for 500 extras. Scenes were shot at one of the Santa Monica ballrooms with the cash customers producing the atmosphere but without getting paychecks. In this case utilization of this method also saved set construction costs. A similar method was used for a picnic sequence in a film. To get that background Warner sent its camera crew to one of the State picnics which were then an institution in Southern California. (Every summer in this area picnics were held, such as the Pennsylvania Picnic, the Iowa Picnic, and so forth. People who had originated in the named states but relocated to Southern California attended such functions in large numbers.) [37]

One extra who had her work profiled, briefly, in print was Merry Fahrney Pickering Von Eiszner, a millionaire Chicago heiress who was, for reasons not really explained, spending some time in Hollywood where she was roused early each day in order to report to Paramount studios so she could be a film extra. She was a handmaiden, in 1934, of the court in the Cecil B. DeMille epic *Cleopatra*. The 23-year-old Fahrney was a girl described in the account as one "with two unfortunate marriages and four airplane crashes behind her." When she first arrived on the set DeMille himself took her aside and reportedly said to her, "You arrive here every morning at 6:30. That's so as to get your makeup and costume on before the cameras begin turning at 8." He added, "Now that you're in the cast you can't quit. If you are going to want to quit you've got to quit right now. Tomorrow will be too late because failure to appear in a follow through scene is one of the unpardonable breaches. You not only wreck yourself as far as motion pictures are concerned, but you wreck the work of others which often takes weeks to plan." DeMille continued, "Don't complain about the treatment you get, the costumes you're told to wear, or any fancied lack of attention. All these things may seem strange, but every one here gets the same thing, even those who fail, and I believe you've got a chance to get on." Fahrney lived with a "retinue" in a suite on the grounds of the Ambassador Hotel in Los Angeles. She had the hotel phone girl wake her every morning and had been turning down parties "because it's hard enough to get up early even when I got to bed early. Before I came to Hollywood I hadn't dreamed about a career, least of all motion pictures. I had just been trying to make myself happy. I never had cared much for the idle life, but on the other hand it had never occurred to me I could do something with proficiency." Fahrney continued, "But I found so many girls struggling to accomplish something in Hollywood that it seemed that even the effort toward accomplishment was well worth while. That's why I'm here, even if I should fail to advance to a bigger part after *Cleopatra*."[38]

Journalist Dan Thomas wrote a second lengthy piece about extras; this one appeared in December 1934 and was specifically about the extra girl. He argued the federal government's efforts, through the NRA motion picture code, to reduce the list of extras from some 17,500 to about 6,000 was a very good thing because when the reduction was achieved those remaining extras would be able to eke out a fair living. But, at the time he was writing, it was financially tough going for extras with almost no money for most of them. Directly across the street from the RKO studio lived Helen Murphy, 19, and Muriel McKinnon, 23, in a single room apartment consisting of one room, a kitchenette and a bath. When Thomas arrived to interview the two extras Muriel had just had a call for two days work at Monterey, about 350 miles up the coast — it was to do some ocean swimming. The job paid $15 a day, $30 in all. Each girl paid half the $55 monthly rent on the apartment, $27.50 each. It was the first work call either had received in a week. "And yet, she [Helen] would rather live this way than to get out of the picture business into something which might pay her a regular salary. So would every other extra girl in the business," said Thomas. "There's something about it that keeps the fires of hope burning eternally. To them each succeeding sunrise brings the possibility that they may be discovered by some director and given a role which will carry them to fame." Thomas went on to point out those girls could not even go out and look for jobs in the movies as they could in other businesses. That was because all extras were engaged through Central. And the only soliciting they could do was to telephone that bureau, as some did dozens of times daily to see if there was a job for them. Some did make contacts at different studios that might help them to some extent. They got on friendly terms with someone in the studio casting office or with an assistant director, so that when the studio ordered its day's extras from Central Casting, they would be requested. That, declared Thomas, was not always as simple as it sounded. "For one thing, there is a lot of competition and for another thing the price of these friendships sometimes is too high. Although there has been a definite decline in such activities during the last few years, propositions still are fired at those girls from all sides." He added, "Some have found that they get along better by saying 'no.' Others are typical 'yes' girls. And still others weaken simply because they get to the point where they figure anything is better than starving." Thomas mentioned the dress extras and their higher pay of $15 a day, but also carrying the necessity of maintaining an expensive and elaborate wardrobe. One such dress extra was Alice Adair, who lived with her mother. Recently she had been working three days a week, but said she had little left at the end of the month, after her expenses of rent, wardrobe, and car payments. "It may sound like I'm doing extremely well to be able to afford a car. But I'm not," said Alice. "It's necessary in order to get to a studio when I have a call. Some of them are miles away and it would take hours to get to them on a bus." She added that most of the girl extras had one, or at least access to one. Sometimes two or three girls chipped in to buy a car that they then shared. "We stick because we hope some day we'll get a break," said Adair.[39]

A journalist by the name of Erskine Johnson produced a March 1935 article that told of the child extras "and their scant rewards, a warning to movie-struck parents who flock to the celluloid capital." According to Johnson there were 1,500 child extras in the Los Angeles area, each clinging to the hope of stardom. High wages were paid to the young ones—$75 a day for children aged from two weeks to one month; $50 a day for those from one month old to three years; and $25 a day for children aged from three years old up to six years. Those high rates of pay were set by the state of California, not the film studios. However, Johnson observed that a child extra was fortunate indeed if his annual income was greater than $300. That was because there were few calls for children—usually they were used for playground scenes, kid parties and for atmosphere on big sets. Probably half of those 1,500, estimated Johnson, worked only one or two days in a year. For Johnson those figures "shout a warning to the hundreds of parents to rush every month to Hollywood to haunt studio reception halls, clamor to the casting bureau, and waylay directors at studio gates." Hardly a day passed in Hollywood, he said, that some director, writer, or producer was not accosted at a studio gate by a mother with a prospective baby star in tow. The scene then unfolded to include a sidewalk performance of ability on the part of the child and some fast talking on the part of the parent but the end came abruptly when the director or producer explained that extra children were employed only through the Central Casting Bureau. Nevertheless mothers and children could be seen waiting in studio reception halls at all hours of the day. Some of the mothers came to seek interviews, while others just sat and waited in the hope that a director or producer would catch a glimpse of their little boy or girl and see a second Jackie Cooper or Shirley Temple. Just one sentence summed up the advice to parents from the woman in Hollywood, declared Johnson, who knew best the trials and tribulations of child extras. Bernice Saunders was in charge of the child extra list at the Central Casting Bureau.

She said, "Stay home; it doesn't pay." Scores of mothers pleaded daily with Saunders, who observed, "But too many mothers bring in their children over groomed. Most of the little ones needed are plain kids, not spoiled, pampered, or sophisticated. Overdressing and marcelling often work to the child's disadvantage." In the files of Central Casting complete information was held about each child who was on that list of 1,500. Noted were features such as freckles or a snub-nose, whether the child was a twin, whether the child could dance, or sing, or cry easily. Listed also were any language abilities the child had, beyond English. Black children were classified according to "degree of color." It was through Central Casting that producers also secured children under six months of age, although they were not listed on the bureau's regular files. When a studio needed a new born child, officials of Central Casting contacted maternity hospitals in and around Hollywood. More than one mother had carried her baby directly from the hospital to some film studio. Under California law infants could not appear in films until after they had been permitted by the attending physician to leave the nursery ward.[40]

When journalist John Scott surveyed the condition of film extras in April of 1935 he found they existed in poverty. He declared that 5,000 picture extras wondered why their pantries contained little or no food and why their rents could not be paid. "They are connected with a business that 'pays off' in big money yet they're hungry," stated Scott. "Here's the reason, in general terms: there isn't enough work to go around. It's a matter of survival of the fittest, yet the unfit won't give up the ghost and seek other employment." At a recent San Francisco conference called by U.S. Secretary of Labor Perkins, the statement was made, said the reporter, that the minimum wage for a single woman should be $17.20 a week or about $900 a year. Yet a recent check made at Central Casting showed that just 373 extras (including both men and women) out of a "known" 6,000 earned $900 or more in 1934. Scott argued, "Actually the situation is a dire one for the day-to-day players. The glamour of pictures holds the aspiring Thespians in a vise-like grip, even to the point of missed meals and shelter." If people wondered why they could not "get on" as extras then Scott felt he had the reason in black and white, backed up by official figures released by Central Casting. Those figures showed that only 42 people (33 men and nine women) made as much as $1,900 in 1934; 18 men and eight women earned from $1,700 to $1,900; 25 men and 22 women made $1,500 to $1,700; 41 men and 13 women earned $1,300 to $1,500; 63 men and 28 women earned $1,100 to $1,300; 73 men and 40 women earned $900 to $1,100; 117 men and 49 women made $700 to $900; 115 men and 81 women made $500 to $700. Thus, just 735 people earned more than

$500 each during the entire year. That was less than $43 a month (at the low end) and should have been enough, reasoned Scott, to convince the other thousands of extras and would-be extras they could not be supported by the available work or given enough income to maintain a bare existence. What was to become of those who continued to hang on, anyway, waiting for the call that did not come, wondered Scott. He posed that question to the head of Central, Campbell MacCulloch, who explained to the reporter that Central tried, whenever possible, to place those extras the bureau knew were not suited to the work in other types of jobs, but employers often balked at hiring them. "The reason is that they know by experience whenever a former extra gets a film call, he will desert whatever he is doing pronto," said MacCulloch. The casting bureau chief observed the studios paid an average of $1,767,642 annually for extra talent, of which $1,237,349 went to registered extras and $530,293 to the crowds and racial groups. "On the basis of the totals there is available for registered players an average of fewer than 400 adult placements each day," added MacCulloch. "We cannot begin to take care of the 6,000 who believe they should be used. It's an impossible task," he concluded.[41]

Although Central Casting Bureau was used exclusively to procure extras for all the film-cartel (MPAA) productions, such was not the case with the independent motion picture producers in Hollywood who could not use Central Casting to fill their needs and instead relied on getting their atmosphere players from private agencies, of which there were several, with the largest two being General and S-K. These agencies charged a 10 percent fee on the extras, for placing them at the independent studios. While those agencies were supposedly licensed by the state of California, many came and went illegally, and many scammed the hapless film-hopefuls. According to reporter John Scott, in 1935, one popular scam was for an agency to demand a sum of money up front (illegal under state law) giving a promise of work to come which, of course, never materialized. Such fly-by-night operations charged what they could get from extras, usually $1 a month, and were difficult to find and close down since they had no headquarters but functioned through "walking delegates" who contacted the extras in unofficial fashion. One of their pitches was in the form of "I have an in with such-and-such a casting director and he'll use the people I name." An estimated 80 percent of all film extras went through Central Casting and into MPAA productions, with the other 20 percent left to find their own way, somehow, into the independent productions.[42]

Film extras were even once briefly used by movie moguls as part of a right-wing political agenda, in the real world. It happened when famed progressive author Upton Sinclair was in the midst of his EPIC (End

Poverty In California) campaign for the governorship of that state in 1934. Right-wing elements in the state quickly condemned his supposedly far-left policies and attacked him on the ground that if he was elected all his socialist-type policies would lead to an influx of the unemployed into California — and there were many of those in America during the height of the Depression. To prove their point newsreels were run in cinemas that showed videos of scruffy-looking vagrants purportedly all streaming toward California even though, said a news account, "some of the pilgrims were later identified as movie extras cast in the role of transients."[43]

Following a 63.6 percent increase in accidents among film extras for the first quarter of 1936 over the same period in 1935, major studios were faced with the cancellation of their insurance policies, carried with private companies. Heaviest casualties were said to be among the riding extras in Warner Brothers' *Charge of the Light Brigade*, Selznick's *Garden of Allah*, and Paramount's *Rhythm on the Range*. Blame for the increase was attributed to Central Casting for sending inexperienced riders out for extra work that required experienced riders. A charge was leveled by the California Industrial Accident Commission that favoritism was practiced by Central Casting and took precedence over actual riding ability and experience. Reportedly, the insurance company used by Warner cancelled its policies with the producer after claims were filed resulting from accidents on the set of *Charge of the Light Brigade*. Where business was declined by private companies a studio's only option was to follow the lead of Columbia and 20th Century–Fox and deposit a $30,000 bond with the state of California, with the latter assuming the risk.[44]

At Hermosa Beach, California, lifeguards rescued 185 movie extras, in 1938, who had become exhausted trying to swim with their clothes on in order to qualify for atmosphere roles in a film that involved a gambling ship. More than 500 people took the test, which was to swim one-quarter of a mile around the pier. A total of 40 lifeguards in two dories and 30 others on surf boards picked up the men and women who became exhausted. In the film the gambling ship would be set on fire and sunk, with 300 patrons on board the vessel jumping into the water.[45]

On a Monday night at the beginning of January 1939, Harvey Burns collapsed and died at the wheel of his car while driving his car through Hollywood. He was 58 years old and said to be a champion of the extras. His widow told his story to *Los Angeles Times* reporter James Bassett. Back in New York's Bowery in a gymnasium in 1896, a 16-year-old boy pushed a nickel into a slot to start a mechanical bag swinging. In a couple of years he was a champion bag puncher. Burns took that specialty into vaudeville and made plenty of money. Then, in 1911, he journeyed to Los Angeles where the cinema was just emerging from its infancy. He got involved in work in boxing and promotion of that sport at Uncle Tom McCarey's Vernon boxing arena, doing such things as refereeing 50-round bouts. About 1914 politicians legislated out of existence the type of boxing Harry was involved in. Burns then turned to motion pictures. He kept props for Charlie Chase and soon he was directing for William Fox, Chet Franklin, and Hal Roach. By 1920 Burns was putting wild animals through their paces for Carl Laemmle at the old Universal zoo. One day in 1923 Burns was involved in a fire that occurred on the set of the film *Souls for Sale*, during which he was seriously injured and confined to hospital for seven months. During that time he developed an idea, and in 1924 he took over the struggling trade paper *Filmograph* and began to champion the "sorry cause" of the Hollywood extra. He was successful in a campaign to get the extras paid daily (previously they had been paid weekly). However, when the Depression arrived, Harry's paper folded. He faced a bleak future. Burns had married Dorothy Vernon (mother of comic Bobby Vernon) in 1915. So, around 1931, Harry Burns became an extra. Sometimes he earned $8.50 a day. A few months before his death Burns had written, "Today I find myself an extra. My loyal wife, too, is among the rank-and-file. She is, if I must say so, as clever a character actress as there is in the business. You can buy either of us for $8.50 a day ... and we will thank any producer who gives us a hand."[46]

In the summer of 1939 the Screen Actors Guild (SAG) announced plans to place a ban on the presentation of gifts by extras to directors and other film executives. A resolution had been introduced in the SAG Council providing for an amendment to the Guild by-laws prohibiting the collection of funds by or from extras on studio sets or on location. The decision to offer a resolution to stop what was called an "old practice" in Hollywood of collecting funds from extras in order to buy gifts for members of the company was reached after a recent location incident when players were called upon to buy a horse and saddle for the director in charge of the company. While the director supposedly had no knowledge the fund was being raised, extras complained they felt compelled to contribute to it. Also, extras had recently been called upon to kick in contributions to buy a $125 watch for another player. SAG executives took the position the extra was entitled to every protection since the earnings of the majority were small and much of that had to be spent to maintain a wardrobe.[47]

2

Central Casting Bureau

Problems with extras being exploited by private agencies who found work for extras in studio films had existed in the industry since its earliest days. A commission was deducted from the already small wage paid to the minor players as well as various other complaints of exploitation and abuse. The MPAA film cartel might have continued to ignore the problem as it had been doing or continue to participate in it (the Service Bureau was cartel-controlled and the commissions charged the extras there were nothing short of a kickback to their employer) except for government involvement. When the California government began to investigate the situation — and make noises about regulations — the MPAA suddenly saw the light and jumped in with self-regulation — better to be seen to regulate, or pretend to regulate, yourself than to submit to government regulations, which might have been real regulations. Thus 1925 through early 1926 marked a period of intense attention to the issue as the Central Casting Bureau was conceived and implemented. Under it, all extras for MPAA motion pictures (about 80 to 85 percent of all Hollywood minor players) would be hired in a strictly impartial manner through Central Casting (CC) with no commissions charged to the players and all other abuse and exploitation ended, or so the story went. The Central Casting website, in 2010, contained the following brief entry in its history section. By 1922, it said, an estimated 30,000 extras were in the Los Angeles area. With no system in place to regulate talent, "many people looking to break into the industry as extras were exploited."[1]

The only reference that appeared to a CC-like agency prior to 1925 was a reference that appeared a decade earlier, an apparent abortive attempt at establishing such an agency. *Variety* reported in a September 1915 issue that representatives of several large film studios had been conferring, with the idea of forming a general employment agency for extras through which each of the concerns that subscribed to the upkeep of that agency would secure all the extra players they needed, without having to resort to the private, independent agencies that had been supplying them. Said the article, "Considerable grafting has been going on in the ranks of the independent agents and it prompted the manufacturers to take this step in wiping it out." Among the candidates to take charge of this proposed agency was John Edwards, who, two years earlier, had a plan for such an agency. It was felt back then, however, that such an agency was not necessary. A number of local film agents who supplied producers with their extra players held a meeting of their own (all these meetings were in New York) to discuss the looming threat to their businesses. Those men denied all allegations leveled against them by film producers, stating the amounts paid to extras were all set by the film men and they, the agents, took only a small commission for their work. However, no move was undertaken to combat the proposed new agency; the agents declared they held their meeting merely to vindicate themselves.[2]

Almost a full decade later *Variety* reported, in its March 25, 1925, issue, that the film cartel was then working on "reforms" to improve the condition of motion picture extras. Under this proposed new system, the agent and his commission would be "entirely eliminated." The MPAA committee working on the concept had to that date held two meetings. The plan was to have all studios in the cartel obtain their extra people from this office. One estimate had it that $40,000 would be required to establish the office and that one of the best agents on the coast would be hired and placed in charge. Also to be implemented under the new system was the regulation of working hours for extras and the establishment of graded pay scales in accordance with the importance of the work done. Also noted by the trade publication was the fact that "before this is put into operation, an endeavor will be made to minimize the list of available extras, to cull the list and strike out the undesirables."[3]

Four months passed before the project was mentioned again, when it was reported that MPAA head Will Hays, the so-called czar of Hollywood, had voted in favor of the agency, the cost of which would be borne completely by the studios who were members of the MPAA, with the new agency, according to this report, to maintain the same wage scale then prevalent among extras. Once established, said the piece, the agency was figured to eliminate the 10 percent commission to agents (effectively giving extra players a raise, if the wage scale remained the same) and also eliminate the questionable agents "with whom the city is flooded. Schools of make-up and the notorious casting offices, which have heretofore existed, would also be wiped out." The specific plan for the central office had been worked out by Fred Beetson for the MPAA and, it was reported, had the full approval of the California Labor Commission. Admitted in this article was that there had been all sorts of complaints from the extras who had been the victims of the gypping agents, who had flourished in the past through obtaining employment for them. "Not only have these agents exacted a commission, but they have in addition gypped on the price. They would contract to furnish extras at $3 a head, pay the extras $2 and then exact their commissions in addition," observed the journalist. Reportedly, several investigations had been made in Los Angeles by the California Labor Commission, in addition to private investigations by the MPAA, and the conclusion had been that a central office operated by the MPAA itself was the only possible way in which protection could be assured to the extras.[4]

In Hollywood on December 11, 1925, plans were announced to "remedy" conditions for employment for thousands of extras through the operation of the Central Casting Bureau. Fred W. Beetson, western representative of Will Hays, was elected president of the agency, while Lieutenant Colonel C. C. Wyman, army reserve officer, was appointed general manager of the organization, which was to begin doing actual work in early January. Plans for the agency were said to have been worked out with the advice of the Industrial Welfare Commission. It was said to have resulted from the many complaints brought by extras to the state Labor Commission and heard and investigated by them. By this account more than 30,000 extras, representing an annual payroll of $3 million, were utilized each year by the studios in Los Angeles.[5]

On January 25, 1926, the Central Casting Bureau formally opened its doors for business in Hollywood. Newspaper headlines about the opening revealed, perhaps, the most important reason for the establishment of the agency, at least as far as the cartel was concerned. "Movie vagrants to be eliminated," declared the *Fresno Bee*, while the *New York Times* asserted, "Hays begins clean-up of Hollywood today." The account from the California paper said, "The doom of the Vaseline-haired sheik vagrant at film's doors and the girls who dance sans clothing on the beach, together with the whole coterie of hangers-on who have surrounded the gates of filmdom here with a spicy and racy atmosphere that has scented the name of Hollywood throughout the world was to be sealed here today by Will Hays." The film czar stated the industry would be purged with one of the main moves in that direction being the formal opening of Central Casting operated by producers. Thus the only entry to film work in Hollywood, at least at the minor player level, would be with a Central Casting Bureau listing card. The 30,000 hopefuls aspiring to film work were to be classified, investigated and segregated (as to only those qualified). There was a massive surplus of people seeking extra work, and the continued employment of extras into the future was to be based solely on merit, with carded records kept of past references and job details. In the *New York Times* much the same story was repeated, with the addition that it was said that Central Casting would establish "conditions that will make employment desirable and clean up and eliminate the misfit."[6]

After spending two weeks in Hollywood, Will Hays returned to his office in New York City where he declared, at the start of February, that he was "perfectly satisfied" with things. Hays said Central Casting was functioning, the extras were receiving the full monetary value of their work and the agents who had been extracting 10 percent of the extras' pay "were out of the running entirely."[7]

After the first six months of operation by Central Casting it was reported that not a single complaint had been filed by an extra against Central or against any of the MPAA studios, with the California Labor Commission. Prior to the establishment of Central an average of from 12 to 20 complaints a day were registered by extras against either studios or private agencies, usually over wages.[8]

As of October 1928 *Variety* reported things were not as rosy as the cartel would have one believe, with respect to extras. The California Department of Industrial Relations was then investigating allegedly large-scale violations regarding working conditions and pay rates for extras, set by the state and recently imposed on the film industry. A separate complaint against a main studio (unnamed) had many extras irate and involved Central Casting. All of those MPAA studios were supposed to take all their extras from Central. However, the studio in question was alleged to have a list of about 60 extra people, not registered at Central, who were given work regularly by individual calls from the studio. When the day's work was over, the checks for those people were said to be sent to Central Casting, which stamped its official okay on the checks and then issued them.[9]

When the talkies arrived Central Casting was ready for the transition, and by then it was apparent that Central had indeed culled the mob. Central manager Dave Allen (what happened to C. C. Wyman, reportedly named manager before the bureau formed, or when it happened, was not reported in the press; however, Allen was manager from the opening day) announced in December 1928 that talking pictures would not hurt the market for extras. At the time, he said, some 11,000 extras were registered. He also noted that registration at Central Casting was closed except for a few particular types of which there was a scarcity. With registrations closed it meant newcomers arriving in Hollywood to take the film world by storm could not get their foot in the door as an extra. With no registration card from Central you could not be hired as an extra for any studio within the cartel. At least that was the official story. Of course, there were always exceptions—for the friend of a friend, say.[10]

By early in 1929 Central Casting was in the process of making a survey of its 11,000 or so people registered to list them according to language abilities and voice type, for the talkies. The organization had prepared a special registration blank that inquired into such things as voice range, whether the voice was trained or not, how many languages were spoken, and so forth. Dave Allen was in the process of engaging authorities on singing, dancing, and dramatic work to pass judgment on the qualifications that the extras claimed to possess. Extras were also to list if they were capable of sound imitations such as animals, what dialects they spoke, and what radio experience they had and at what stations.[11]

Toward the end of 1929 the requirement that extras speak the foreign language of the locale in which the film was set had reportedly set mob-casting back 15 years. Long before Central was established extra mobs were frequently recruited by classified ads setting a meeting place at some corner just out of the downtown business section. The assistant director would arrive and pick out the specific individuals for his mob, load them in trucks and take them to the studio. At the end of 1929 a Central Casting representative went into one of the foreign colonies and, with the help of one or two who could speak the language, lined up the mob for a talking picture. Using this method, 300 Russians were recruited in East Los Angeles for one talkie and contact information was taken from them and maintained. A few weeks later another Russian mob was wanted but only half of the original group were interested for a second time — the others apparently having satisfied their curiosity the first time. When a call went out for a third Russian mob hardly anyone was interested. Most of those Russians worked in small factories earning $4 a day. Production had been disrupted at those plants from the first two calls to the extent that those factories took to posting signs that said "Anybody who takes work in the movies is fired." Thus, when the Russian workers weighed the very occasional $7.50 per day in a film against the very regular $4 a day in a factory, motion pictures rarely won.[12]

Campbell MacCulloch, described as "a leader in State organizations under the National Recovery Administration" was, on September 11, 1934, named as new general manager of the Central Casting Bureau. He succeeded Dave Allen, who resigned in July 1934 following his indictment on a morals charge (see chapter 3). MacCulloch was named following a meeting of the Central Casting board of directors and the board of the MPAA, of which Jack L. Warner, vice president, was acting as president in the absence of Louis B. Mayer, who was then in Europe. Allen quit his post to clear his name, he said. Until this appointment MacCulloch was executive secretary for the National Recovery Administration's State Recovery Board, and of the Los Angeles Regional Labor Board.[13]

As part of a publicity effort for Central Casting, radio listeners got a chance to hear about the inner workings of the Bureau as part of Kate Smith's *Variety Hour*, produced in New York City and released over station KHJ at 12 noon, on October 17, 1934. Charles Bulotti Jr. of the KHJ announcing staff broke into Smith's program at 12:30, interviewed the Bureau's main executives and then turned his microphone to the switchboards of Central so that listeners could hear the actual calls that came in. Requests made to the operators of the multiple switchboards included "We want 500 bearded men and fifty blondes in street clothes. On the set at 9 o'clock tomorrow morning."[14]

Later that same month reporter Hubbard Keavy wrote an article about a new initiative at Central. Specifically he said that in order for extras to voice their complaints, a complaint bureau had been established for them, as part of the Bureau. MacCulloch was reported as wanting to know if the extra believed he was getting a square deal. What he soon learned after assuming his post was that there were many extras who said they were not being treated fairly — not getting enough work was one common complaint. As a result he set up a formal complaint department. However, Keavy reported, the new department unexpectedly became almost exclusively a welfare or rehabilitation department instead of one for complaints. Allan MacDonald (once an actor and once in welfare work) was head of that new department. When an extra complained to MacDonald the latter checked into his background, and if he believed the man deserved more than the one day a week of work he had been averaging, he tried to get him more. But the maximum MacDonald would give was three days a week, to maintain a reasonable distribution of jobs. Keavy reported the main part of MacDonald's work was in looking after the "needy family man" who was a qualified extra. A typical case was Mr. Doe, who had a wife and three children. He had been averaging three days work a month as an extra, at $5 per day. An unnamed welfare organization was giving him $45 a month. According to MacDonald's estimate, for a family of that size to live properly it needed $72.91 a month. Thus, MacDonald saw to it that Mr. Doe got six of those $5 days of work each month, instead of three, to make up the difference.[15]

When journalist Douglas Churchill did a piece on extras in July 1935, he stated there were then 17,000 extras listed on Central Casting's rolls. But less than half of that number were regarded as active. Of the 8,000 active people, just 2,500 were said to depend on the studios for a living. During 1934 extras (all) averaged a weekly wage of just $8.97 each. Churchill's article was written about the last 2,500 he mentioned. They were divided, he wrote, into classes; dress extras, atmosphere people, racial groups, and character men and women. Those people all earned from $5 to $15 a day — when they worked. "There was a day when these people had reason to hope. Twenty years ago the ranks of stardom were filled with people who came out of the mob," said Churchill. "Those days are gone forever. Today an extra is lucky to make a living." A few years after that, extras were hired through private agencies, and they paid out of their $3, $5, or $7.50 a day, 10 percent to the agency. "A natural evil that grew out of this was the 'cut back.' The casting director and picture directors in the studios began taking theirs for throwing their employment needs to agencies with whom they had understandings," explained Churchill. Thus, extra work became a "racket," and that caused influential people within and without the industry to begin to look into it. "Coupled with the abuses of employment was the matter of morals. There were many stories relating to the requirements placed on extras; many of them were true," continued Churchill. "So the studios bought one of the largest bureaus and organized Central Casting, an employment agency that hired all extras and which was supported by the producers without charge to the workers." However, Central wasn't in operation long before charges were made that a favored few got all the work. "The head of the bureau [Allen] was forced to keep a gun in his desk. Often, when things got tough, he was protected by a bodyguard," wrote Churchill. "Riots occurred in the Central Casting office. Eventually, after nine years of dissension and accusations, the whole thing blew up in criminal charges which are still pending in the courts." (This is a somewhat fanciful and exaggerated account of Allen's tenure as head of Central.) Then a year ago, in 1934, Central hired MacCulloch to head the Bureau, related Churchill, "a Scotsman with a reputation for fanatical honesty and an old timer in the town." He had attempted for almost a year to bring order out of chaos and put extra work on a business basis. But "with nine years of suspicion of corruption attached to the bureau, he has the almost impossible task of creating a feeling of honesty in the bureau's dealings." During 1934 the top paid male extra worked 224 days and was paid $2,447 ($47 a week). To earn that sum he had to maintain (cleaning and repairing) an extensive wardrobe — at a cost of $750 in 1934 — which reduced his average wage down to $36.50 a week. In addition, to earn that sum, he spent another $920 on additions to his wardrobe.[16]

The joys of automation at Central were celebrated in a piece that appeared in the *Los Angeles Times* in September 1935, in which the reader learned a studio needed only to describe its extra needs and a machine would produce them. The machine had been installed at Central and sorted cards upon which the characteristics of the extras registered with the Bureau had been marked. An example given was a request for eight soprano-singing Russian women, all 40 years or more in age. To fill this request the registration cards were fed into the machine and the code number for Russian women was pressed. Out popped the cards for 36 Russian women. Those cards were returned to the hopper and the code number for sopranos was pressed. That produced 25 cards, representing Russian female sopranos. When the remaining cards were put through for a third time, with the age requirement code punched in, a total of 10 cards remained. Each of those cards contained all relevant information as to appearance, type, and experience, and contained a photograph pasted in one corner. The International Business Machines Corporation (IBM) had installed the automatic sorter. "We used to depend on memory. Someone had to recall who were soprano-singing Russian women or we couldn't find them," explained Campbell MacCulloch. "This machine does it automatically. Each card is marked for between 500 and 600 characteristics, such as brown hair, platinum hair, blue eyes, grey eyes, fat, skinny, speaks Abyssinian, and so forth." Those cards were hole-punched and sorted on the holes.[17]

Reporter John Scott remarked in September 1935 that Central had not taken any new registrations since February of that year. He said Central had 12,400 players on file but couldn't find work for a third of that number. Casual workers, consisting of racial types, were not listed as regulars but, it was said, Central could lay its hands on 5,000 in less than 10 hours. Players listed with Central had signed agreements with the Bureau that they understood that there was no guarantee of work. In fact, during the registration process, each applicant was asked whether he expected to support himself by doing extra work, "and if he answered in the affirmative, was given no consideration." In other words, remarked Scott, playing atmosphere roles in films should be considered a "hobby," or as one Hollywood wag put it, a "disease." Of those thousands registered fewer than 120 earned as much as $29 a week in 1934. Central Casting received some 11,000 calls a day from those wanting extra work. "It is estimated conservatively that there are some 50,000 would-be film extras in and around the celluloid capital, persons who would jump at the opportunity to appear as atmosphere in pictures," Scott concluded. "From this it can readily be seen how rackets can flourish in Hollywood."[18]

As of February 1940 it was reported that thousands of film extras had started a drive to crash major studio casting offices. That move followed an announcement that producers had abandoned the "no request rule" in placing calls for atmosphere people and were submitting preferred lists to Central Casting. (In theory, a studio was supposed to place a request to Central for, say, a 40-year-old Swahili-speaking Italian — not one for a 40-year-old Swahili-speaking Italian, John Doe preferred). That move by the major studios meant that the majority of extra jobs in the future would be set by the studio casting offices. Producers would continue to place calls through Central but lists of names furnished by a studio would be exhausted before other extras were called for the jobs. If calls could be completed from studio lists, any extra who was not on a studio list was out of luck. If the new plan became generally implemented, Central Casting officials estimated that as high as 70 percent of extra jobs would be filled by studio casting offices from their preferred lists with Central acting only as a telephone agency to see that phone calls reached the designated extras. Studio executives were reported to feel that abolition of the "no request rule" would enable producers to get more experienced players and a "better class of extras." It was also argued that the studios could be able to steer more work to the regular extra and the occasional player and "freak" extras would gradually be forced out of the industry, enabling regulars to earn a livelihood. It was noted by this article that the new method of preferred list was simply a reversion to an earlier time when all extras were hired directly by studio casting directors.[19]

Then the situation at Central was reported as much worse as, among other things, there was an unexpected change at the top of Central Casting. In the middle of April 1940 it was suddenly announced that Howard R. Philbrick, a former agent for the Federal Bureau of Investigation, had been named head of Central Casting and would assume that post immediately, meaning that MacCulloch must have been fired, although he was barely mentioned at all in most of the news accounts except to the extent he was named as the man replaced. It was said Philbrick was sponsored by California Governor Culbert Olson and that "a financial settlement will be made with MacCulloch." Philbrick reportedly had been one of a "corps of former FBI men" called in to investigate Central when extras made recent charges that jobs were being passed out in return for bribes being paid to Central employees. As a result, Central had been under fire from a variety of sources since that time. The MPAA film cartel and SAG (Screen Actors Guild, representing the actors) issued a joint statement that Philbrick's appointment met with the full approval of both organizations. In part, that statement said, "Neither producers nor SAG expects Philbrick to solve overnight the problems on which the energies of the industry have been concentrated for several years. Extras should not expect reorganization will mean that all work that is wanted will be made available. The appointment has not changed the mathematical problem of trying to spread approximately 900 average daily jobs among more than 7,000 extras." Both the producers and SAG expressed confidence that Philbrick would establish maximum efficiency in the operation of Central. Aside from his experience in the U.S. Department of Justice, Philbrick had more recently served in California as State Director of Motor Vehicles.[20]

His tenure as California Director of Motor Vehicles had been mired in controversy and he had resigned that position, only days before his appointment at Central, as the outgrowth of a state capital wiretap scandal in Sacramento. Philbrick had steadily denied any responsibility for the placing of a listening device in the hotel room of Assembly Speaker Gordon Garland. He admitted, however, hiring private detective Paul Rowe, who in turn hired R. E. Voshell, the central figure in the case. Philbrick said in the resignation he submitted to Governor Olson that the wiretap scandal was one of the factors responsible for his resignation.[21]

A different account reported Philbrick had been given the job of reorganizing Central (at a salary of $1,000 to $2,000 per month) after he resigned his Motor Vehicle post (where he was paid $500 a month in salary) after he assumed responsibility for the hiring of investigators who, it developed, planted a listening device in Garland's Sacramento hotel room. Reportedly, Garland had been the target of a campaign to oust him from his office because of his reputed opposition to certain policies of Governor Culbert Olson. According to this account, Philbrick "will have an opportunity to assist the offices of the district attorney and other law enforcement officials in ousting from the ranks of movie extra players any hoodlum and racketeers who reportedly are attempting to collect tribute from the actors and actresses." SAG had recently launched its own investigation of Central Casting following rumors of job-buying and favoritism in distributing work to the atmosphere players.[22]

Toward the end of April it was observed that Philbrick had begun his task of "humanizing" Central Casting — the staff was always saying "no" to the extras. As a start Philbrick removed the front door of his internal office. Central Casting's locked front door had a peephole with a sliding cover to allow inspection from within. "It used to take an act of Congress to get past that door," remarked Philbrick. "From now on every effort will be made to bring the human element into the administration of the casting bureau. No legitimate complaint will go unheeded. All will be handled in a tactful human manner." According to the article writer, "Philbrick already has abolished nepotism from Central Casting."[23]

2. Central Casting Bureau   41

Still at the end of April a news account declared that on April 30 Philbrick enlisted the aid of the sheriff and the District Attorney in "weeding out" Eastern hoodlums and gangsters from the ranks of film extras. "We have agreed upon close cooperation in cleaning up this situation," said Central's head. "There are thousands of good, honest, law-abiding movie extras. We don't intend to let gangsters and hoodlums invade their ranks." Philbrick stated he was roughly familiar with SAG's report "detailing inroads made by hoodlums and was confident undesirables could be weeded out quickly."[24]

One of Hollywood's high-profile female gossip columnists weighed in at this time with a column on Central's new boss. Louella Parsons called Philbrick a political power during two California state regimes and said that he conducted investigations of various state agencies and departments over that time. "I thought he was strange company indeed for the Screen Actors' Guild," at first, she admitted. However, she decided snap judgments were not always right and so decided to interview him. She found him slim, blond, and about 33 years old. When he first came to Central, he told Parsons, "the place was run like a speakeasy, with a small hole in the door. Extras who applied for work had the door slammed in their faces and were told there was no work today. I have opened all the doors and every extra who comes up here is given a hearing." Central opened for business each day at 5 AM. When Parsons asked him how he planned to keep all those thousands of extras happy he admitted it would be difficult. "However, we are going to divide the work as much as possible. We are definitely not going to show any favoritism."[25]

At the beginning of June 1940, reporter Paul Harrison pointed out the "extra problem" had existed for producers from the very beginning. However, lately there had been added such new problems as "gangsterism, job-selling, union troubles, and some delicate questions of moral racketeering." A rough idea of the complexities, wrote Harrison, was provided by the fact that inquiries were being conducted, or had been conducted, by the Federal Bureau of Investigation, the district attorney's office, the sheriff's department, the state Labor Board and a detective agency retained by SAG. That SAG report, said the journalist, "is such a sensational document it will not be released and couldn't be printed if it were." He said MacCulloch had been dismissed by the MPAA, which acted after SAG had presented it with a copy of its own report on the conduct of the casting agency.

According to Harrison, one thing Philbrick wanted to do at this time was to fingerprint all the extras. While the Central head acknowledged such a move would bring a great hue and cry with respect to invasion of privacy and constitutional rights, he believed it would "result in the swift exodus of a lot of hoodlums who are getting into the movies."[26]

Later in June 1940, when it became known that Philbrick had compiled a list of extra players who had earned in excess of $700 within the previous five months and had distributed the list to Central's casting personnel, the extra players complained to SAG and urged the trade union to investigate the memorandum. Philbrick advised SAG that he did not intend to blacklist anybody and indicated the list of top-money extras had been tossed "into the ashcan." SAG members, however, told the Guild they were not satisfied with that explanation, pointing out Philbrick's memorandum stated, "Be conscious of these names and their earnings for the first five months of this year. Wherever and whenever possible, try to select other individuals in place of those listed." Following protests from SAG extras, Guild executive K. Thomson sent a memo to Philbrick that said, "Members of the Screen Actors Guild have made inquiry at the executive offices concerning a purported list of extras said to have been prepared at Central Casting for the purpose of having casting directors withhold calls from those on the list." SAG asked Philbrick two questions. One was why the list was prepared, while the second asked why, if the list was intended to cover all extras earning $700 or more during the first five months of 1940, certain extras whose earnings were above that amount were not included in the list.[27]

Philbrick's reply to SAG gave his personal assurance the list "was in no way intended as a blacklist, and simply set forth facts with which I felt the casting personnel should be familiar. Many persons included on the list have telephoned this office and, after discussion, realized the true significance of what the list represented and had no quarrel therewith." In his reply Philbrick went on to say that soon after assuming his post at Central he observed that a small number of extras year after year were the top earners. It was his thought that those top earners, through frequent use, were established in the minds of the casting personnel to the neglect of many similarly highly competent and well-equipped extra players. "This situation was the subject of constant and articulate complaint. Favoritism was the charge. Spread the work was the answer." He did acknowledge in his response that a few extra players who had earned $700 or more for the period were "inadvertently overlooked" and left off the list. According to Philbrick the memorandum in question contained no "blacklist feature. It did not suggest any such thing. It simply recommended that the casting personnel use some judgment in an effort to spread the work among other equally competent extra players." And, "The matter had been fully discussed with the casting staff, and my intention made clear. They stated they were in thorough accord. They were specifically instructed that the individuals named, when best qualified to fill studio requirements, were most certainly to continue to receive assignments."[28]

If SAG was annoyed with Central not long after Philbrick took charge, it was not alone. Around the same time, according to a report in *Variety*, the film producers were none too pleased with the recent publicity emanating from or revolving around Central Casting since Philbrick was installed as general manager. Already annoyed because of a 20 percent "arbitrary" assessment increase in the cost of maintaining Central, the film executives contended there had been no improvement in the service to studios, despite the increase. They insisted that with work calls 40 percent less than in the previous year, the cost of maintaining Central should have gone down proportionately. Several changes in the methods of distributing jobs were to be inaugurated by Philbrick in the coming days and weeks. It was announced that no calls would be received from "racial types" asking for work in order to cut down the incoming telephone calls that then averaged 4,000 to 5,000 per hour. When jobs were available for the racial types, they would be called directly instead of having to call in for work. Other extras would be given certain numbers to call, and when they attempted to get through on a different switchboard their calls would be ignored.[29]

Central Casting continues to function today but it is nothing like it was, but then, neither is Hollywood. It continued to be an MPAA-funded and -controlled bureau until 1976 when it was, in its own words, "sold to private interests."[30]

3

Morals and Corruption

Life for film extras was difficult enough when the letter of the law and the various agreements in place such as wage scales were honored. But such things hardly ever were, making life for film extras even worse. A news account in March 1923 remarked that the atmosphere players had been the center of excitement in the motion picture studios during the previous few weeks. Enough of a fuss had been made to cause a California state board to take notice of their grievances. The major complaint from the extras was that they were the victims of graft. For the most part those players received their work through the Service Bureau, a private agency. By the connivance of the studios, it was charged, they were forced to cash their checks at a discount at the Service Bureau, and that was on top of having a commission deducted from their checks. That alleged systemic gouging had led the California Labor Board to promise a thorough investigation of the Service Bureau and every similar employment agency that had set up operations around the motion picture studios. Names of the accusing extras were all being kept secret to save them from having their names added to the blacklist.[1]

Journalist Robert Donaldson wrote a piece in August 1923 for the United Press news agency in which he said a campaign was then under way in Hollywood to raise the dignity of extra work and "to form a colony of extras so that all may obtain a reasonable living and form a substantial part of Hollywood life." Actually, his article was only about female extras. Donaldson declared that Hollywood wanted "fewer drifting girls—girls who are given to chance acquaintances and who, because of lack of proper environment, are tempted to listen to improper advances by men influential in the studios." Several years earlier the YWCA in Hollywood started the Studio Club, a temporary residence for girls coming to Hollywood to go into the movies. It housed 20 girls. They were supposed to stay only for two weeks, while they made more permanent living arrangements,

3. Morals and Corruption

although even after they had moved out they were encouraged to make the Studio Club their social center. From the time it first opened the Studio Club had always been filled to capacity. The two-week rule had never been enforced, and girls were housed there for periods ranging up to several months, until they could get on their feet financially. Membership in the Studio Club was not limited to girls who aspired to be actresses but was open to all girls who worked in the film industry, from stenographers, to film cutters, to scenario readers, to secretaries. At the time he was writing, said Donaldson, a campaign headed by Will Hays and the major studios was under way to raise $150,000 for a new Studio Club building to house 100 girls and serve as a recreation center and clubhouse for all film girls in Hollywood. At this proposed new facility residents would be permitted to live for as long as a year.[2]

One of the Studio Club's secretaries told Donaldson, with respect to the girls who came to Hollywood, that most of them were from small towns and were generally girls who had gained some fame in hometown amateur theatricals. Most of their families were said to be in modest circumstances. "Of course, a large number of them are quite unsophisticated as to the ways of the world and the dangers that beset a single girl in the motion picture or any other large business," said the secretary. "I feel sure the club has saved a great many girls from going astray. Where girls have told us of improper advances we have taken the matter up with the studio heads and usually have put an immediate stop to such a man's activities." According to the secretary, many of the girls ran out of money after a few weeks in the film capital and had to confess that fact to the YWCA, which then tried to find them work in other occupations instead of the movies, as secretaries, say, if they were so qualified. And if they weren't qualified for some other specific occupation then the YWCA tried to get them work of some sort in Los Angeles stores. Any girl that planned to come to Hollywood to work in the motion picture field, this secretary advised, should arrive with enough money to live on for at least six months, and "she should also have a good wardrobe, as a girl without plenty of clothes for all occasions, cannot qualify for the wide variety of scenes which require extras." A final thought from the secretary was, "Of course, we see only a part of the girls who come to Hollywood. There is a fast set, who hope to win success in another way, and the last place they would think of coming would be the Y.W.C.A."[3]

Evidence, perhaps, for that "fast set" could be found in a news account published on September 4, 1924. Twenty members of Hollywood's film colony were arrested on that date at a Laurel Canyon residence when police broke up a "wild party" and held the film people on charges of prohibition law violations and disturbing the peace. Among those lodged in the Hollywood jail were Jules Lebaron, film company president; Robert Conville, film director for Lebaron; and F. A. Datig, a casting director. All of those arrested gave assumed names, including five female film extras. That party was held at the home of former film director Jack Sherrill. Neighbors complained about the noise of the party, which had been going on all night.[4]

When he was head of Central Casting, Campbell MacCulloch declared, in a national magazine, that reports of immorality in connection with the hiring of girls for work as film extras "have been greatly exaggerated." He said the most common complaint was that casting directors and their assistants offered girls work on the "one-thing-for-another basis." Admitting that instances of that sort had existed and that he did not doubt that they still occurred, he added, "But I have known them to exist in other industries also, and the labor reports of a dozen states have dealt voluminously with similar conditions." MacCulloch went on to state the California Labor Department was fully aware of the conditions surrounding the extra girl and that much legislation had been enacted in her behalf. "I think the studios are inclined to lean backwards in their efforts to protect women — as much for business reasons as anything else," he concluded. "In a business where the supply of embryo talent is twenty times the demand, it is surprising that conditions are not extraordinarily bad."[5]

Legendary film director David Wark Griffith was charged with criminal assault in a civil suit filed in Superior Court in February 1931 in Los Angeles by Fern Setril (perhaps Setrill), a 22-year-old film extra. She asked for $601,000 in damages. In her complaint Setril said she met Griffith (around 50 at the time) when she was touring the studios looking for work, and he told her she was of an "unusual type of beauty, unspoiled, and that she had remarkable features that would film well in motion pictures." She added she visited the director in an apartment on June 25, 1930, on his promise to employ her in the role of Ann Rutledge in the film *Abraham Lincoln*, and alleged he forcibly attacked her. She asked for $500,000 for actual damages, $100,000 for punitive damages, and $1,000 for medical treatment. Griffith described the charge as "absurd" and "without foundation in fact." He said he could not recall having met Setril, although she could have been among the thousands he interviewed every year. As to the date of the alleged assault, Griffith said *Abraham Lincoln* had been completed before June 1930 and that he would have had no reason to summon her for a part at that time.[6] One day later an amended complaint was filed by Setril. That altered complaint was identical to the original except it omitted reference to an assertion that Griffith wanted to give her an important role in *Abraham Lincoln*.[7]

The day after that Setril was summoned to the District Attorney's office. Investigators were also ordered to bring in Earl W. Taylor, a friend of Setril, for questioning. Shortly after the suit was filed, Taylor was alleged to have called newspapers and attempted to sell a story of the girl's life. District Attorney Buron Fitts said, "If the facts develop sufficiently to justify a prosecution on the charge of a conspiracy to commit the crime of extortion, or attempted extortion, this office will prosecute." However, nothing more was reported on this case.[8]

The highest profile case involving morals allegations began in May of 1934. In that month Dave Allen, 48 and married, of 2000 North Curson Street, Los Angeles, manager of Hollywood's Central Casting Corporation, was named in a grand jury indictment that charged violation of Section 288-A of the Penal Code, a morals offense. On May 17 he appeared in Superior Judge Bowron's court for arraignment and denied the truth of the statements made against him before the grand jury. Allen was released under $2,500 bond at the request of his attorney, Jerry Geisler. At that time officials were still seeking Miss Gloria Marsh, a film extra, who was named as a codefendant in the indictment. It was reported that she had disappeared from her Hollywood apartment. According to Allen, the charge against him was a deliberate frame-up fostered by personal enemies who were seeking to destroy his reputation and to injure Central Casting. "I have obtained evidence bearing on this case from numerous persons of irreproachable character which I am positive will lead to a prompt acquittal when my case goes to trial," he declared. The alleged offense was said to have occurred in the apartment of Miss June De Long, Allen's accuser, who lived at 3342 Oak Glen Drive with a friend, Mrs. Pearl Owings. De Long was then being held in custody as a material witness guarded by Marjorie Fairchild. The matter was brought to the attention of the grand jury by a Los Angeles attorney. Another comment by Allen was that he was the victim "of the dirtiest, lowest, most despicable frame-up ever perpetrated."[9]

About one month later a grand jury report on the affair was released that contained charges that young girls aspiring to film careers were forced to submit to "affairs" with studio "courtiers." County officials made public the testimony of a "feminine bit player" that she and others who came to Hollywood were forced "to surrender their charms" and become "partygirls" in exchange for minor film work. While the extra was not specifically named in the report it was, presumably, De Long.[10]

Seated in defendants' chairs in Judge Rey Schauer's courtroom on July 11, 1934, Gloria Marsh, 26, and Dave Allen reportedly "fidgeted with the gaze of a dozen representatives of women's clubs, civic and reform organizations fastened upon their backs." Arthur Veitch, deputy district attorney, was prosecuting the pair under a section of the California penal code "involving an offense not publicly detailed." Charles Ostrom was the attorney for Marsh while Jerry Geisler continued as attorney for Allen. June De Long had been constantly guarded by a policewoman since the "sensational episode" first reached a grand jury investigation in the previous May, said a report. According to the two defense attorneys; "Dave Allen and Miss Marsh were framed. We intend to prove that certain prosecution witnesses, for reasons of their own, made things appear to exist which did not exist." On the other hand, according to prosecutor Veitch, De Long's sworn story would show that extra girls were compelled to submit to men, to persuade other girls to do the same, and to lend their apartments for use as meeting places in order to obtain work as $7.50 and $10 a day film extras. Allen had then headed Central Casting for many years.[11]

During the jury selection process each side used up all of its challenges before settling on a jury composed of four women and eight men. In challenging and selecting the jury Geisler asked them whether they had ever worked as extras in films or had any prejudice against Allen because of the fact he was a Jew or if they or anyone related to them belonged to any society, club, or organization opposed to Jews. Attorney Ostrom asked the prospective jurors whether the then current nationwide agitation by religious organizations for "clean pictures" and the recent demand for the removal of Will Hays as president of the Motion Picture Producers Association (the Hollywood cartel's lobby group), would influence them against Allen and Marsh. Veitch objected to that line of questioning and was sustained by Judge Schauer. On that first day of the trial in the packed courtroom were three representatives of the Women's Christian Temperance Union, who made copious notes. Bailiff Forrest F. Blalock said he had promised to reserve seats for them daily throughout the trial. Mrs. Jessie B. Smith, assistant morality director of the WCTU, announced that it was the policy of her organization to report the proceedings of trials involving morality. As that first day moved along Marsh was said to have appeared nervous and dejected, while Allen "nervously chewed gum and eagerly studied the faces of the prospective jurors."[12]

The trial testimony began a day later with the first two witnesses being Mrs. Grace Whittier, manager of the apartment house in which the incident took place, who testified about the room and the lock on the door, and Mrs. Pearl Owings, film actor, who related "intimate details" of the scene of which she actually became a witness when she walked unexpectedly through the unlocked door of De Long's apartment on April 26, 1934. She said De Long and Marsh were nude and Allen was partly undressed and that she stood still for several seconds too amazed to speak. When Allen saw her he rushed at her shouting, "It's a frame-up," she testified. Then Marsh and De Long ran into the dressing room while Allen asked Owings if Pat Harmon or Allen Garcia, both film actors, had sent Owings to the apartment, she said. "I said I had merely come to get some photographs from Miss De Long and no one had sent me," she told the court. Allen then demanded to know, she testified, if she "was a spotter for a women's club," which she denied. After Marsh had departed Allen offered Owings and De Long $200 to "keep quiet," Owings asserted. The witness said Allen demanded of De Long, "Haven't I paid for every party I've had in your apartment." De Long, she said, replied, "No. The first party in my apartment was when you promised to register me for picture work at Central Casting Bureau. The second party was after I visited you at your office in search of employment." Allen then suggested, the witness said, that "everybody knows what I do; the kind of parties I like, let's you and Miss De Long and I have a party and forget the whole thing." Owings said she declined and Allen left the apartment followed by De Long, who promised to obey his demand to "get out of town." In the course of speaking to the jury, Veitch said he would prove De Long had been placed under pressure to lend her apartment for use as a meeting place between girls and men in the movie business before either she or the other girls could be sure of getting work through the casting bureau that Allen managed.[13]

With respect to Owings' testimony, another account reported that spectators in the courtroom leaned forward, "almost in a body, some cupping their hands to their ears as Mrs. Owings was asked by Veitch to 'describe thoroughly'" the scene she saw when she entered De Long's apartment unbidden after her knock had gone unanswered. Meanwhile, "outside the courtroom hundreds of persons strained at barricades." Owings testified, "I stood there speechless until Mr. Allen leaped up and approached me, his face angry, and demanded to know who was responsible for the 'frame-up.'"[14]

When he cross-examined Owings, Geisler thundered at her, "Didn't you talk over the possibility of catching Dave Allen in an incriminating position before you walked into Miss De Long's apartment last April 26?" To which Owings replied, "I did not; I had never met Dave Allen before, and did not talk with anyone about him." When he asked her if she lived with Pat Harmon as his common-law wife, Pearl said he was only a boarder and had been so at her home for some time. Owings did admit that Harmon drove her to the De Long apartment on April 26 and that he accompanied her to the grand jury room on May 15. Both denied they had taken part in plans to appear in a stage production based on the story of the

Allen/Marsh scandal, although Geisler insisted he had been informed that an actor to play the part of Allen had been engaged, "and I am informed the funds taken in from the 25 cents admission fee are intended to be turned over to a legal fund for the prosecution of Mr. Allen." Geisler continued to hammer away at Owings, trying, unsuccessfully, to have her say that she, De Long, and Harmon plotted to get Allen into the De Long apartment and that the door to the unit would be deliberately left unlocked so Owings could later burst in.[15]

June De Long came out of seclusion on July 13 to testify in court about the incident. Prior to the start of the trial and ever since she had told her story to the grand jury, she had been under constant guard. As well, she had been absent from the courtroom for the first days of the trial. Each day of the trial all the available seats in the courtroom had been occupied long before the session began and hundreds stood in line outside, waiting and hoping for an opportunity of seizing some vacated seat during a recess.[16]

Prior to De Long taking the stand, Pat Harmon, film "heavy" and former policeman, admitted he boarded at the home of Pearl Owings at 3342 Oak Glen Drive. Harmon testified he drove Pearl to the apartment of De Long in which Owings testified she found a "wild party" in progress. He also said he did not depend for his film work on Allen or the Central Casting Bureau but obtained most of his screen engagements directly from the studios. In a dogged cross-examination of Harmon by Geisler, the actor emphatically and repeatedly denied he and De Long and Owings were the instigators of a plot to frame Allen. The attorney further tried to discredit Harmon by implying the actor wanted to smear Allen and put Central Casting out of business because he, Harmon, had received no work through them and that he would go so far as to instigate a frame-up, if necessary, to accomplish his goals. According to the news account Harmon "admitted he was a member of a 'secret society' of actors organized to fight discrimination and other abuses charged against the casting bureau."[17]

When Geisler asked Harmon if he had ever been convicted of a felony, the actor said he had served a term of 14 months following his 1911 conviction for receiving stolen property. Asked to explain why he and Pearl went to attorney Carl Kegley, both Harmon and Pearl testified, over the objection of Geisler, that Mrs. Grace Whittier, manager of the apartment house where De Long lived, telephoned to find out whether the pair was in jail. The witnesses testified Whittier told them that the day following Owings' unexpected visit to the De Long apartment, police had visited De Long and threatened to throw her in jail unless she got out of town. Those officers, Whittier said, told De Long that Harmon and Pearl were already in jail. Angered by what they declared was an attack on their characters, Pearl, accompanied by Harmon, according to their testimony, consulted J. C. Dahlen, secretary of the Motion Picture Alliance. Pearl said she told Dahlen she had accidentally walked in on a "shocking scene" involving Allen, De Long, and Marsh, and then reported what Whittier had told her. Dahlen, the witnesses declared, advised them to consult Carl Kegley, attorney for the Motion Picture Alliance, which they did the following day. Kegley, after hearing Pearl's story had her repeat it to Superior Judge Bowron, in charge of the grand jury. Pearl admitted she telephoned De Long in San Francisco on June 2 and advised her to return to Los Angeles at the request of the District Attorney's office. De Long returned to Los Angeles two days later and remained at Owings' home in the custody of Marjorie Fairchild of the District Attorney's office for several days before taking an apartment in Hollywood. Both Harmon and Pearl were emphatic in their denial that they planned to stage or participate in a play based on the trial of Allen.[18]

Finally, June De Long took the stand. A journalist wrote, "She entered the courtroom smiling and hatless, clad in a smartly tailored pink silk sports dress with pumps and handbag to match. The nails on her shapely hands, which have been used in close-up film shots as those of film stars, were deeply tinted." Jurors were described as looking "embarrassed" as she revealed details of what she described as a "wild party" in which she participated with Allen and Marsh. June De Long, whose real name was Ann Snyder, testified she had registered at the Central Casting Bureau on December 5, 1931, the day after she had met and been at a party with Allen and another girl. On April 19, 1934, she said, she went to Allen's office and asked him for work. One week later, on April 26, she again visited Allen at his office, seeking work. Returning home after that meeting, De Long testified she had hardly closed the door of her apartment and removed her hat before Allen arrived. As a result of his request, she said, she phoned Gloria Marsh, who was a stranger to Allen. Soon Marsh arrived at June's apartment.[19]

Allen, according to June, made a tour of inspection of her apartment. She said he personally locked the door to her apartment. Said De Long, "I didn't know that my girlfriend Pearl Owings had walked into my apartment until Allen ran toward her. Gloria and I then ran into the dressing-room. We could hear Pearl and Dave arguing. Gloria left and Allen accused us of framing him." De Long continued by testifying Allen threatened to call the police. He said he had told a friend that there was a plot in the works to frame him and that he had been advised to go through with it. June added that she left later the same night for San Francisco after two police officers visited her and threatened to put her in jail if she didn't leave town. During his cross-examination Geisler tried, unsuccessfully, to get De Long to admit the whole affair was a frame-up. The actress with the "most beautiful hands in Hollywood" did admit, after being confronted with her grand jury testimony, that she expected Pearl to call on her on the afternoon of the alleged party. June stated she had left the door of her apartment unlocked during the morning hours of April 26, when she visited Allen at his office but that Allen locked the apartment door when he arrived at her apartment.[20]

Then things got really dramatic. De Long had begun her testimony on Friday, July 16, 1934. Geisler had just begun his cross-examination of her late on Friday when court was recessed for the weekend. On the next day, just before noon on Saturday, June vanished from her apartment at 1760 North Wilcox Avenue, leaving a note behind her in which she intimated she planned to destroy herself. Eight hours later she was found wandering in a dazed condition on Western Avenue near 8th Street and was taken to the District Attorney's office for questioning. Needless to say, her disappearance created a furor of excitement in the prosecution team. She was discovered by car salesman Frank Gerard and his wife while police officers throughout Southern California maintained a blockade of all highways and conducted an intensive search for the missing witness. After her discovery June explained by saying, "I wanted to die. I felt that my life was ruined and that I had hurt my girl friend Miss Marsh. I felt there was nothing left for me to live for." She added that she could not bring herself to go back into that courtroom. "It all turned out so different from what I expected after watching film courtroom scenes. I just couldn't go back there and hurt Gloria anymore. She was my best friend. But, of course, I see now there is nothing else for me to do. I must go through with it now that I've started."[21]

On Sunday, a day later, she told Deputy District Attorney Veitch that she did not swallow poison as she said at first when she was found on Saturday night. She said she had two tablets of a deadly poison tied up in her handkerchief when she fled from the apartment house. According to Veitch she wandered around for a long time, climbed into the Hollywood hills for a last look and then, resigned to suicide, she reached for the poison pills only to find she had lost them out of her handkerchief. After weeping for a time she decided to return to the world, and was soon found by Gerard and his wife. June had continued to be under the guard of Marjorie Fairchild, an investigator for the District Attorney's office, in June's apartment. On that fateful Saturday Fairchild left the apartment to buy some food for a late breakfast. While she was absent De Long slipped out the back way leaving a suicide note that read, in part, "Dear Marge — when you read this I will be dead." In that note June expressed contrition for having made trouble for her friend, Marsh, and left her automobile and other possessions to her accused friend. After a conference with June that lasted nearly three hours on that Sunday, Veitch said June had not changed her story of the alleged party and the events leading up to it. She had run away to commit suicide because June did not want to take poison in the apartment, as she thought Fairchild would soon return and thwart any such attempt. After she was found on the Saturday De Long was placed under the guard of Fairchild and a police matron.[22]

Back in court on Monday, July 16, June admitted she had testified falsely the previous week when she denied having been arrested in Los Angeles in March 1931 on a morals charge. "I figured I had already disgraced myself," she explained, "and I couldn't see where the question had anything to do with this case." While no mention was made in court about the weekend's disappearance and recovery, the largest crowd to date to seek admission to the trail started forming outside the courtroom three hours before the hearing convened.[23]

June continued her testimony on July 17, and the story got still stranger as the state's star witness hinted at tampering. De Long testified she had been offered $100 "to meet a bunch of lawyers" after she had told the grand jury of a "Babylonian revel" in which she had participated with Allen and Marsh. Mrs. Serena Rowland of San Francisco made the offer, according to De Long. Rowland previously had urged her not to testify against Allen and Marsh, said June, who added that Rowland told her Allen could do a lot for her in pictures if she dropped the matter. According to a journalist attending the trial, "Much of Miss De Long's testimony, which has shocked a crowded courtroom, has been unprintable and upon it the state has built its hopes for a conviction." That reporter also observed that the trial was revolving around "the question of whether pretty girl movie extras must sacrifice their honor to get jobs." June's morals conviction in 1931 had caused her to be fined $25 and sentenced to five days in jail.[24]

On July 17th the prosecution closed its case, and the defense started its case, calling a number of witnesses whom, Geisler declared, would prove the charge was a frame-up. One called was Mrs. Myra McKinney Russell, secretary of the Motion Picture Supporting and Extra Players' Association. She testified that June came to her office and wanted to "make a statement concerning the morals of Dave Allen," four months before he was indicted by the grand jury on charges of an offense against public morals. Russell declared that June discussed the matter with her for three hours and that she finally told her to go to the district attorney.[25]

A parade of defense witnesses took the stand on July 18, all making an effort to prove Allen was framed. The names of De Long and Marsh were not mentioned by any of them. Some of them said they had heard Pat Harmon, described as an officer of two organizations composed of extra players, utter threats against Central Casting manager Dave Allen. One witness, Jack Lloyd, actor and publisher of a casting directory, said Harmon telephoned him following the indictment of Allen on the morals charge. He quoted Harmon as saying, "I've tried for three years to get that ____ ____ Allen, and now that I've got him, he's going up for a long time." Harmon, of course, denied making such a statement. Carl Faulkner, an extra, testified he once met Harmon on Hollywood Boulevard with Harmon telling him he was "still after that bunch at Central Casting" and that he was going to "have them all tarred and feathered and run out of town."[26]

Another who testified for the defense was Detective Lieutenant Robert L. Griffen of the Los Angeles Police Department, who said De Long had intimated to him the possibility of a frame-up in the case. Also called for the defense was Blayney Matthews, chief special investigator for the district attorney's office. Matthews told of an interview he had with Harmon when he called the actor to his office on April 30 in connection with a complaint made against Harmon by Allen. When Matthews asked Harmon what the trouble was out there in Hollywood the latter told him he had been in the movie business for many years but he was not getting the work to which he was entitled. It was a situation that he blamed upon Allen. According to Matthews, Harmon said he had called on Allen several days earlier at his office but Allen refused to see him. Later, Harmon continued, he was standing on the sidewalk in front of the Central Casting office when two of Allen's associates came by. He admitted to Matthews that he asked them if they were "plug uglies" for Allen and that if they were his car was just around the corner and that his "old equalizer" was in it. Matthews said he told Harmon to go back to Hollywood, that he wanted no violence and that if he felt he had a grievance against Allen he should take it up with the proper authorities. Harmon denied all such statements attributed to him but admitted he felt Allen was preventing him from obtaining any work.[27]

Carl Faulkner, Edwin G. Parker, Monte Vandergrift, and John Gibson were other prominent film extras who testified they had heard Harmon make threats against Allen at various times. Mrs. Ursula Green, wife of Jack Green, president of the Motion Picture Alliance, testified that she had heard Owings, whom she knew as Mrs. Harmon, call Allen "vile names." J. M. McCarthy, proprietor of a dress shop, also testified he knew Owings as Mrs. Pat Harmon.[28]

From the witness stand on July 21, Dave Allen denied that he had ever participated in an immoral party with De Long and Marsh. He admitted he went to June's apartment on April 26 and there met the two women. However, he denied emphatically that any of the three had performed immoral acts. "Miss De Long did come out of her dressing-room nude, except for an open slip or kimono," he testified. "But Miss Marsh did not remove her clothing." Allen was then on a "leave of absence" as manager of Central Casting. He claimed he went to June's apartment that day because she had come to his office that morning with information that she knew a girl who had heard of a plot against him.[29]

Continuing with his testimony, Allen said that after June came to his office to say she knew of a girl who had heard of a plot against him, "I was extremely worried at the time because I had received several threats against my life." In fact, he added, one day about noon he received a telephone call in which he was informed he was "on the spot," and at 12:30 a hearse drove up in front of his office and an undertaker came up and asked for his body. Several minutes later a florist drove up with flowers, he testified. Allen said he was particularly afraid of Pat Harmon and recounted several instances in which he said, Harmon had threatened his life, instances he said he reported to the authorities. "Harmon once told me," he continued, "that if he ever came across him again he would 'run my tail off' so I stayed out of his way for a long time, driving in the opposite direction when I saw him, or crossing the street to avoid him. Harmon was angry with me because he thought I was keeping him out of film work." He had tried to explain to him that this was not the case but had failed to convince him. The casting director also said he knew Pat Owings as Mrs. Pat Harmon.[30]

According to Allen, he went to June's apartment only a few minutes after she called at his office. When he knocked she let him in whereupon he asked her where the other girl was. June said she would telephone her. She then phoned Marsh who soon arrived. The two women then went into the dressing-room and they came out several minutes later. "When I saw how Miss De Long was dressed, right away I knew something was wrong, I was scared to death," he testified. "Just then there was a knock at the door and Miss De Long opened it. There stood Mrs. Harmon." Allen added that Owings said, looking at the occupants of the room, "Isn't this nice" and "Won't your wife like to hear of this." Then Owings told him she knew of two people who were now "going to get all the motion picture work they desired." When Allen asked her who she meant Pearl replied she meant Pat Harmon and June De Long. When Gloria Marsh took the stand she said; "I went into the bathroom and when I came out June had all her clothes off, with the exception of a black crepe wrap, which was quite revealing." Gloria asked her what she meant by the way she was dressed and she replied, "Never mind, just follow me." With that the two women went into the living room where Allen, whom Marsh said she had never seen before that day, was sitting. When he saw them Allen jumped up and asked, "What's the meaning of this?" And just at that moment Marsh heard another voice at the kitchen door—that of Owings. Marsh said she heard considerable talk between Allen and Owings in which the word "frame-up" was prominent. Gloria said she left the apartment as quickly as possible. Her real name was Turner, and she was a former resident of Salt Lake City.[31]

Marsh joined Allen in his claim the whole situation was a frame-up. She also stated she was never unclad while at June's apartment. In this account it was said that Allen had been lured to June's apartment under the pretense that a woman was there who would tell him of a threat against his life. As court recessed on Friday, July 21, for the weekend Harry Adams, a former screen extra who was to be called as a rebuttal witness against Allen and Marsh, asked for police protection. He claimed he had been threatened with harm if he persisted in testifying.[32]

The trial began on July 9 and ended on July 24. In his argument to the jury Veitch demanded a verdict of guilty. Conviction on the charge carried with it a prison sentence not to exceed 15 years. He described Allen as "the one man who with a mere nod of his head controls the film fate of 17,000 men and women." Ridiculing the defense contention of a frame-up, the prosecutor declared the "scenario writer who got up Allen's defense didn't have much experience with lawsuits." Veitch then detailed how the casting director discarded his bodyguards and, without even telling his secretary where he was going, hurried to the apartment of De Long, where he contended he was to receive information concerning a plot against him. Yet, the prosecutor emphasized, at no time did Allen seek to ascertain from Gloria Marsh whether she was the girl June De Long allegedly said had important information for the casting director. Charles Ostrom, attorney for Marsh, criticized lawyer Carl Kegley for taking the case directly to the grand jury instead of going to the district attorney's office. Had the case gone to the district attorney, declared Ostrom, there would have been an investigation "but the trial would not now be going on because there is absolutely no basis for a trial." Ostrom described June as an unfortunate, misguided girl, a pawn in the hands of others who were, he stated, the instigators of a frame-up.[33]

At 5:40 PM on July 24 the jury retired to deliberate. Two days later, at 4:00 PM on July 26, the jury requested further instruction from the

3. Morals and Corruption   57

judge. To that point ten ballots had been taken with each one standing at eight votes to four in favor of conviction. Each of the 12 jurors voted the same on each ballot, with the minority four being Mrs. Katheryn C. Hughey, Mrs. Dora Veith, Edwin A. Williams, and Joseph Oberwise. Each of them later said their interpretation of the evidence led them to believe the contention of the defense that Allen was the victim of a frame-up. When they met with the judge at 4:00 PM, jury foreman Knox explained the nature of the deadlock since the first ballot. Judge Schauer asked the members of the jury if they were willing to continue to deliberate. Since each of them said yes, the judge sent them back to deliberate. Four more ballots were taken that evening but each ended as the ones before. At 10:10 PM on July 26, Knox reported to the judge that the panel was hopelessly deadlocked. Judge Schauer dismissed the jury at that point and tentatively set August 20 as the date for a new trial. June's apartment on April 26 was given in this account as located at 1057 South Western Avenue.[34]

In the middle of September, 1934, it was announced that the Central Casting Bureau had a new director—Campbell MacCulloch. Nothing was said as to whether Dave Allen quit or was fired; however, since MacCulloch was to take over his post immediately it would appear Allen had been sacked. At that point the retrial was slated for October 1. In the recap of the situation in this news account it was said, of the first trial, that "sordid stories of indescribably immoral acts involving two comely film extras" were aired. Prosecutors were unable to bring out during the trial, said the report, the testimony of June De Long before the county Grand Jury, before which she described what she said were the "problems" of an extra girl in Hollywood. She did testify in open court at the trial to "intimate details" of the alleged "Babylonian wild party." Up to the time of his selection to head the Central Casting Bureau, MacCulloch had been acting as executive secretary of the NRA State Recovery Board and of the Los Angeles Regional Labor Board. Previously he had held executive positions with many large business organizations, and his identification with the film industry was said to date back to 1915 when he served as business manager, studio manager, scenario editor, and advertising and publicity director of Triangle Film Corporation.[35]

No second trial was ever held and dismissal of the morals charges against Allen and Marsh was ordered on December 2, 1935, by Superior Judge Henry M. Willis. The dismissal was recommended by Arthur Veitch, deputy district attorney.[36]

On October 19, 1936, Allen was divorced from Mae Evelyn Allen, who had charged him with desertion. She was granted a decree after she accused her husband of staying out nights and leaving her for weeks at a time. In this account it was reported that Allen resigned as head of Central Casting "after being acquitted" in the Hollywood morals case.[37]

On January 3, 1955, Dave Allen, 68, described herein as "founder" and first manager of the Central Casting Bureau, "which helped eliminate racketeering in the booking of movie extras in the silent film era," died in hospital in Los Angeles. The brief obituary mentioned nothing about his scandal or about leaving Central Casting under a cloud, just that he "left the post in 1935." For the 19 years after that he worked for Columbia Pictures, although no details were provided, and he continued to reside at 2000 North Curson Avenue. Prior to the establishment of Central Casting in 1926, said the account, "extras usually were booked at studios by individual agents. Many were exploited by racketeers representing themselves as established agents." Dave Allen had started his theatrical career as a pianist in a New York theater some 50 years earlier, but he had lived in the Hollywood area the previous 45 years.[38]

In October 1934, when the Allen trial was still fresh in the news and the retrial still pending, and MacCulloch was new in his post as Central Casting head, that bureau made a move that just possibly was a response to the potential negative fallout of the Allen case, yet another Hollywood morals scandal. It was announced that an advisory council, membership of which was selected from people prominent in church, business, sociology, and education, would augment the scope of the bureau. According to Central Casting officers the council's purpose was to consider the sociological and economic aspects of the work of the film extra. The council was to pursue any inquiry and make such recommendations as it deemed necessary. For its part the Central Casting Bureau pledged itself to aid and conform to any recommendations of the council.[39]

The advisory council's inaugural meeting was held on October 25 in Los Angeles with its 20 members in attendance with the meeting presided over by Campbell MacCulloch. He told the council that 8,000 extras were registered at Central but the average daily work call provided work for only about 350 a day. Following MacCulloch's talk, several members of the council made short addresses pledging their cooperation in realizing the purposes of the new body. Members of the council were Rev. Harold Proppe, Rev. James H. Lash, Rev. Neal Dodd, Rev. Stewart MacLennan, Rev. J. George Dorn, Rev. Glenn R. Phillips, Rev. C. J. McCoy, Donald Price, Mary Pickford, Dr. Gordon Watkins (UCLA economics professor), Rabbi Isadore Isaacson, Dr. John R. Buckley (foreman of the Los Angeles County Grand Jury), D. C. MacWatters (Community Chest), Dr. H. A. Waggener, F. A. Hartwell, Mrs. Henry J. Wright, Mrs. Marian Bachart, Mrs. Sadie Gill, Mrs. Wilma Bashor, and Mrs. Lillian Toomey. Other people present at that inaugural meeting (but not on the council) included Mayor Frank Shaw of Los Angeles, Mr. Cohn (Collector of Customs), Superior Judge Bowron, Fred W. Beetson (ex-secretary of the Motion Picture Producers Association), and Carl Bush (secretary of the Hollywood Chamber of Commerce). The advisory council seems to have left no more traces on the public record.[40]

At the very start of 1935, on January 1, Central Casting laid down an edict that drinking, gambling, and "other tomfoolery" by film extras on the set was henceforth barred. Formal notices to that effect were posted on bulletin boards of all the studios that were members of the Hays organization (the MPAA cartel). Those notices indicated that offenses had become so rampant among that group of workers that only "drastic threats" could take care of the situation. Extras, it seemed, had been getting drunk, playing bridge and pinochle to excess, shooting dice and indulging in various other breaches of discipline, such as leaving the set without permission. According to a report in *Variety*, Central Casting, which since MacCulloch took charge had evolved more rules and regulations "than a field has mice appears determined to emilypost the throng element into being refined; at least, while on the set." Penalties for offenses were to be as follows: first instance of getting drunk or gambling during the work period would result in a warning to the offender; second violation would bring suspension from the call list for a week, with consequent loss of earnings; a third breach would result in the offender's name being removed from the extra rolls, apparently for good. Until MacCulloch's order was issued, it was not generally known intoxication and gambling had become an issue among extras. It had long been the custom for extras, during the long waits between scenes, to indulge in cards or other games to pass the monotony. But such activities were never taken seriously because extras, as a rule, did not have enough money to gamble with. Part of the new edict from Central Casting was that extras were not to leave the set without the permission of the second director. That had always been a rule but enforcement had been lax or nonexistent, with the result MacCulloch felt a need to reinforce the seriousness of the rule.[41]

Another incident that provoked national media attention took place in Los Angeles in the spring of 1937. On June 4 it was announced that a far-reaching investigation was in progress into what happened the night 100 "beautiful Hollywood film extras were asked to entertain delegates to a motion picture studio convention." That probe was precipitated by 19-year-old Patricia Douglas, who demanded the arrest of a film executive, one of 100 or so, on charges of criminal assault. While checking out the Douglas girl's story, investigators for the district attorney said many of the other extra girls at the party claimed to have been similarly attacked. District Attorney Buron Fitts said he wanted more information before deciding whether to lay the case before the grand jury or to proceed against individuals as the females involved identified them. Douglas said she and the other female extras received a regular studio call to report for extra work and were outfitted in cowgirl and Spanish costumes. Then they were driven in buses to a ranch where convention delegates awaited them. Whiskey and champagne flowed freely at the party, where the girls soon learned it was not required of them to give a dancing performance, as they had been led to believe when they received the work call. According to Douglas she was persuaded to take a drink, became ill, and went to a car where she said the executive attacked her.[42]

One day later the investigation of what was called in a news account a "$35,000 Hollywood hayloft party" had reportedly become national in scope. Besides the complaint from Douglas there were a dozen other film extras who had complained of mistreatment. Ginger Wyatt was the only other extra named specifically as a complainant. The probe led investigators to the office of a film distribution agent in Chicago. In a sworn affidavit, Wyatt said she was called to the studio with 125 extra girls, fitted with an outfit and driven to a ranch on the outskirts of Los Angeles, believing that she was going on location for a motion picture shoot. A large barn at the farm was fitted out as a banquet room, said Wyatt. Those extra girls were assigned to tables immediately and then it developed that each was expected to become the partner of a visiting motion picture sales executive and entertain him for the evening. Wyatt said she refused numerous drinks of liquor and with some difficulty managed to escape from the premises later in the evening when a "well-known" actor volunteered to take her home. The party had taken place on May 5.[43]

Facing David Ross, Chicago film sales executive, for the first time since she met him at a Hollywood ranch party on May 5, Patricia Douglas, on June 16, identified him as her attacker—the man who beat and raped her after she repulsed his advances. The identification took place in the grand jury room. Ross denied the allegation. Douglas said that when she arrived at the party and found she was expected to entertain one of the assembled film executives, instead of appearing as an extra in a film as she had expected and been led to believe, she attempted to leave. When she tried to leave, she said, she was followed from the building and was beaten and attacked. Vincent Coniff, casting director for Hal Roach studios, was the one who made the call for the 100 or 125 extra girls. Coniff claimed there was neither heavy drinking nor any sexual activity at the gathering.[44]

3. Morals and Corruption 61

Following its investigation the county grand jury took no action against Ross, or anyone else. Demands for the arrest of Ross, after his exoneration by the grand jury, were made later in June by William J. F. Brown, attorney for Douglas, in telegrams sent to District Attorney Fitts and Sheriff Biscailuz. The latter said he would take no action unless a warrant was turned over to his office. Brown declared he had received two phone calls from two extra girls in San Francisco who said they attended the party and that they would be glad to testify as to the nature of the party, to back up Douglas. They were then on location in San Francisco, and Brown said he would fly there to get their affidavits. In the meantime Ross had flown home to Chicago.[45]

Patricia Douglas filed a $500,000 lawsuit on February 10, 1938, in Federal Court for damages incurred in the alleged attack during the party. Named in the suit as defendants were: Davis Ross, Chicago film salesman; Hal Roach, comedy producer; Edward J. Mannix, screen executive; Vincent Coniff, casting director; and 50 John Does. Although Ross alone was originally charged by Douglas with the actual attack, in her subsequent suit filed for $500,000 in Superior Court the previous fall, the extra added the names of the other men as having been present at the party. Because of the diversity of residence, the case had to be moved to Federal Court; Ross was a resident of Illinois while the plaintiff was a California resident. Still pending, the suit was delayed when Roach, Coniff and Mannix obtained a ruling that Douglas' complaint had to show specifically how they could be linked to the case. Patricia's suit demanded $100,000 for actual damages and $400,000 in punitive damages. Nothing more about this case appeared in print.[46]

More controversy and complaints leveled against Hollywood over the treatment and conditions of extras surfaced in the summer of 1936. That had to do with what was alleged to be salary chiseling on the part of the producers. Central Casting issued a report showing that for the first six months of 1936, of the 15,275 people given work as extras, 13,463 earned less than $200 for that period. Screen Actors Guild (SAG) had filed some lawsuits and was contemplating others, charging that studios were paying extras $7.50 a day for speaking parts in defiance of the producers' agreement to pay $25 a day for such work. Reportedly, SAG had gathered data and had a "wealth" of evidence to substantiate its chiseling charges against the studios. It was SAG's contention that when the producers agreed to continue the provision of the NRA code agreement after the death of the act when it was deemed unconstitutional by the courts, their resolution to honor it in any case caused it to become a labor contract. And in that contract it was specified that people speaking lines germane to the plot would be paid $25 a day. But with the studios trying to cut costs in the Depression they were demanding the extras do the bit work for the usual $7.50, and the players, "rather than be blacklisted," said journalist Douglas Churchill, complied. It was pointed out that the savings to the studios of such practices were infinitesimal, amounting perhaps to $100 on a $150,000 production.[47]

On the heels of SAG's threatened barrage of legal test cases and salary suit claims against the major film studios, the MPAA (the Hollywood cartel lobby group) decided to get tough with any cartel member who continued to short-change extras. With this response it was expected the scores of complaints would be dropped. Reportedly an MPAA official met with the casting directors of all the major studios and put them all on notice to end the practice.[48]

A week later it was announced that all court cases being prepared by SAG and alleging short-changing on pay would be dropped following a promise by studio executives to adjust all bona fide player complaints. About 100 such cases had been prepared by SAG, and it was felt all would be settled satisfactorily within the next few days. Producers also agreed to adjust any such complaints in the future within 24 hours. Complaints in the future would be handled by a board of three, with the power to recommend the discharge of studio employees found guilty of violating the NRA regulations regarding extras and bit players. That board was composed of Edwin Loeb, Fred Beetson, and Campbell MacCulloch. The two suits that had been formally filed in court — for violation of the $25 rule — involved Rex Alexander against Warner Brothers and Victor De Camp against Columbia.[49]

Los Angeles District Attorney Buron Fitts made it into the news again in November 1937 when his "Gang Busters" squad questioned studio casting directors in a widening investigation of reports racketeers were collecting thousands of dollars weekly from movie extras. Investigator John Klein stated he had information that various extra "clubs" had been formed under the purported control of racketeers. Reportedly, the inquiry was an outgrowth of the murder one week earlier of Hymie Miller, bit player and former prize fight manager that, Klein indicated, may have resulted from a war over control of extra work. Supposedly these groups levied tribute from the extras amounting to thousands of dollars weekly. Klein added that the illicit sale of extra jobs, if true, was by organizations not connected with the Central Casting Bureau.[50]

Within a few days investigators looking into the sale of extra jobs separated it from the Miller murder, claiming no connection between the two cases. Various extras and film executives were questioned to see if they were aware of any extra players having been forced to make payments to gangsters who falsely claimed to have control over bit jobs in the movies. Nevertheless, Klein was forced to concede, at the end of November, "So far we have been unable in a single instance to pin the sale of extra jobs on any individual or group, but are tracking down every report to determine if such a racket exists." And nothing more was heard of this investigation.[51]

About one year later, in December 1939, a report in *Variety* stated that definite evidence of job sales to extras had been uncovered by investigators for SAG. Kenneth Thomson, SAG executive secretary, said former government agents hired by the Guild had uncovered several cases of actual job purchases, in addition to the passing of gratuities with such regularity as to constitute bribery. A report was then said to be in the works from Edwin Atherton, who had recently been in the news for his exposing of a graft scandal in San Francisco. That report, said the news account, would be cited by the actors in their forthcoming demand for a general housecleaning at Central Casting. Speculation was that this expose would also involve casting offices of several studios that had been making hundreds of direct work calls to preferred extras independently of Central, a violation of the cartel rules, as all hiring of extras, in theory, had to go through Central. Nothing more was seen in print about this supposed scandal.[52]

In September 1940, Central Casting announced a determined drive to eliminate "goon squads" and questionable characters from the extra ranks. Charging that casting directors had been threatened with physical violence, Central head Howard Philbrick appeared before the SAG board of directors to urge SAG cooperation. Initially SAG took the position they were not concerned with "outside quarrels" by their members, that such quarrels were matters for the police and the district attorney. Later SAG reconsidered, deciding the alleged tactics might give certain extras an unfair advantage in the job market, with the end result that SAG determined to call a meeting to investigate Philbrick's charges. In the meantime, alleged members of the goon squad were finding it difficult to get work. They were receiving no calls through Central Casting and were having to depend for work upon the jobs they were able to land themselves through friends in the industry. Nothing more was heard about this situation.[53]

4
A Surplus of Extras

One of the greatest problems faced by extras in Hollywood was the overwhelming number of them, all struggling to make it in the film capital, first as extras and then, hopefully, as stars. The Hollywood cartel was highly ambivalent about the number of extras on the west coast. On the one hand they wanted a huge number in Hollywood — it meant producers would never have a problem with finding willing bodies, and the wages paid to extras would be kept down. Appearing in the national media from time to time were rags-to-riches stories about extras that had made it big. If it happened on rare occasions, it was about as likely as getting struck by lightning twice in a day. On the other hand, once those tens of thousands of extras were assembled in Hollywood the film cartel became sick of them, as they constantly harassed film executives and laid siege to studio gates in an effort to get work. Central Casting came into being for many reasons. One of those was to remove that pressure as no hiring of extras, at least in theory, was done through the studios then. It all went through Central, and thus would-be extras laid siege there. But at least it was removed from studio gates. Efforts to deal with the problem of surplus were dealt with by studios, Central, unions, and the federal government over time and never really ended; they just took a rest from time to time. Such efforts never succeeded.

Back in February 1915 the show business periodical *Variety* observed that according to all reports there were more picture supernumeraries (an early term for "extras") charging around the local studios begging work than at any other time. "Almost any morning and afternoon, generally the former, the studio offices are deluged with men and women looking for 'extra jobs.'"[1]

A little later in 1915 a reporter named Kitty Kelly wrote a story set at Selig's film studio, at Irving Park Boulevard and Claremont, where *The Millionaire Baby* was being filmed. Among those gathered on the lot were about 100 extras. Kelly asked Colin Reed — whose job it was to oversee those extras — how he managed to get all those people when he wanted them. "Oh, I have them on my list. They are always coming in and asking for jobs as extras and we keep a list of them for when I need them," he said. "I pick them out carefully when they apply because there are a lot that wouldn't do at all so I don't bother to register them." Reed added that it was a lot harder to get men than women. "Those we have are mostly from shows that are playing, or that have gone under here, and then we have some young fellows, boys that are well-to-do and well groomed and have good clothes. We use them quite a bit." People just came on the lot and asked for Reed, who then looked them over. "We have some days as many as a hundred applicants, other days, only ten maybe. Probably tomorrow we'll be swamped because news of this will have gotten out [meaning Kelly's story] and everybody will be flocking over here," exclaimed Reed.[2]

Kelly asked Reed if he thought it was a good thing for so many to be trying to get in as extras. He said he did, if they were of a certain kind. The kind Reed wanted were the really good-looking ones and the really good dressers. "We can use blondes or brunettes or almost any type and kind except that they must be good looking and well dressed. They furnish all their own clothes for ordinary scenes and they get from $3.50 to $5 a day." When Kelly asked Reed how he gauged the pay, the film executive explained to her that it depended on what they did. He did admit that some of the women extras would not work for less than $5 a day. "A lot of people can make a nice little thing of it, if they work two or three days a week," concluded Reed. "And I don't mind all the applicants, because you never know when you are going to find something especially good."[3]

Early in 1924 an article commented on the extra situation by writing that when any one of the big film studios in Hollywood sent out a call for extras "that particular studio at the appointed hour generally looks as if a swarm of locusts had descended upon it. From every point of the compass in the city, from every walk of life, of all types and ages they come, usually a motley but interesting army of hopefuls." The account added that it was a rare experience for a casting director to find a scarcity of extra people for his big mob scenes. "His task is usually the reverse — getting rid of the besieging clamoring surplus that responds to his call." One such famine had occurred recently in the New York studio of Fox during filming of *The Fool*, explained the reporter. Five hundred extras were needed for a big scene inside a fashionable Fifth Avenue church. Those extras needed had to be a certain type — they had to represent high society on a Sunday morning in church. They had to be gray-haired, dignified banker types, well-groomed, silver-haired dowagers with their lorgnettes, and a sprinkling of debutantes, sub-debutantes and "sleek morning coated young men with their inevitable gardenia boutonniere." When the call went out for those extras, with all the wardrobe specifications, few answered it. So the producers went around to half a dozen of the most fashionable colonies in and around New York and recruited likely candidates. After 10 days of hunting, 500 of the most "notable" extras were assembled.[4]

A brief news account in March 1925, datelined Sacramento, stated 50,000 jobless movie girl extras were searching for work in Hollywood then, many of them in destitute circumstances, according to Mrs. Amy Steinhart Braden, secretary of the California State Board of Charities and Corrections. That body had issued a warning to girls in other states not to migrate to the film colony in expectation of securing employment. Of course that figure of 50,000 female extras was grossly exaggerated.[5]

Six weeks later an account used that figure of 50,000 applicants for positions in Hollywood, saying they presented to the studios a great problem in the selection of competent, experienced extras, according to B. P. Fineman, a film studio manager in Hollywood. However, in this report the 50,000 referred to men and women extras and not just to females (but still remained an exaggeration). The problem, in Fineman's view, was that many of those people, unused to work before the camera, often spoiled expensive scenes that then had to be discarded. A plan had been evolved, he said, whereby the extra problem would be solved, at least for his studio (unnamed). Fineman had arranged to guarantee groups of experienced extras at least 12 days work a month. Few extras averaged more than six or seven days' work a month then, Fineman asserted. The great problem for the beginner, he remarked, was to get enough to pay bare living expenses.[6]

"Hollywood as it is" was the headline of an article produced by a reporter named Doris Blake that appeared in the *Washington Post* in October 1925. It was largely a warning to film hopefuls to stay away from Hollywood as there was too little work and too many people. Mostly the piece was directed toward actresses, as opposed to would-be extras. "The greatest lottery game in the world is this moving picture fame, if you would know the truth. The good fortune of the few lucky ones is given wide publicity," said Blake. "The unlucky ones, the countless numbers of them, you never hear about." Blake then discussed the subject with Fred Beetson, the West Coast representative of the Motion Picture Producers Association (the film cartel — the Hays office, as it was often called). Beetson declared it was "impossible" to succeed in Hollywood as there were only 12 big stars with the lesser satellites of good incomes fleshing the list out to a number that was still less than 100. "This gives an idea of the opportunities open to the thousands and thousands who are either here or plan to raid the community before the year is out." Continuing on, Beetson said there were then more hopefuls in Hollywood than could be handled. Adding to the problem, he pointed out, was the lack of industry in Los Angeles, with no telephone jobs, no stenographic jobs, and no mail order houses to turn to when the movie career failed. "The experience of looking for employment is as heartbreaking here as for a girl anywhere."[7]

When reporter Blake wondered why so many came to Hollywood, she answered herself by saying the lure of the stage had always existed and that brought some of them. Some came because they wanted adventure, some because they were conceited, and some may have been attractive enough seemingly to justify the attempt to break into films. "But the rattlebrains do not think of the hard work, nor those periods of financial and physical depression when there is no work." Blake declared the beauty contest winner had more chance than the complete unknown, in the opinion of Beetson, and that opinion was endorsed by several casting directors of large studios to whom the reporter had talked. "Some few years ago, before these contests became a feature of every town fete and county fair, an interest may have been evoked — enough for a hearing at least. But not any more," stated the reporter. Added Beetson, "My secretary on $50 a week has a better job than most of the girls working on the lots. Her hours are regular. She has two weeks' vacation with pay. Her expenses are less." Concluded Blake. "Without money to tide you over well for six months you are urgently requested to keep away from Hollywood. And a wardrobe! Without a wardrobe a girl is useless. Clothes are to her as tools to the workman." Then she told the story of a girl she knew who came out to Hollywood with little money. When it was almost exhausted a call came for her to take part in a mob scene. She was asked to bring evening dress and wrap. The pay for the day was to be $7.50. It cost the woman almost that much to rent the evening dress and coat. On the following day the extras were ordered to appear dressed in golfing apparel. Once again this unnamed woman had to rent the clothing, using up most of the day's earnings. "Then came a long pause when there was no work and no place to turn to for work," ended the story.[8]

Another 1925 article was a brief piece that boasted about the fact that many types of extras could be found easily in the film capital and that there was not a single type in all of the varied populace to be found in America that could not be produced at a few hours' notice by Hollywood casting directors. "They must be experienced before the camera, have their own wardrobe and know makeup secrets," ended the report, almost bragging about one of the benefits of a surplus.[9]

By 1926 most of America's film production by the main studios had migrated to Hollywood from its original base in the New York–New Jersey area. That year it was reported that there were an estimated 2,300 out of 3,500 people in New York identified as extras that did not belong. That estimate was said to have come from "experts" who for years had been in close touch with the hiring of extras for the films made in the eastern studios. Some blame for the surplus was laid, in this article, on film schools turning out "atmosphere" (a term used for "extra") graduates. Another problem was a director on location who recruited, say, 300 extras at the remote spot — of which 100, say, would go on to try and become regular extras. Casting agencies for extras still existed in the East.[10]

The first hard data, presumably more or less reliable, on the work situation of extras was released by Central Casting Bureau in October 1927. According to this report 11,000 people were registered with the bureau, 6,000 women and 5,000 men. Of the 6,000 females, only one averaged as much as five days' work a week for the previous six months. Two men averaged six days' work a week in the same period; two men averaged five days of work each week. Eight females averaged four days; 21 received three days of work each week; 20 men got four days' work, and 36 averaged three days' work. All of those people who drew three to six days of work per week (30 women and 60 men) drew from $8 to $10 for each day of work because they were known as "dress extras"— people maintaining very complete wardrobes that enabled them to dress suitably for any occasion. Those figures were the first of their kind ever released and showed that only a few of the extras were able to work three or more days a week and that the majority of extras who worked at all got nothing more than an average of one day a week. While hundreds depended on film work for a living, the majority had other means of support. According to this account the major film producers in Hollywood hoped to cut down the total of registered extras to a figure that would assure each one a living wage. No new registrations had been taken at Central Casting for months, reportedly, and new names would not be added to the lists until the total was reduced to less than half the current figure.[11]

Also in 1927, Fred Beetson issued another alert. It was a renewed warning to people throughout America who aspired to motion picture screen fame "via the extra route" not to come to Hollywood with the hope of joining the group at the foot of the film ladder. Beetson pointed out that the registration lists for extras at Central Casting were still closed because of the oversupply of candidates.[12]

That same year the union Actors Equity conducted an investigation as it tried to formulate a strategy to reduce the surplus in Hollywood

4. A Surplus of Extras

including, perhaps, trying to restrict foreign players. Equity's investigation revealed there were 120 film directors in the various studios in Hollywood who required, if all were actively engaged at the same time, a daily maximum of 1,200 players. Yet in the entire film colony there were said to be 4,000 principals (all players from stars to supporting to character, down to bit players—but not including extras). A normal average day for the previous 12 months, Equity discovered, had seen 60 directors working, calling for 600 principal players, leaving 3,400 principals, on average, idle at all times. That did not include the 11,000 extras "who are continuously idle."[13]

The Hollywood Studio Club was an organization maintained for the welfare of female studio workers, from actors, to extras, to clerical workers in the studios. It offered various welfare assistance including running a residence building where a small number of those females could be housed. At the start of 1928 the Club released a report stating the number of female film extras requiring charitable assistance in 1927 was almost negligible as compared with previous years, according to its own records. National publicity given Hollywood's unemployment problem and "propaganda" circulated by local civic organizations were said to have reduced to a minimum the number of penniless girls. Formerly they poured into Hollywood yearly expecting to find immediate employment. During 1927, the report continued, most of the migrating women seeking film fame arrived with sufficient funds to care for their needs until jobs were forthcoming. "Of those who came to the coast with movie aspirations, less than five percent succeeded in getting inside a studio. The other 95 percent, it is estimated, secured work in other fields or returned home."[14]

At a 1929 meeting of the Governor's Council in California, Will J. French, director of the California Department of Industrial Relations, spoke about the situation of film extras. French reported that out of 11,000 film extras registered in Los Angeles in 1928 an average of 756 worked each day for an average daily wage of $8.84. Only 133 men and 87 women worked more than two days a week. He concluded, "This stationary picture of unemployment gives reasons why would-be movie stars should consider all angles before embarking for Southern California."[15]

During the summer of 1933 an article appeared in *Variety* that stated that bums that came to New York were just that. But in Hollywood bums, along with show-struck clerks, waitresses, and so forth, immediately became extras. When they got hungry or got into trouble they described themselves as film extras, "And filmdom gets blamed." The reporter went on to applaud any and all moves in the film industry that would separate the wheat from the chaff "and make the title of 'extra' as tough to get as a policeman's badge." According to the reporter, if all the people calling themselves extras "roughly estimated at around 200,000" could get into studios, there would not be a day's work for each of them. For that matter, he added, according to official figuring, if only the "18,000" people then officially registered with Central Casting Bureau were to have all the extra work evenly divided among them each person would not draw pay for over 11.5 days per year. At that point, it was said that it was being suggested in various film quarters that the state of California or the city officials of Los Angeles be asked by the industry to enact some kind of a law that would have the effect of an immigration gate which could be opened or shut. However, the reporter admitted such an idea as a brake to immigration was not a serious idea but believed the industry's own machinery (Central Casting) needed to be adjusted. His idea of the future was that all persons entering Hollywood with the intent of pursuing a career as an extra make their desires known immediately to Central Casting. That Central, instead of asking about film experience, submit each applicant to a carefully selected talent-picking committee. Finally, if that committee decided the applicant demonstrated qualifications to become a performer as well as an extra, then he or she be officially awarded the title of "extra."[16]

One year later, in the summer of 1934, a warning was issued to a certain group of extras—babies. Well, the warning was delivered, of course, to the parents. Reportedly, among the people clamoring at the gates of Hollywood for movie jobs were thousands of parents. A Baby Leroy or a Shirley Temple came along, made a tremendous hit in films, and immediately fathers and mothers (but mostly moms) all over America imagined their offspring were needed in the studios. So huge had that army of fame and fortune seekers become that one company in Hollywood had issued a warning to parents everywhere to stay at home. "Doubtless you have a budding genius in your happy home, but don't bring him (or her) to Hollywood! The motion picture capital is already over-run with infant sensations," went the warning (from an unidentified source). In a single studio, it was said, there were on file close to 3,000 names of children available for film parts. When a child character was needed, the casting director started working on that list.[17]

Franklin Roosevelt's administration launched the National Recovery Administration (NRA) in 1933. It was designed to establish employment codes in all industries across America. Each industry would hold meetings and negotiations between employers and employees to set wages and working conditions for that industry—subject to government oversight and approval. The idea was, in the heart of the Depression, to spread work around as much as possible (by limiting the maximum hours of work, for example) and to establish floors below which wages could not fall. The film industry was just one industry involved in setting its own NRA Code. In the end none of it mattered after the U.S. Supreme Court struck down the idea as unconstitutional (the federal government not being empowered to impose specific wages on industries) in 1935.

However, hearings toward a motion picture code were held for a period of time. Late in August 1933 representatives of film extras and bit players appealed to film superstar Mary Pickford to take their side in Washington hearings on the film NRA Code. A telegram was sent to the actress in New York saying many of the extras and their families were on the verge of starvation and that the proposed code submitted by movie producers would "cut our wage scale sixty percent." Pickford responded to them by saying that business engagements in New York would prevent her from making a personal appearance at the hearing. She added, though, that she would seek to help the extra through telephone and telegraph messages to the National Recovery Administration.[18]

Hollywood's NRA Code was presented in Washington, D.C., by a committee of men from the MPAA and Dave Allen, head of Central Casting. According to one account it seemed to be a policy of the industry's code to keep wages down to the lowest level and to take advantage of the distress of unemployed players, even though the point of the NRA Code for industries was to set standards to try and keep wages up and to spread the available work around as broadly as possible. This news account in *Variety* pointed out that the pay of extras had been "radically cut" in the past few years and that those then getting between $7.50 and $15 a day had been sliced on average 20 percent. While two years earlier $2 and $1.50 per day extras were unheard of, such low salaries were found to exist in 1933. It was also found that during the past year many former well-known names in films had been reduced to working as extras for $3 a day and that the average pay per day for an extra in 1930 had been $9 but during 1932 that sum had been reduced to $7.48. Only 69 extras averaged as much as two days work a week in 1933; no one averaged three days of work per week or more. Charges of graft had been heard but none substantiated, "although there was plenty of evidence that favoritism and discrimination at Central Casting office was in existence, with relatives and close friends being given the breaks."[19]

New code rules requiring all extras to be picked from those registered at Central Casting were announced at the end of 1933 (although Central had been supposedly following that method from its inception). It was reported that requirement knocked out the relatives from getting pay checks but also a big group of part-time studio people who counted on the additional work as extras to help them out in the Depression. That part-time group of studio people included assistant directors, assistant cameramen, stenographers, scenario readers, drivers, carpenters and others who did not have steady work in their usual studio occupation. They induced friends in the studio to get them the jobs as extras to help eke out a week's salary. According to this account about 20,000 were then registered at the Central Casting Bureau, and Central refused to register new people except by "special request" from a studio casting director or a film director who claimed he wanted a certain player for an extra part. Studio officials were not even supposed to ask for specific players, unless for a good reason, with Central doing the specific selecting. That is, under Central rules, a film studio could send a request to Central for a male extra, under 30, Irish, but not a request for Sean Smith.[20]

Early in January 1934 a committee to conduct an investigation into the possibility of limiting the work time of extras under the motion picture code was appointed on January 12 by the National Recovery Administration. Definite outlines of matters to be examined were to be given to the investigators later that month by Divisional Administrator Rosenblatt when he arrived in Hollywood. Behind the plan was the idea to spread employment around for extras and to wipe out abuses of that class of players. The NRA designated 13 people to participate in drafting those regulations to supplement the code. Five of the 13 formed an executive committee to direct the work: Mabel E. Kinney, M. H. Hoffman, Ben B. Kahane, Charles Miller, and Larry Steers. The other eight members of the committee were Dr. A. H. Giannini, Fred Pelton, David Werner, Mrs. Una J. Hopkins, Pat Casey, Allen Garcia, Lee Phelps, and Fred Burns.[21]

One month later most of the extra community was likely made uneasy when a report surfaced that more than 15,000 of the registered extras soon might be erased from the ranks of registered hopefuls. An unofficial (and unnamed) spokesman for the NRA screen code subcommittee said a reclassification of the 17,500 extras, as provided for in the code, probably would begin in a week or so. This subcommittee composed, of extras and studio representatives, would, it was generally believed, reduce the registration on the Central books to just 2,000 names. That number of people could earn from $7.50 to $15 a day doing just extra work, and work every day, Sol Rosenblatt, NRA screen code administrator was told, when he was in Hollywood. "The casting bureau, which hires extras for all the major studios, attempts now to rotate the work which 2,000 persons could do among the 17,500. The result is that few receive enough from this source to live on," observed a reporter.[22]

Under NRA film code regulations made public in Hollywood on

March 18 by Charles Cunningham, NRA executive assistant for Southern California, film extras would receive from $5 to $25 per day. Extras speaking individual or "atmospheric" lines would earn the top rate of $25 a day. Women with elaborate, modern wardrobes of evening gowns, formal afternoon and street clothes, including fur wraps, and men with full dress "boulevard" clothes and riding habits, not overlooking silk hats and canes, were in the next highest class—$15 a day. In the $10 group were men and women of good physical qualifications with smart but not formal clothes, to include bathing suits and lounging pajamas. They could be professional dancers. The women playing character parts had to have wardrobes that enabled them to appear as spinsters, waitresses, hag beggars, or the like. Corresponding males in the category had to be able to appear as gangsters, detectives, waiters, butlers, and so forth. Next category down was the group at $7.50 per day wherein costumes were furnished but the individuals had to supply ordinary street clothes, sport clothing, and bathing suits. Lastly, at the bottom was the $5 a day group to be composed of men only, with no interviews required or any clothing qualifications.[23]

Another attempt was made by the NRA extra committee in early April 1934. This time the Code Standing Committee on Extras was reported to want to reduce the list of extras to 1,500 names. The plan arrived at by the committee was to get from Central Casting and from the studios the names of all extras then doing extra work in films. From that list 3,000 names would be chosen as prospective extras. Investigation would then be made of all 3,000 of those people, with the number reduced to 1,500 for reclassification as permanents. It had also been decided to allow for a 20 percent increase in the number of names on the list during the first year and a 5 percent increase the following year. Thus it was anticipated the list would start with 1,500 names in 1934, move to 1,800 in 1935, and then to 1,890 approved extras on the roster list in 1936.[24]

Still, the NRA struggled on. In June 1934 it was reported the NRA was then in the process of whittling down the list of film extras from an estimated 25,000 to what was an unannounced number but that unofficial estimates placed at somewhere between 3,000 and 10,000. Reportedly, the committee was working faster then and hoped to have the list completed by September 1. It was another try in a continuing process to reduce the extra list of 25,000 who struggled over the 500 to 600 extra jobs available per day and left almost no extras that could actually make a living from the work. While the process to select the names to remain on the list went unexplained, the committee, mindful of storms of protests over earlier attempts, took pains to emphasize the current elimination was "purely a mechanical process with no personalities entering into the question. That much is assured." This reregistration committee consisted of seven members, headed by Mrs. Mabel E. Kinney. In this process the committee called for lists of recommended extras from each of the major studio casting directors, from each independent casting group (such as Central) and from each association in the film business that had connection with extra placements. None of these solicited lists was allowed to have more than 3,000 names on it, listed alphabetically. While unexplained, it appeared an extra got points for each list his name appeared on, with total scores used to determine the master and final list.[25]

Around that same time it was revealed that 17,000 people were registered for extra work at Central Casting, 10,000 of them being females. In 1933 the average number of extras used per day was 805; 485 men, 287 women, and 33 children.[26]

The 13 proposed rules and regulations for extras working in Hollywood, as drawn up in the film capital by the NRA standing committee on extras, following numerous West Coast hearings, were passed by the Code Authority in September 1934 and sent on to Washington to Divisional Administrator Sol Rosenblatt for his approval. Rule 1: Location in Los Angeles territory meant employment outside a six-mile radius of 5th Street and Rossmore; 2. Within that radius was the "studio" zone; 3. Employers were not to provide transportation within the studio zone, except if dismissal from work was at a time when public transportation was not available. If more than 30 minutes was consumed after dismissal for checking of wardrobes, the added time had to be paid for; 4. When extras remained on location overnight they were to be paid for half of the time consumed in travel to and from the location; 5. Hazardous work called for added compensation; 6. If an extra's wardrobe was damaged during production the employer had to provide compensation; 7. Extras that were required to have wardrobe fittings were to be paid not less than a full day's wages if they were not given full employment in the picture for which they had a fitting; 8. In "weather-permitting" calls no wages were due if a notice was posted at the call hour. If extras were instructed to wait they were to be paid one-quarter of a day's full rate for each two hours they were kept waiting. If during the waiting period they were filmed then a full day's pay was due; 9. If a call was cancelled at the reporting time extras were to be paid one-quarter of the day rate; 10. Meal periods were to be not less than 30 minutes or more than 60 minutes. There was to be only one meal period in the first eight hours and had to be given within 5.5 hours of reporting; 11. Food and hot drinks were to be provided for all extras working after 11:30 PM; 12. In emergencies extras could be employed more than eight hours but the total within 24 hours was not to exceed 16 hours; 13. Employers to pay for one-half of the time actually consumed in traveling to and from locations.[27]

As Kinney led the seven-person panel in the task of cutting the list of names, it was emphasized all seven had been hired by the NRA and that they had no film industry connection whatsoever, and no axes to grind. If an extra's name appeared on eight lists that person got eight points; if the name appeared on only one list, the person got one point. Before the list was forwarded to Washington a meeting would be held of all concerned and challenges to the list would be permitted. Said Mrs. Kinney, "Extras will be re-registered because of merit alone. Personalities absolutely will not be involved in the issue; this is a business proposition and while many will undoubtedly feel discriminated against, I am sure that those who have worked at all as extras and have been satisfactory to their employers will find themselves re-registered." Kinney asserted that extras left off the list would have to go elsewhere than the studios to find work. She pointed out that since none of them could possibly have made a living as an extra under the old registration they must have been working elsewhere or had an income of some sort. "Films will require all types in the future just as they need them now. Pictures run somewhat in cycles, so naturally, all the various types will be in demand at one time or another," concluded Kinney. "But there is no consistent demand for 30,000. We hope, when the job is completed, to provide living wages for the full-fledged extras who are, after all, real necessities in the picture business."[28]

Late in September 1934 a report in *Variety* declared the list of extras had been reduced to about 8,000. Also, the NRA had derived a questionnaire to be sent to each one of those 8,000 extras. Apparently, the questionnaire had been designed to test and measure the moral fitness of those extras on the newly reduced list. Among the questions to be asked: Do you own your own home? Are you an American citizen? Are you married or divorced? Do you live with your husband or wife? State your husband's weekly income? What allowance do you receive? Are you related by marriage or otherwise to anyone employed by a picture company? Have you ever been arrested? If so, how many times? Have you ever been under the influence of intoxicating liquor or had such in your possession while working in a picture? What have your earnings from extra work averaged in the last three years? What other remarks, in your opinion, entitle you to extra work as a preference? A footnote to the questionnaire declared that the standing committee had the right to reject any application where the statements on it were proven false or made in an attempt to mislead the committee. A misspelling of the word "questionnaire" caused a delay of several days in the mailing of those sheets to the prospective extras, as the entire batch of 10,000 questionnaires had to be returned to the printer.[29]

A few days later a story in *Billboard*—the other bible of show business—declared the standing committee had boiled the list down to about 7,000, from 17,000, and would continue until the list was reduced to about 2,500. Also, this report said all the 17,000 were mailed the questionnaire, containing 29 questions, as part of the process. Each person filling out the form was required to sign it twice, once at the bottom attesting to the truth of the answers, and once at the top agreeing that the answering of the questionnaire "does not guarantee that I shall be employed as a motion picture extra." Questions listed here, but not in the above paragraph, included: For what reason? [if arrested] Have you any source of income other than from extra work? How many dependents? Do you own your own home or rent? Have you had parts with screen credits? How long in pictures? What type of work are you best qualified for? And what other points do you consider in your favor for consideration for extra work?[30]

Early in November 1934 it was reported that assistant casting directors and other studio employees who had found their immediate dependents and friends struck off the extra lists through a "non-favoritism" clause in the NRA industry code were leading a campaign to have that clause removed through revision of the code. Those people, after several weeks of discussion, had presented a petition carrying about 35 signatures, asking that the Code Authority revise the particular clause to allow wives and other immediate relatives of studio workers' families to act as extras in studios other than the one in which the family member is employed. Many of those behind the petition claimed lower salaried assistants and clerks in the various casting offices had married girls who were working as extras, and the combination of the two incomes allowed the couple to get by. The code clause, they argued, prevented the women from doing any extra work and was putting undue hardship on a number of competent atmosphere players. However, the journalist who wrote the piece said it was known that many assistant casting directors drawing good salaries were annoyed at the NRA code provision that prevented their wives from getting extra calls and hoped that by appealing to the NRA with a sham financial hardship argument they might get the non-favoritism clause removed. It read, "No one shall be employed as an extra player or atmosphere worker who is a dependent member of the immediate family of any regular employee of a motion picture company, or any person who is not obliged to depend upon extra work as a means of livelihood, unless the exigencies of production, reasonably construed, require an exception to be made." That section of the code was included to prevent nepotism and padding of the extra list by studio officials and other employees of the studios.[31]

In a break from her work on paring down the extra list, Mabel Kinney, as chair of the NRA standing committee on extras, laid down a warning to casting offices in November 1934 when she warned that stiff fines and possibly jail sentences would be meted out to studio executives that cheated extras. Kinney was said to know most of the "tricks" that were played on the atmosphere players, and she told the executives personally they would have to obey the letter and the spirit of the code. She gave the following as an example of cheating: An extra is called to a set at the usual rate of $7.50 a day. Later he is given a speaking line and offered an additional $7.50. The worker was entitled to $25 a day as specified in the NRA code. That example was said to be one of the "more prevalent evils" that had to stop, or the executive responsible would be punished. There were said to be other "off color practices" used on extras, but no details were given.[32]

Resentment against the secrecy that had surrounded extra reregistration proceedings under the NRA film code, on the order of Sol Rosenblatt, flared out into the open at a Screen Actors Guild (SAG) meeting on February 28, 1935. Members of SAG dispatched a telegram to their president Eddie Cantor, a member of the Code Authority, branding extra reregistration as "star chamber action" and asking that he get the Code Authority to hold up the process. SAG wanted to scrap the existing process and, instead, have public hearings in Hollywood. The union had over 1,600 members in Class B (extras and bit players), while only 1,004 of those names were on the list okayed by the Code Authority and then pending before Rosenblatt for the final approval. At that point the local Code Authority was ready to put the list into effect and planned to pass out Code "work cards" to accredited extras the minute Rosenblatt okayed the final list and sent it back to Hollywood from Washington. Despite the secrecy with which the Code Extra Committee's work had been done, details of the scoring system used to qualify extras for the coveted work cards had begun to leak out, drawing bitter criticism of the system and charges of favoritism.[33]

Writing in the *Los Angeles Times* a week later, journalist John Scott stated that Hollywood sighed with relief when the NRA took over the problem of cutting down the list of film extras, but that sigh was apparently going to be short-lived because the NRA had failed to take action and could throw the whole matter back into the industry's lap. From unnamed NRA sources Scott had learned it was doubtful the government would carry out its intention of dramatically reducing the extra list. Much publicity had surrounded the NRA's aim to decide who should and should not be an extra, and the final list had been sent east to Washington for final approval some time ago. And there it stayed. An unusual situation had resulted from the delay since there was a law penalizing studios for using any except the NRA-approved group of extras with NRA work cards, but no such approved and authorized list was then available. According to Campbell MacCulloch, Central head, the bureau was continuing to work along as it always had in the past. Major Donovan, in charge of the NRA Hollywood office had adopted a "watchful waiting position" in the matter. His work would begin when, and if, the reduced list arrived from Washington.[34]

SAG, it was revealed in April 1935, had strengthened its report of conditions filed with the Code Authority Administrator, Sol A. Rosenblatt, the previous April, with a new and stronger protest over the current treatment of the extra players. Officers from SAG met with the registration subcommittee of the Extra Standing Committee of NRA and went over its list of complaints. Meanwhile, the Hollywood Picture Players' Association, the Picture Players' Alliance, and the Troupers, Inc., organizations representing extra and bit players, forwarded to Rosenblatt a protest stating that the action of the Extra Standing Committee in selecting only 1,004 extras from the list of several thousand was a direct violation of the National Recovery Act. That is, it would not spread work out reasonably. Those three groups also argued the manner in which the names had been chosen by the Extra Standing Committee was grossly unfair, for no statement had been made by that committee as to how it used whatever information it had extracted in order to generate its list. That is, no objective standards as to how the names were selected had ever been made public and available, so the groups argued. SAG was opposed to putting the present list of extras, as compiled, into effect and in its statement to Rosenblatt denounced the setup as unfair. Furthermore it was intimated that the Guild might resort to court procedures if necessary to see that the matter of qualifying extras be carried out in open hearings.[35]

Less than three weeks after the above described plan to reduce the number of extras it was declared in a news account that it had been "virtually abandoned." A storm of protest arose over the idea, leading the Hollywood Players' Association to send attorney Eugene Marcus to Washington to oppose the proposal. With respect to that list Mabel Kinney, chair of the committee compiling the list, said, "We have recalled the proposal for further consideration. We are awaiting further word from the national administrator [Rosenblatt] as to what we should do now." The committee had sent to Rosenblatt a list of about 1,000 names of extras with the intention of expanding the list by 50 percent a little later. While

Rosenblatt had declined to comment publicly he was reported to have given a "distinct understanding" he would not under any circumstances approve a report that placed any rigid limitation on the number of extras who could be employed. Apparently, that Rosenblatt objection had led to the shelving of the proposal.[36]

The *Los Angeles Times* ran an editorial on "the extra problem" on April 25, 1935. It started off by stating, "Seventeen thousand separate howls of protest from the film extras of Hollywood have drowned the timid suggestion of the industry's code committee that for the extras own sake, the list of registered eligibles be cut from 17,000 to 1,000 or at most 1,500." Abstractly, the editor thought those extras had a justified complaint because if there was any unassailable principle in America it was that everyone was entitled to get ahead in the line he or she chose to follow. Actually, he said, the situation was much as if 17,000 people were trying simultaneously to crowd into a theater seating only 1,000. Theoretically, every one with the price of admission had equal rights with all the others. However, "Practically, the chance of the majority to get trampled to death in the scramble is so large as to justify police interference."[37]

The studios, the editor continued, then paid an average of slightly more than $1.7 million a year for extra talent, meaning that if it were evenly divided among the 17,000 registered extras each would get a little less than $2 a week. What actually happened was worse. Less than 1,000 of the best qualified on the extra list received more than half of the total paid; the rest was more or less unevenly divided among the other 16,000 or so. Assuming $500 a year to be the minimum on which a person could exist in Hollywood, exactly 735 extras earned a living wage at it the previous year, or about one in every 23. The rest of them squeezed out some sort of an existence at other odd jobs or on the dole. Few of them, it appeared, held regular jobs for any length of time since, according to Central Casting, the great majority would instantly quit any other kind of work to answer a call for extras in film production. Apart from the drain on relief funds, the editor added, the situation presented a social problem of serious dimensions. Many of the extras for whom there was little or no work were inexperienced young girls drawn from all parts of the world by the hope of capitalizing on their good looks to get into films. And "various agencies are doing yeoman work in caring for these babes in the woods but the task is an impossibly large one." He acknowledged that if the extra list were cut to 1,500 half of them could get along, "but where is the Solomon to pick out the 1,500 and banish the other 15,500 from the sacred lots."[38]

Fewer than 120 of the 12,146 extras registered with Central Casting

Bureau earned as much as $29 a week in 1934. In September 1935 Central Casting sent a letter to each of its registered extras containing that statement as a warning. Said a news story, "A year ago Central embarked upon a campaign to try to turn the hopes of the extras from picture work to some surer, though less romantic means of livelihood. For the most part the attempt was abortive." Besides those 12,146 registered extras, said the reporter, there were 11,500 bit players who, if they could not get work in minor parts in support of the 318 stars and featured players under contract to the major studios, would accept extra work; in addition to those 23,916 people there were "uncounted thousands" who were listed at Central for mob, atmosphere and racial work. "Probably 35,000 men and women sit in their homes waiting for the telephone to ring, waiting for the magic call of romance and glamour," said the reporter. During 1934 one male of all the extras earned as much as $2,800. He had invested about $2,000 in a wardrobe and spent an additional $700 during the year for replacement and upkeep. In 1934 four extras earned $2,400 each; 115 earned $1,500; 363 earned $900; and 1,100 earned $400. Thus, the figures from Central showed that out of the 12,416, only 1,583 had earnings exceeding $40 a month. Despite the fact that Central Casting had closed its registration books some nine months earlier people still came; 25 to 75 people showed up every day at the Central office in the vain hope of getting listed. When Campbell MacCulloch took charge of Central he harbored a dream, it was reported, that he could divert many of the extras to other vocations. But, of all the thousands registered, he managed to place only 350 in other occupations. "Most of them were back at Central Casting in a few weeks." Each day Central received telephone calls from registered extras to see if any work was available for them. In discussing the surplus of extras situation with a reporter, MacCulloch remarked that if all extra casting could be confined to 1,000 people their average earnings would be $1,350 a year, a little less than $26 a week. "As it is, there are more than 20,000 surplus persons in Hollywood whom the studios probably will never be able to absorb. They must find other employment, although 90 percent are incapable of doing other work, or they will become public charges," concluded MacCulloch. "Unless they have had screen credit they are ineligible for help from the Motion Picture Relief Fund. Fully half of the registrations at Central are from people who have passed their meridian. Their future is deplorable."[39]

On the last day of 1935, Edward Nolan, California State Labor Commissioner, released a report prepared for him by Dr. Louis Bloch, principal statistician of the California state division of labor statistics and law enforcement. It stated there were too many film extras in Hollywood and as a result "very few of them are able to derive a livelihood from their work." Bloch's report was based on a study of the work done by Central Casting since its formation some 10 years earlier. He said the organization had accomplished all the objectives for which it was established, except the "decasualization" of the work. Recommended by the report was that Central should substantially reduce the number of extras registered and thereby regularize the work of the men and women depending upon that occupation for their living.[40]

In the spring of 1936 Central launched another of its stay-out-of-Hollywood campaigns, with respect to extra work. Campbell MacCulloch made it clear to reporters that joining the ranks of the extras was pretty much hopeless, as getting registered was impossible, and even if one was in the extra ranks any advancement upward from there was more than hopeless. Admitting each studio selected from 15 to 20 new feature players each year, MacCulloch stated that practically every one of them was "discovered" in New York or some other city distant from Los Angeles. The head of Central went on to give grim statistics as to the low wages received by extras. In conclusion a gloomy reporter said, "As for earning their living out of an extra's pay envelope, well, MacCulloch says most of them don't."[41]

This campaign was still on the go as the summer of 1936 ended. Women's clubs and parent-teacher associations, among other organizations, in the East and Midwest of America were sponsoring radio programs featuring transcribed talks by MacCulloch. He had made several radio disks through which he described the working conditions of extras and how difficult it was to earn a living from that occupation. Seven radio stations were then using these recorded talks and other stations were being sought.[42]

Early in 1937 a news account appeared that announced the chances of a movie extra winning fame as a star was one in 100,000. That was because only 13 lucky extras had succeeded out of 1.3 million who had registered with Central (the 1.3 million figure was unexplained). Despite such poor odds, the reporter declared, "Yet daily the casting office is besieged by between 35,000 and 50,000 extras." One thing that fueled such activity was the successful film *A Star Is Born*, about the rise of an extra to stardom. According to this piece the 13 lucky ones were Janet Gaynor, Clark Gable, Jean Harlow, Frances Dee, Carole Lombard, Ann Dvorak, Randolph Scott, Sally Eilers, Edwin Booth, Raquel Torres, Adrienne Ames, Karen Morley, and Gary Cooper. Reportedly, Jean Harlow was the only one of those 13 to rise from the ranks of extra to star since the advent of the talkies in 1928. With respect to the hordes that, nevertheless, still besieged Hollywood in search of work as extras, Ethel Callis of Central Casting remarked,

"They can't realize the extra ranks are now the end of the trail, not the beginning. In the old days more extras were used and fewer registered. The situation is now reversed."[43]

Hollywood's gossip column heavyweight Hedda Hopper added her opinion on the extra situation with an article under her byline that appeared in newspapers on July 31, 1938. It was her report of a chat she had with her old friend Campbell MacCulloch (although she managed to misspell her old friend's last name as "McCullogh"). He observed that the influx of people from all over America after *A Star is Born* was released was tremendous. "Even though they're perennially warned — and were in that picture — not to come here, each individual is certain he or she will be the one out of thousands chosen," said Hopper. "Public hasn't yet digested the fact that the Cinderella girl of today doesn't come up through the extra ranks," she continued. "Yes, she did in the old days. That was before pictures talked. Norma Shearer, Janet Gaynor, Clark Gable, Charlie Farrell were all extras. I could go on until your eyes got tired reading names. But that day has gone forever." Hedda argued that at the time she was writing stars that emerged did so from small parts, but not the extra ranks. Those small parts may have had only a line or two but the parts were not simply "atmosphere." Hopper said that out of the 16,000 extras fewer than 1,800 exceeded an annual income of $500 from film work. Ninety got $2,000 a year and about 600 made $1,000 a year. Only three made $3,200 a year. Of those in the top financial bracket of the extras, she wrote, "Those are world-famous models who dress better — in some instances — than the stars. In fact their wardrobes are insured for $5,000. And at least $1,000 goes into replacement of wardrobe" each year. Some male dress extras, she added, made as much as $1,600 a year, but that was top money. Hedda's message was for people to stay out of Hollywood because one could not make it in the film capital as an extra.[44]

Another piece was published in the press in June 1940 that warned readers to stay away. The prospects were bleak, said the account. "Take it from the men and women who are extras — that's not the way to crash the movies. That's the way to starve, they say. That's the way to see uncertainty and poor food and irregular hours, destroy looks and weaken self confidence." Central Casting head Howard Philbrick declared, "We don't want any more extras. We already have 7,000 and that's far too many. Our aim is to whittle that group down, not to admit extras."[45]

Two years later *New York Times* reporter Thomas Brady wrote, "The motion picture extra players, who constitute Hollywood's worst sociological problem, growled more than usual this week before an incident that underlined their growing difficulty in earning a living." Paul Cook, an extra, made a stump speech on the set of Samuel Goldwyn's *Pride of the Yankees* because some of his union friends could not get work, while SAG had granted Goldwyn waivers to employ nonunion extras to fill up the grandstands in his baseball picture. Eventually Cook was evicted from the set, and news of the fracas "stimulated the chronic unrest of the extras all over town until some of their casual gatherings outside casting offices were described as 'protest meetings.'" Brady said the reason Cook's friends were not employed was that they were women while the shortage that necessitated waivers existed among male players, according to Central Casting. The complaints were loud enough that SAG directors met to discuss the possibility of the union abandoning all jurisdiction over the $5.50 a day extra calls— the lowest rate of pay then and used only, more or less, for extras that were part of large mob scenes such as a sports crowd. Brady said there were 6,000 extras in SAG, while the film industry could provide a decent livelihood for only 2,500. Two years earlier a SAG committee that surveyed the problem recommended that at least 2,000 extras be dropped from the Guild but SAG had never acted on the proposal because no formula could be found for selecting the 2,000 to be eliminated. Although the labor market was glutted, only 350 men and a few more women out of the 6,000 would work for the minimum pay of $5.50 a day.[46]

5

Unions

While the struggle to unionize was long and difficult for all actors, stage and film, it proved to be even more difficult for film extras. When motion picture actors finally unionized under the Screen Actors Guild (SAG) the extras found new problems to deal with. Finally, the extras broke away from SAG to form a union of their own, the Screen Extras Guild (SEG). However, that also would be found wanting and eventually the film extras returned to SAG.

Back in 1913, in New York City, it was reported that an attempt to organize actors into a union failed in July of that year, after several months of effort. Organizing had been conducted covertly, and the plan had to be abandoned when it became apparent that a blacklist would be applied against any actor attempting to unionize. Word got around that film producers were then aware of the covert plan, probably from a studio spy in the ranks of the players. A similar plan to organize had been attempted one year earlier but had also aborted after a few months. That fledgling group that failed in July 1913 had hoped to form a union as solid and effective as the stagehands' union and to seek affiliation with the International Alliance of Stage Employees. One of the goals of that proposed union was to help extras. They wanted directors and studios to systematize their work so that movie extras would not needlessly spend their small financial resources on bus fare to studios on the "frontiers" without final assurance of a day's employment. "The small pay for the extra work per day often makes it imperative that some of the movie fillers-in walk to and from the markets for their wares," wrote a reporter in *Variety*. "For many this means rising at dawn to arrive at the studio in time for selection."[1]

In New York City, in February 1916, fed up with the impositions placed on them by agents, a mass meeting of extras was held on a Monday night that month, and plans were proposed for the formation of an organization for mutual protection and to affiliate with the American Federation of

Labor. This was all brought about, reportedly, through the actions of several agents who had been receiving orders from the producers for extra people and instead of taking a nominal fee for their services, had been paying the atmosphere players only about 40 percent of the money received from the producers. Then again, these agencies would advertise in the daily papers for extras and, after tentatively engaging them, would keep them calling at their offices for three to four days prior to telling them of the picture location, or that the work call order had been cancelled by the producing company. A flagrant example of such behavior was to be seen, said a *Variety* report, in an advertisement inserted by William A. Sheer, an extra agent, in one of the morning newspapers about five weeks earlier for experienced horsemen to be used in a film production. More than 500 men called at the Sheer office and left their names and were tentatively engaged at a salary of $1.75 a day to begin work on a film to be shot at Whitestone, Long Island. They were told to call at the office a few days later and at that time were told to call again the next day. They were then told no word had been received about the start of shooting but if they called again in a few days they would positively be put to work. However, that stalling kept up according to several extras, for about 10 days, at which point Sheer's brother George told them they would receive a postal card when needed. Many of those extras said they were compelled to forego looking for other positions and were also put to the expense of spending car fare to get to the Sheer office.[2]

Another example of poor treatment of the extras also came from the Sheer office. About three weeks earlier Sheer dispatched one of his aides to Tenth Avenue in New York City to get a number of men of the "yegg type" for a film. These men, numbering about 20, were taken to Sheer's office and then sent to the studio. There were only six of them who were accepted, and the rest insisted that Sheer either put them to work or pay them for their time. He refused to do either, and as a result they threatened to "clean up" his place. But one of Sheer's aides called the police and had the men arrested for disorderly conduct. They were all fined (an undisclosed amount) in the Magistrate's Court the next day. When a *Variety* reporter called at Sheer's office to ask about the extras for the film at Whitestone, William said, "I know why *Variety* is doing this; it's because they sent a bill collector around here a dozen times to collect. They are sore and want to get even." The reporter said he was not interested in the business side of his paper and if Sheer would make a statement about the conflict with the extras, *Variety* would print it. Sheer then said he had been asked by the director of the studio to get 500 men and hold them in readiness for a film that would start "most any day." He said he only took their names and addresses and did not ask them to call until they were notified of the location. He admitted, however, that a great many of those people came into his office every day to ascertain when they would be wanted, and did complain about the stalling. When an official of the studio producing the Whitestone film was seen, he said work on the interior scenes of the film had commenced just four weeks earlier and that exterior work had only started the previous Monday. He said he did not know whether his director had ordered Sheer to engage the people so far in advance and could not make any definite comment on that point.[3]

It was cases such as the ones cited above, remarked the *Variety* journalist, that had spurred the extras to try and organize. They proposed to have a membership assessment of $5 a year and maintain offices from where extras would be supplied, as the proposed organization planned to do business with the producers directly. Their proposed scale of wages was to be $3 per day per person in films using 100 extras or less, $2 a person for motion pictures using over 100 atmosphere players, $5 a day for full dress and fancy dress extras, $7.50 a day for "hazardous" extra work, and time and a half for night work, defined as beginning at 6:00 PM or later. As well, this proposed organization declared that no commission would be deducted from the extras' wages for work obtained through its own office. Reportedly, several producers had been approached on the subject and indicated their willingness to employ their extras directly from the proposed group instead of from the agencies. Lewis J. Selznick was one of the first approached and stated he was heartily in accord with the movement and that he would not only employ all of the atmosphere players he needed from the new association but that any concerns he was associated with would also cooperate with him in that respect. Selznick said he was sending out a letter to all film producers in New York City urging them to cooperate with him in the movement to pay the extras what they were worth and to "exterminate" the agencies from the business.[4]

Agitation by the extras against the treatment they received at the hands of agencies or contractors continued through 1916. In September of that year it was revealed that Hugh Frayne, general organizer of the American Federation of Labor (AFL), and Harry Mountford, an executive with the White Rats (a union of vaudeville performers), had held several conferences with leaders of the extras and arranged for the granting of a charter to an organization that was tentatively formed and would be known as the Motion Picture Extra People's Association of Greater New York, Local 30, White Rats Actors Union of America. The following were elected temporary officers: J. Stern, president; Jack Snyder, vice president; Fred Von Strange, secretary; Allen Law, treasurer. Those people would hold office until a mass meeting could be held at which the permanent officers would be elected. As word of this development spread it was reported the offices of the agents and contractors were "greatly perturbed" over the steps the extras planned to take. Word was conveyed to those extras from those offices "that any of them that joined the organization need expect no work through the offices." A representative of William A. Sheer was in front of the Leavitt building (where extras congregated) all week telling the extras there was no possibility of an organization and that they should keep away from the union agitators or they would be blacklisted.[5]

Just a few days earlier a woman had stationed herself around 46th Street in Manhattan, engaging extras to play Indian characters in a Fox motion picture to be shot at Fort Lee, New Jersey. She did this without any authorization or sanction from the Fox company, and as a result she had more than 100 people at the 130th Street ferry one morning. Word was conveyed to the Fox office and a representative was sent out who, after explaining to the assembled extras that no commission had been given the woman to hire them, reimbursed them for their car fares. As the woman engaged the players she told them she would pay $2.50 a day, and when they completed work on that picture she would take them to the coast for six months and pay them $4 a day and expenses. The Fox studio was one of the few producers that hired its people directly instead of through contractors and consequently was very much upset when it learned of this woman's behavior. It was also said that a man named Parker, who was described as an extra captain for a contractor, assisted the woman in her work. Attempts had been made by the extras to determine the legal status of the agents and contractors. One of the things they had done was to call on New York City Commissioner of Licenses George H. Bell. He informed the players there was no provision for those agency and contractor people in the city charter as far as his department was concerned, and therefore he was powerless to assist the extra army.[6]

In this account the majority of the film studios were said to be in accord with the movement to do away with the middleman agents. William A. Brady (of the World Film Corp.), J. S. Blackton (Vitagraph), Lewis J. Selznick, W. L. Sherrill, and Frohman Film Corporation informed Stern (representing the extras) that they would be glad to employ the extras directly, as they were paying a good price for all the atmosphere players and believed that it would do away with a great evil in the industry. It was also reported that individual directors at the studios were powerless to hire extras directly; though they might have been willing to accept them they would have to obtain their employment from the agencies. Just such an incident happened a week earlier when word was conveyed from the

Rolfe studio that 20 men were wanted for the retake of a scene. The men applied to the director and he informed them they could work for him, provided that they accepted the employment through Ben Weiss, an agent, who was providing all the extras for Rolfe productions. When interviewed by a *Variety* reporter, B. A. Rolfe, president of Rolfe Picture Corporation, stated that all the extras under the $5 a day scale were hired through Weiss, because Rolfe found getting the players in that way saved the studio a great deal of trouble and at the same time they were able to get better character types through the agency than if they hired directly. As to the fee that Weiss was said to have exacted from the people, Rolfe said he understood the agent was getting 50 cents on each $2.50 a day extra, and believed Weiss was entitled to that amount.[7]

Just two months later it was reported the affairs of the newly formed Motion Picture Extras' Association, affiliated with the White Rats and known as Local 30 of that organization, were in a muddled condition owing to several rival factions arising within the organization. The weekly meetings held by the extras on Sunday nights at the White Rats' clubhouse "on most occasions end in riots with the last [meeting] barely escaping termination in a gun fight," said *Variety*. Main trouble in the group was said to center around Isador Stern, its financial secretary and organizer. Stern had been charged by Joseph Scott (president of the local) with being incompetent to manage the affairs of the local owing to his being a minor. Stern was due to turn 19 about a week or so after the meeting in question. Acting under the advice of Harry Mountford, leader of the White Rats, Stern sent in his resignation as organizer but his withdrawal was not voted upon for several weeks, and when finally brought up he was deposed but still retained his position as local secretary. Then, on a Sunday night when Stern followers were in the minority another vote was quickly taken and Stern lost his position as secretary. That meeting broke up in "a riot" with Stern sympathizers swearing vengeance. However, Stern retained the backing of the White Rats, although the local was then on the point of breaking up.

Mainly, that union had been formed to clean up the business of supplying film extras that had gotten into the hands of agents who were alleged to be securing exorbitant commissions for supplying atmosphere players to the studios. It was also intended to make the organization an educational one, and to teach its members new skills, such as dancing for the females and camera operation for the men. "The trouble which has been going on since the start of the organization is laid largely to the agents who, it is believed, are trying to break it up," said a journalist. "Members of the organization who are forced out are offered positions with agents to secure people for them, and have been making it a custom to work among the members of the union in order to cause internal disorder in that body."[8]

Nothing more was heard about efforts by film extras to organize for a full decade. A report published in September 1926 remarked that movie extras in the East might become unionized. At least that was the trend of thought among their ranks since several production companies had reduced the generally accepted $7.50 daily scale down to $3. However, the account admitted there was no definite plan for unionization at that time but only a popular agitation due to the sharp pay decrease. Reportedly, the studios were standing firm and refused to budge on the wage issue.[9]

A few years later, in the summer of 1929, Actors Equity was making one of its attempts (all unsuccessful) to organize film actors into a union. For the most part there was no overlap in show business unions. The White Rats organized vaudeville players, but not stage or film people. Actors Equity organized legitimate stage people but not vaudeville or film players. Some individuals belonged to more than one union, either separately or simultaneously but that was usually because they worked in more than one area. Film actors would ultimately organize themselves from within through a new group — Screen Actors Guild — which did not organize vaudeville or legitimate stage players. During this attempt by Equity, Frank Gillmore, president of the union, was in Los Angeles for a time and while there said film extras were not, at that time, being invited to join Equity and no effort was being made to organize them. At that time, explained Gillmore, Equity did not have enough to offer the extra player to warrant his spending the money necessary to become a member and pay the dues. According to Dave Allen, head of Central Casting, insofar as working hours were concerned the extras had long had extra pay for overtime "on an even more liberal basis than that which Equity is demanding in its contract."[10]

One week later, as part of its unsuccessful organizing drive, Equity held a mass meeting in Los Angeles, presided over by Frank Gillmore. At that affair he read out a letter from a female extra complaining of unsanitary conditions at the James Cruze studio and saying females were worked 16 hours a day on the sets of *The Great Garbo* and *The Broadway Melody*. Sometimes those extras were compelled to even work 20 hours at a stretch. Later in the meeting William Dyer, whom Gillmore introduced as a representative of extras, denounced the Central Casting Bureau, saying conditions there had to be corrected as the bureau was not being fair with extras. While Dyer reportedly told the meeting of various methods that he considered unfair, no details were printed.[11]

Joseph M. Casey, American Federation of Labor organizer working out of San Francisco, spent several weeks in Hollywood during August 1933, again attempting to organize the extras and bit players under the AFL banner and using the NRA code as a selling point. According to this article, this attempt marked the third time that efforts had been made to unionize the extras. He met in conference with Charles Miller of Equity and proposed a plan whereby the extras would come in under the Equity banner instead of organizing a separate union. At that time the "extra problem" was being investigated by the Academy of Motion Picture Arts and Sciences special extras' committee, which was probing alleged favoritism on the part of Central Casting toward certain extras to the detriment of the average atmosphere player. Today the Academy is best known as the sponsor of Hollywood's Oscar awards. However, when it was first formed, its main function was to be a company union and, the film cartel hoped, a way to forestall actors from organizing a real trade union. Such efforts failed and the Screen Actors Guild was officially formed in 1933.[12]

On October 26, 1933, class distinctions among actors were forgotten—at least in theory—when SAG announced that extra and bit players would be taken into the organization in its fight against "salary control" features of the proposed NRA motion picture industrial code. "For the first time in motion picture history," said Ken Thomson, SAG secretary, "there are no class distinctions and no castes among the players. The star and the extra will work together to solve their mutual problems."[13]

Despite such pronouncements the Guild had, apparently, worries about treating the extras as equals. As of March 1934, it was reported actors above the atmosphere and bit ranks were in SAG proper, while the extras were in their own "special" part of the organization called the Junior Screen Actors Guild.[14]

Later in 1934, in October, the Screen Actors Guild membership consisted of 400 or so in "Class A" (everybody above small part players, extras, and bit players); "Class B" (about 200 small part players); and the Junior Screen Actors Guild, consisting of 1,750 or so extras and bit players. In matters of SAG policy and elections only Class A members had a vote, with a motion being carried on a 60 percent or higher approval vote. Thus, 240 SAG members could effectively speak for, and impose conditions and set policy for, a union that had some 2,350 members.[15]

Some extras apparently were not happy with their position in SAG, for it was announced in March 1935 that a new organization for extra players was in the process of formation, featuring an antistrike policy and with an announced aim of protecting the professional extras from incursions made by nonprofessionals. Patterned after the American Society of Cinematographers in setup, it planned to have a group insurance plan. Membership was to be open only to "recognized" extras that got on the NRA preferred list, if and when that document was finalized and produced. It never was. The nucleus of the new group was a faction that was an offshoot of the Hollywood Picture Players Association. J. Buckley Russell (a member of the NRA's Extras Standing Committee) was president of this fledgling group — which was not heard from again.[16]

Initially, when SAG was formally recognized as the bargaining agent for film players, recognition did not extend outside of the Hollywood-area studios. Then it was announced that extras and bit players in the few active studios left in the East would receive the full Hollywood wage scale and all benefits guaranteed under the SAG contract with producers, effective August 1, 1937, stated Kenneth Thomson, secretary of SAG. Although SAG provisions automatically applied to any leading screen player who took part in a New York production, the announced extension would mainly benefit the extras, members of the Junior Guild (who paid $5 a year for dues). Some of the daily guarantees extended to the East included $25 a day minimum for speaking lines, $16.50 for dress extras, and $5.50 a day for the "crowd" extras. Principal studios then active in the New York area were Warner Brothers, Vitaphone, Paramount, and Fox Movietone.[17]

A revision of the "weather-permitting" clause in the employment of film extras, allowing the player one-quarter of the day's pay if calls were cancelled because of the weather, took effect in August 1937 as the result of conferences between SAG and the film cartel — the MPAA. Approximately 7,500 extras were affected by that change. Extras signed up for "weather-permitting" calls were obligated to refuse other assignments, and in the past had received no pay if rain, fog or other unsuitable weather cancelled shooting plans. Often they had to travel long distances to a studio and then to the location and even kept waiting for an hour or more to see if the weather would cooperate. Not only did they receive no pay at all, in early times they were not even reimbursed for their car fare.[18]

SAG continued to fight to improve the conditions of extras, at least to some extent. What was expected to amount to a new registration of thousands of extras listed at Central Casting was a resumption of the interview department, to be limited to members of SAG in good standing. Simultaneously, Central would establish a special department for racial groups, headed by a man experienced in the business and knowing problems of racial players. In addition to the interviews, extras would be permitted to write Central on any matters pertaining to film work, with letters considered on merit and each to be answered personally. That deal, negotiated with Central by a SAG committee headed by Aubrey Blair, was expected to give extras who received most of their work calls in the lower wage brackets an opportunity to qualify for more desirable calls, if they were specially qualified. SAG was said to have pursued this plan with the idea of giving extras the opportunity to renew personal contacts at Central, which had been lost when interviews were discontinued earlier and Central's registration books closed.[19]

Bitter complaints from extras that most of the calls emanating from the studios were only for the lowest pay scale of $5.50 surfaced late in 1937 and caused the Junior SAG to appoint a special committee to investigate this newly arisen situation. The Guild made that move when producers placed calls at that low rate, then attempted to dictate what costumes the players should wear. When the producers agreed to abolish the $3.20 pay level under their agreement with the union a few years earlier, it was stated that a $5.50 check would replace it, applying only for persons recruited for mob scenes. A check for "regular" extras was increased at the same time from $7.50 to $8.25 and $11.50 (each having wardrobe requirements) with a $5.50 check (no wardrobe requirements, come-as-you-are or studio-supplied apparel).[20]

A couple of weeks later SAG was preparing to draft demands for improved working conditions for extras. It was mulling the idea of asking producers to abolish the current $5.50 check for extras, moving that minimum to $8.25. Many of those players were still complaining that since the $3.20 check had been abolished the producers had been placing most of their calls at the $5.50 a day level.[21]

At the end of 1937 SAG declared it would make a formal demand to producers for a closed shop for extras and a gradual slashing in the number of extras until a workable level of 4,500 to 5,000 players had been reached. The method of decreasing the extra ranks was to cut from SAG membership all those extras who failed to pay their quarterly dues. Under this system SAG figured all the remaining extras would be able to earn a good livelihood. For the first six months under operation of the Guild union agreement, extras were paid $249,382 more in total in 1937 than for the corresponding six months of 1936, which was an increase of 23 percent in dollar volume.[22]

As 1938 began a fight for control of Junior SAG was under way. It was a question of two factions: One favored the organization's current board of directors while the other faction wanted them out. At the same time SAG wanted a closed shop for extras with permission to close the registration rolls. Meanwhile the film studio cartel had proposed SAG take over Central Casting — an idea that was reportedly to be discussed at SAG sessions. Several SAG executives were said to favor the proposal if producers would grant the demand for a closed shop, grant permission for the union to hold registration of extras at around the 4,000 mark, and help defray the cost of operating the SAG call bureau, which was envisioned to take the place of Central Casting. SAG then had more than 10,000 Junior members.[23]

In April 1938 negotiations between the Hollywood film cartel (via the MPAA) and SAG on amendments to the current collective agreement got under way with actor Robert Montgomery (SAG president) heading the actors' committee. SAG had already asked that extras that received a $13.75 call out and were instructed to bring dress clothes, on the chance they might be used, be paid the dress scale of $16.50 per day. Certain studios went so far as to admit players might be entitled to some bonus but objected to paying full dress scale unless the extra in question was actually used in the latter classification. Extras then had five pay scales, with an additional one of $6.50 a day for stand-ins. The lowest rate of $5.50 was largely for players in crowd scenes. A regular extra was paid $8.25 (the rate having been increased from $7.50 when SAG contracts became effective on June 1, 1937). Special types was a category used for extras that played military leaders, detectives, waiters, gangsters, and so forth, and paid $11 a day. Special types who furnished their own uniforms were paid $13.75, while the dress extra scale was $16.50 a day. Extras that had a speaking line were then paid $25 a day, but were classed as bit players rather than extras. According to this story extras continued to squabble and fight among themselves, in factions, for control of Junior SAG, through elections to its board of directors. A total of 164 candidates had been nominated for the 33 posts of the Junior Council for the upcoming election.[24]

A contract settlement between the producers and SAG was reached in September 1938 that would remain in force for eight years (there was an option to open the contract once each year but only for money, no other issues). Approximately 1,200 members of SAG and 10,000 members of Junior SAG were involved. Put in place in the contract was an arbitration mechanism to settle all disputes past and present. The MPAA would pick one person; SAG would select one; then those two would pick a third, and that trio would arbitrate. Both sides resolved to study the situation with respect to extras—to investigate and to seek facts. Other than that there was nothing specific for extras in the agreement. There was no change in salary, for example; no change in Central Casting (or switchover of the bureau to SAG); no closed shop for extras; and no specific limitation on the number in the extra army. One gain was a provision for time and a half for extras required to work on Sundays along with a few minor points dealing with rest periods and transportation to locations. That contract went into effect on November 1, 1938.[25]

Infighting at SAG reached a new height on November 15, 1938, when SAG officers declared that the 3,000 extras who were then threatening to bolt from their own union, SAG, faced expulsion. Bylaws of the organization required a member to notify SAG in writing of any application made for membership in any other trade union. The Congress of Industrial Organizations (CIO) (this was a rival group to the AFL, with the two groups fighting for dominance in the trade union movement. In the end they merged into the AFL-CIO) denied any interest in the extras' reported move, as it was pointed out that 90 percent of the unionized film industry was in the AFL. A formal announcement of a hands-off Hollywood policy was expected to be issued by the CIO at its forthcoming convention in Pittsburgh. A move to split SAG and form a separate union of extras had been launched by two groups of players claiming to represent more than 3,000 members of SAG. That fight had been carried before the National Labor Relations Board (NLRB), with one of the two groups, Cinema Players, Inc., petitioning to be certified as bargaining agent for extras, bit players, dancers and singers. That petition had the support of several former leaders in the old Junior SAG, who resigned from the SAG Council because of differences in opinion with the board of directors over policy. Cinema Players, which had opened temporary headquarters in downtown Los Angeles, claimed SAG had never been recognized by the NLRB as the bargaining representative for the extras. The other petition, filed by the other group, which was headed by Edward Dahlen and Art Taylor, extras, asked that the producer-SAG agreement then in effect be cancelled. Copies of the two petitions were taken to Washington by Dr. Towne Nylander, regional director of the NLRB, for discussion with board members.[26]

In a statement released by the fledgling group, Cinema Players, through its attorney Don Lake, declared it had filed its documents with the National Labor Relations Board pursuant to Section 9 of the National Labor Relations Act, a petition for recognition and certification as the sole collective bargaining representative for extra players, bit players, riders, singers, dancers, atmosphere people and all other workers who came under the jurisdiction of Section 3 of the NRA code of the motion picture industry. With a stated membership in excess of 3,000, Cinema Players claimed it represented the majority of the qualified workers at the time the producers and the Screen Actors Guild entered into a 10-year agreement. Lake, in speaking for this group of extras, stated the members, the qualified extra players, wanted a union of workers of the extra, by the extra and for the extra.[27]

Dahlen and Lake, in their petition, charged that a conspiracy existed between the producers (the MPAA), SAG, and Central Casting Bureau. They charged that SAG was fraudulently designated as bargaining agent for the actors and that more than $1 million had been collected in dues and fees from them since May 15, 1937, of which all but $100,000 had been unlawfully disbursed. Further, their petition charged, the extras had no vote or voice in the affairs of SAG, except to pay the dues and fees as set by the senior SAG. Petitioners claimed that as a result of that alleged conspiracy "following unlawful acts of interference with a restraint of the Junior Guild and the actor employees; the extras lost the following rights"—the right to strike; the right to vote or choose a collective bargaining agent; the independent right to engage in a concerted movement of any kind or character; or to initiate any movement of any character or kind for their own mutual benefit and protection; the independent right to fix or regulate fees and dues of their membership in the Junior Guild, and to make rules or regulations governing the affairs of the administration of the Junior Guild; the right to limit the membership of the Junior Guild, and the right to regulate and control the disbursement of the funds derived from the said membership. As well, the petition charged the Junior Guild was further interfered with and had been "exploited" by building large memberships, increasing the dues and fees, "therefore the membership exceeds the demand for the employees in the industry by more than 6,500 and the ... more than 6,500 members have not and never will benefit from said memberships, and all of which was and is discriminatory to said members' rights, and the actor employees of said industry, and ferment unrest and strikes." Kenneth Thomson, SAG executive secretary, and other SAG leaders, indicated that SAG would not oppose an NLRB-ordered election to designate a bargaining representative for extras, provided such a request was made by a substantial and representative group of players. They pointed out, however, that 30 percent of the extras could force an election in SAG, and that the extras could withdraw from the Screen Actors Guild if 51 percent of the membership voted for such a withdrawal.[28]

Conflict within SAG continued into 1939 when in May of that year several film stars found themselves defendants in a suit brought by three extra players to test the validity of an election of the SAG Council members in the Class B division of the union. The defendants in the action were all on the SAG board of directors and included Robert Montgomery, Joan Crawford, James Cagney, and Edward G. Robinson. Eddy Aquilina, Ed Heim and Paul Cook said in their petition that they and 14 others were elected to the Class B Council, which governed some 7,000 extras and bit players, but that SAG directors declined to recognize them on the ground that no quorum was present when the election was held on April 16, 1939. They asked that SAG be enjoined from holding a new election.[29] When a vote was finally held on the question of extras staying with SAG, later in May 1939, the atmosphere players turned thumbs down on an offer of autonomy from SAG. The vote in favor of retaining the current affiliation with SAG continuing to act as bargaining representative for the extras was overwhelming, on the order of 60 to one. Out of 5,800 ballots mailed to Class B members, returned ballots totaled 3,962 to 65 in favor of retaining SAG. That action by the extras paved the way for the dismissal of petitions then pending before the NLRB for certification of other organizations as bargaining agent for the players. It was also said the ballot would call for a stricter policy by SAG officials in controlling activities of the extras. A campaign was already being mapped out to eliminate "the undesirables who have been attacking Guild leadership. Charges are being preferred against more than a dozen who have been agitating for formation of rival organizations." The first move was slated to be the enforcement of a SAG bylaw against a member holding a card in another trade union. May 20 was set as the deadline for members to surrender such cards or drop their affiliation with SAG. Executives with the Screen Actors Guild estimated that between 500 and 1,000 players would be eliminated from the extra ranks when a check of cards was conducted and the new policy became effective. Ralph Morgan (SAG president) and Kenneth Thomson (SAG executive secretary) expressed pleasure at the overwhelming endorsement by the extras of SAG. The extras, in addition to rejecting the autonomy offer, selected 17 members to fill vacancies on the SAG Council.[30]

Union regulations regulated the conduct of a union. That was in effect the decision of Superior Judge Emmet H. Wilson in November 1939 after listening to the plea of Ed Heim, extra, for a preliminary injunction against SAG. Heim sought to have the court restrain the operation of a union bylaw whereby only Class A members (stars and featured players) were entitled to vote in the running and operation of SAG. Wilson denied the petition for a preliminary injunction directing officers of SAG to give some 6,000 extras the right to vote on union matters. He held there was no emergency (and thus no justification for a preliminary order) and that the injunction proceedings of Heim should in due course by disposed of by the court. While Heim challenged the right of the union to discriminate in respect to voting, SAG lawyers pointed out that with 51 percent in favor the nonvoting (in affairs of the union) extras were able to form a new and separate union, which they had not done, in emphatic fashion, in the previous May.[31]

On other fronts, the Screen Actors Guild continued to fight to improve the conditions for extras. In October 1939 the union announced it had launched an inquiry into charges by film extras that favoritism was shown in the distribution of work assignments from Central Casting. Ralph Morgan (president of SAG), then representing some 7,000 extras, said the investigation was an attempt "to clear up the long current reports of favoritism and other irregularities in Central Casting's distribution of work."[32]

Nearly five months later SAG filed a report with the MPAA (on March 8, 1940) charging employees of Central with assigning work to film extras who were willing to pay a percentage of their earnings in return. The report, said to be based on an 18-month investigation by a private detective agency, was accompanied by scores of affidavits giving details of such alleged transactions. Accompanying the report was a demand that the film cartel (MPAA) that operated Central Casting eliminate the practices it described in its report as job-buying, favoritism, and nepotism. Campbell MacCulloch, head of Central, said he knew nothing of the alleged practices and had no comment to make on the report. It was alleged that extras had been required to pay a commission, usually 10 percent of their earnings, to 10 to 20 members of the Central Casting staff and varying amounts to assistant casting directors and other studio employees who had supervision over the hiring of atmosphere players.[33]

However, the battle by extras within SAG remained a dominant issue. At the start of 1940 it was announced that film extras would have the authority to order a strike of atmosphere players and would be able to negotiate wage scales and other items with the film producers under a form of autonomy drafted by SAG. The Class B players would also be permitted to sit in on arbitration of all disputes with studio executives. That proposed bylaw amendment had already been approved by the SAG board of governors. It still had to be endorsed by the Class A membership, but a reporter observed that a tabulation of early votes indicated the proposal would have an easy win. In details of the proposed amendment, Section 1 declared that no collective bargaining agreement affecting the rights of the B membership could be made or amended by the Guild without the approval of a majority of the B members voting on the question. Section 2 declared that in any collective bargaining negotiation affecting the rights of the B membership, the B membership was to be represented on the Guild negotiating committee. Section 3 dealt with the rights of the B membership in any collective bargaining arbitration affecting them, that Guild demands in such matters be subject to the approval of the B membership. In Section 4 it was detailed that the SAG council had the right to call a strike of the Class B members against all producers or against a given producer provided that the Class B members voted at least 75 percent in favor of such action. Any such strike vote would be effective as to Class B members without any vote by the Class A members, but would not affect the Class A members. In a letter advising Class A members that the SAG board of directors recommended immediate adoption of the proposed bylaw amendment SAG, president Ralph Morgan said, "From time to time enemies of the Guild make the charge that the extras are deprived of any voice in the collective bargaining matters affecting their destinies. This charge, of course, is untrue, because in practice the extra members of the Guild have been consulted about anything done which affected their future destinies." Morgan added, "However, in order that the charge may not be made, the board of directors has decided to codify into the by-laws the existing practice which has been followed by the Guild." Leaders in the extra ranks expressed the belief that adoption of this amendment would practically mollify the test suit started by a small group headed by Ed Heim in an effort to force SAG to extend full voting privileges to Class B members. That case was slated for court soon, and speculation then was that it would be dropped before the hearing date.[34]

As the battle by the extras for greater autonomy within SAG played out, the union went after pay increases for the extras. It was reported later in January 1940 that major film companies would be asked to allocate an additional $1 million to $1.5 million for atmosphere players if the present negotiations on reclassification of pay brackets failed to lift the annual earnings of the extras. Dress extras had rejected a 15 percent wage increase demand submitted by SAG. Players believed that an increase in daily checks would result in fewer actors being used and that their average earnings would be even less than at present. Players and SAG officials, however, believed that an additional allocation for employment of extras would result in spreading the work more evenly and should increase the individual take. The demand for a pay increase was to be held in abeyance pending the completion of negotiations on reclassification of pay brackets, with the idea of virtually eliminating the $5.50 check and minimizing the $8.25-a-day work call in favor of the $11 check. Out of total salary payments to extras in 1939, $751,410 was for placements in the $11 bracket. That was divided between 22,149 placements for women and 68,310 for men. There was that year a "decided decrease" in the number of $5.50 work calls. Those figures, however, did not include calls made directly from major studios and by independent producers (not part of the MPAA cartel). It was estimated total expenditures for extras was around $4 million. SAG, in cooperation with the producers, was then arranging tests for 2,300 dancers to provide Central Casting with a master file classifying the specialties of all dancers affiliated with SAG. Dance and casting directors from the various studios would attend the tests and act as judges. When the totals were tallied the vote of the Class A members of SAG in favor of granting modified autonomy to extras was 420 to 31. It was also reported, though, that certain leaders who were trying to drive a wedge between the actors and extras were trying to persuade the membership to continue its fight for full voting privileges and equality with the Class A membership.[35]

During a week in April 1940 a drastic slash in the 7,000-strong extra list was started by SAG, with the transfer of 600 Class B members into the Class A division, with a classification of Class A Juniors. Automatic transfers provided for in the SAG bylaws meant that number could shortly increase to 1,000 or more. Class A Juniors would continue to pay dues of only $18 a year (the Class B rate, which was much cheaper than the Class A rate), but would enjoy all the rights and privileges of stars and other Class A members. They would not be permitted to accept extra calls except upon special authorization of the SAG board of directors. No reason was given for initiating this policy but it had the appearance of being a move by SAG to control and appease the ongoing infighting between SAG and the extras. At the same time the Screen Actors Guild notified all studios that extras could not be hired to drive automobiles as part of their work. Kenneth Thomson told studio transportation heads that such practices infringed on the jurisdiction of Studio Transportation Drivers Local 399, and that extras could be engaged only for "work before the camera." Aubrey Blair, former executive secretary of the Junior SAG was hired as chief casting director at Central Casting. The appointment had been made by Howard Philbrick, who had recently taken over as head of Central. Philbrick had also announced an open door policy at Central, stating that executives on staff there would be available to extras who desired an interview. He had ordered the locked front door of the office and its peephole be removed. For much of its history the Central Casting Bureau operated much like the legendary speakeasies. The windowless front door was locked all the time. A visitor had to knock and was then scrutinized by someone on the other side who looked through a peephole, before admission to the office was granted.[36]

The question of extras breaking away from the union surfaced again in April 1940 when SAG announced that idea had been once again turned down by the atmosphere players themselves. At a meeting of the SAG Council it was declared that extras did not want any separation from the Guild. The Council issued a statement saying that a plan proposing autonomy for extras was presented to the Class B Council of SAG by Morgan Wallace, Guild director, and Kenneth Thomson, under instruction of the board. The SAG Council previously had requested an opportunity to examine any self-government proposal before it was submitted to the full membership. Before hearing or considering the plan, the Council passed a motion placing itself on record as being definitely opposed to any autonomy plan for the Class B membership. Certain members of the Council expressed the belief that at least 80 percent of the membership would vote against autonomy, if the extras got as far as having a Class B ballot. The SAG Council also voted to request its board of directors to reopen negotiations with the film producers for the new code of fair practice and the revised wage scales for extra players, which were postponed pending a decision on the autonomy question.[37]

Delving into the operation of SAG, a suit seeking to obtain equal voting rights for film extras with those of stars and feature players began on June 10, 1940, in Superior Judge Charles D. Ballard's court in Los Angeles. This was the suit launched by Ed Heim in his own behalf and for all other Class B members of SAG. According to the complaint, labor and contract negotiations for SAG were made by a board of directors that was selected by Class A members only. Class B members were permitted to vote only on matters pertaining to themselves. Kenneth Thomson took the stand for SAG to explain how the Guild operated. Sitting in the courtroom waiting to be called as witnesses were other Guild officers, including Ralph Morgan, Edward Arnold (vice president) and Walter Abel, a member of the board of directors. Thomson declared that about 75 percent of the extras were dependent on some other means of livelihood, whereas members of the Class A groups were entirely dependent upon the film industry for their living. He argued there was a major difference between the Class A and Class B groups, in that the Class A members could be classed as skilled workers, while most of the B members might be considered as unskilled workers. Attorneys Stanley Lagerlof and Marvin Freedman, representing Heim, contended that it was against public policy to have a labor union in which the overwhelming number of members had no right to vote. According to this account Class A contained an estimated 1,200 members while Class B had better than 5,000 members.[38]

During the summer of 1940 it was announced that approximately 2,000 extras were scheduled to be dropped by SAG on August 1 under a new ruling that eliminated one-day work permits and provided for the suspension of players who fell 90 days behind in their union dues. The new pruning order was declared to be in line with SAG policy to eliminate occasional extras from the industry and provide more jobs for regular extras that depended more on the motion picture industry. With respect to the new move, Kenneth Thomson stated, "Our present adjustment and leniency policy is clearly inconsistent with our expressed intention of reducing the number of casual extra players in the industry. By revising that policy now and substituting much more stringent rules we can bring about a sharp decrease in our Class B membership. Thus our problem of spreading work will be cut." Simultaneously, SAG announced that extra calls into Central Casting for jobs would be limited to one in each 15-minute period and that SAG would not permit unfair discrimination against any member or group of players. That announcement was interpreted to mean the "ban" on 119 top-earning extras at Central, as well as a ban on extras with relatives employed at Central, would be eliminated. Reportedly, Central sent a memo to studios listing the top-earning extras and suggesting that studios think twice before using them again, to try and spread the work around. Leaders at SAG were reported to have been highly annoyed by reports that one of its executives aided in the preparation of a blacklist of those 119 extras, an accusation the union strongly denied.[39]

Following a conference between a committee representing the 119 extras and a committee appointed by the SAG board of directors, the latter group issued a statement saying the Screen Actors Guild board of directors never had and never would countenance any unfair discrimination in the obtaining of employment. It was a policy, the statement continued, that applied whether the unfair discrimination was directed against any individual or group, or whether it took the form of favoritism in behalf of an individual or group. "In reference to the list of 119 extra players, the Screen Actors Guild had no advance knowledge of or any part in the preparation or in the alleged deletions, if any, from the list, nor in the publication of this list," went the statement. It went on to say the SAG board was aware of the economic problem of the extra player who was attempting to earn a living in an overcrowded field and that the board also was aware that problem may have caused Central Casting to prepare the list referred to in an effort to spread the work. However, the board contended it believed the only sound approach to the problem had to await the report and recommendations of the Producer-Guild Standing Committee, which at that point had been over a year in the process of making a detailed study of extra work. In conclusion, the SAG board statement said, "Extra players whose names appeared on the list of 119 have asked the board for a complete list of extras who earned more than $700 through Central Casting during the first five months of this year. The Guild does not make public figures on earnings of its members.[40]

Still in July 1940, SAG notified more than 2,000 Class B members that they would be suspended effective August 1, if their current dues were not paid up by that date. It was a move the Guild argued was in line with its policy to eliminate casual extras and provide more jobs for the regular extras that had no income outside the industry.[41]

True to its word, SAG dropped 2,035 extras from membership in SAG at the start of August, with the possibility that up to 3,000 more would be dropped, said a reporter, "as soon as SAG devises a means of doing so without incurring legal responsibility." The Producer-SAG Standing Committee that had been investigating the extra situation felt that all casual extras should be eliminated. Those 2,035 people dropped by SAG were suspended for being 90 days in arrears in their union dues. They could be reinstated only by permission of the SAG board of directors. "It is certain, however, that leniency will be extended only to oldtimers who, because of financial reverses and lack of work, have been unable to maintain their dues," concluded the news account. With the reduction in numbers this account still listed the paid-up Class B membership as about 6,500. With less than 800 jobs available daily, officials believed the extra list should be slashed to about 4,000. One idea was that the extras who had not been earning as much as $500 per year would be kept on an emergency list, to be given work only when regular extras could not be secured. Meanwhile a fight for control of the union continued to be fought, at least by some of the extras. When the Class B annual membership meeting was held on August 11, the winners of 15 Council seats would be announced. Two full slates were in the running. One was selected by the SAG Council nominating committee and the other by a group of extras who continued the fight for autonomy.[42]

Thomas Brady, a journalist for the *New York Times*, commented on September 15, 1940, about the continuing reduction in the extra army from the joint effort by the producers and the Guild: "The primary step toward raising the income of motion-picture extras to a civilized level was taken this week when film producers approved a plan to drop approximately 2,000 players from the extra list. The move would reduce the number of extras from 6,500 to 4,500 and in round figures increase the average annual individual income from $350 to $550." That joint standing committee had finally finished its study and reported that around 2,000 extras worked less than 10 days a year, and it was reportedly that low-earning group that was cut from the ranks. The recommendation of that standing committee was understood to have included an eventual reduction in the number of extras to 3,000. Action in the matter had long been recognized as desirable, wrote Brady, but the prospect that "purged supernumeraries would bring suits because of the curtailment of their livelihood has blocked the reform." SAG, unwilling to act against its own members, even in view of the standing committee's report, had left the initiative to the producers, argued Brady, on the theory that an industry has the right to decide whom it will employ. Even the producers were described as proceeding with caution, however, and lawyers were working out details of the plan to obviate the possibilities of appeals to the National Labor Relations Board. It would then be submitted to the Guild for approval. Meanwhile, SAG was developing an education project whereby the dismissed extras would find employment in other fields. "A prospectus is being prepared with the object of persuading as many members as possible to abandon their screen ambition," concluded Brady.[43]

No sooner had the extra army been decreased than there was agitation for an increase in the extra army. In fact, it took only some five weeks or so for the storm to erupt. In the middle of October 1940 it was reported a demand that SAG reopen its membership books to extras was being mulled by the producers. A turndown of numerous applications, by SAG, of people proposed as extras by film studio executives was said to have caused enmity in the industry and led to talk of opening the then existing closed-door policy for atmosphere players. Annoyance among the studio executives was reported to have followed a meeting of the SAG Council admittance committee a week earlier in which a request application from E. H. Goldstein, general manager of Republic studios, was tossed out. At that meeting only three applications out of 50 were accepted (and granted admission to SAG), and those three were old-timers seeking a return to pictures. Other producers, riled by the rejection of their application requests, at various recent times, pointed out that the basic SAG-Producer agreement provided for the continuance of open books for extras. It was pointed out in this account, however, that there was no objection when SAG, swamped with newcomers who were trying to break into motion pictures, notified the producers that the books would be closed. Several of the studio executives, noting a tightening of admittance acceptances, suggested making a demand that the registration rolls be thrown open to anybody who wanted to be an extra. The SAG Council, fearing that the jobs of professional extras would be jeopardized by a flood of new people if the producers had their way, reportedly was preparing an appeal to the American Federation of Labor for protection. But several AFL leaders were understood to have been approached to assist the producers in the opening up of the Class B membership list. To keep the B membership down to "reasonable limits" the SAG-Producer Standing Committee had fairly recently adopted a resolution that extras who worked less than 10 days in 1939 be dropped from the books. According to this account another reduction was indicated among the Western (genre) extras, who had all been ordered to take and pass riding tests, or face removal. Among the 3,000 listed by SAG in the Western category, it was reliably believed that from 1,500 to 2,000 would be eliminated on the sole basis of being unable to pass the riding tests. Some tests called for cowboy riding, some for fox hunting, some for steeplechase abilities, and others for riding using an English saddle. Those tests were to be administered by John Burger (head of the SAG work relations department), assisted by a committee of riding judges "to eliminate any possibility of favoritism." When the final scores were tallied from the riding tests those who passed would be registered with Central Casting as recommended for riding jobs, while losers in the tests would retain their full standing as extras but would be removed from the horseman or horsewoman category.[44]

And the autonomy struggle continued. With employment in the film industry said to be at its lowest mark in five years, 6,500 Hollywood extras appealed directly to the American Federation of Labor, in October 1940, for aid in their fight to force SAG to grant them full voting privileges and authority to negotiate their own deals with the producers. When the SAG board of directors removed Class B members from the admittance committee, which controlled new admissions to the extra ranks, several members of the Guild Council immediately contacted the office of Meyer Lewis, western director of the AFL. It was understood the extras were told their complaint would have to be forwarded to William Green, AFL president, who, if he thought the evidence warranted it, could place the matter before the AFL Executive Council with a request for an investigation. The extras claimed they were the only craft in the studios that had not received a wage increase and that nothing had been done to improve their working conditions. Those extras were insisting that they be given the same voting privileges as Class A members, which would automatically give them control of the Guild. Officials in SAG claimed the complainants did not represent the desires of a majority of extras and pointed out that when the extras were offered autonomy (meaning a separate SAG local) they turned it down overwhelmingly.[45]

It was a situation that was recently aggravated when the SAG board ignored a request from its Council that they be permitted to elect a representative to work with the Producer-SAG Standing Committee in carrying out its recommendations, including the elimination of 2,000 extras who worked less than 10 days in 1939. The SAG board of directors announced the Standing Committee recommendations would be submitted to a direct vote of the Class B membership for approval, after the Council had declined to okay it unless the extras were allowed to name the SAG representative who would cooperate with the committee in executing its recommendations. Members of the Council who had been particularly active in urging autonomy for the atmosphere players also claimed they had been blacklisted by Central Casting and were not being given work calls. They had asked SAG to initiate an unfair labor practice charge before the NLRB in behalf of Ed Heim, the man who had recently sued SAG in an effort to force through a bylaw amendment permitting the extras to vote and have a bigger voice in Guild policies. Because of the big decrease in total extra work calls, Howard Philbrick, head of Central, had ordered a reduction in bureau personnel. First to go were a janitor, three clerks, and a stenographer. It was reported that Harold Melniker, executive assistant and storm center of a recent row with extras, when it was charged he was trying to get rid of old-timers, was also on the way out.[46]

When all efforts to achieve autonomy failed, Hollywood's 6,500 extras (or some of them) appealed to the U.S. government in February 1941 for aid in forcing SAG to give them a voice in the affairs of the union. In a letter to Thurman Arnold, assistant U.S. Attorney-General, members of the ousted SAG Council asked if the election of Guild officers by the 1,200 top players did not fall within the same category as the American Society of Composers, Authors and Publishers (ASCAP), which had been ordered to give the entire membership a vote in their elections. The SAG Council, headed by Harry Mayo, contended that the officers were then selected by a small group of stars, many of whom it was claimed shared in production earnings, making them an employer within the meaning of the Wagner Relations Act. The communication to Arnold stated the atmosphere players, through payment of dues and initiation fees, contributed most of the upkeep of SAG, yet were denied any voice in the selection of personnel, the policies, or the wage agreements. They argued further, that worked to the detriment of the extra player and to the advantage of the producing companies. Complaining extras were anxious to have their affairs made a part of a grand jury investigation that had been ordered by the U.S. Justice Department into the efforts of James C. Petrillo to force all instrumentalists to join the American Federation of Musicians (AFM). They contended their situation was even more distressing than that of the concert artists who, even if forced to leave the American Guild of Musical Artists and affiliate with the AFM, would be given a voice in the affairs of the latter organization.[47]

As the fight for autonomy continued off and on, so did the efforts to reduce the size of the extra army. An October 1942 news story dramatically declared that 4,000 film extras could soon be looking for jobs in some other field. SAG president James Cagney said that the Guild would support a proposal made by Commissioner L. L. Livingston of the Federal Conciliation Service to reduce the number of regular, vocational extras down to 1,000 or 1,200, which would allow the remaining extras a living wage of $150 a month. According to the SAG statement there were 20,000 extras in 1936, and through a series of moves since then the Guild and the film producers had reduced the number to about 5,200, but that number was still too high.[48]

Yielding at least somewhat to the demands of the extras, SAG announced on March 30, 1943, a decision made by the board of directors to establish a separate, self-governing organization for extras, who remained Class B members of the Guild. Under the new plan the 4,500 extras would have their own officers, governing board, administrative staff, offices and control of their own finances and would conduct their own collective bargaining negotiations. Thus, SAG (what was left of it) membership would be restricted to qualified motion picture actors who spoke lines and specialty performers.[49]

In October 1943 demands for wage increases for extras were filed by SAG with the major film producers and the American Arbitration Association. Filing of the demands constituted the first step in the arbitration scheduled to be held under the auspices of the association. Highlights of the demands, the results of weeks of conferences with Class B members, included increases for extras from $10.50 a day rate to $12.75 daily, an increase in the rate for stand-ins to $12.75, and a reclassification of work performed by dancing, ice-skating and swimming extras to professional extra work to be paid at the minimum daily rate of $16.50. The Guild also sought to abolish "weather-permitting" calls; extras who spoke lines would be paid a minimum of $29 a day, under the demands.[50]

Meanwhile on the autonomy front, the National Labor Relations Board held a hearing in March 1944 before Board Chairman Charles M. Ryan, with respect to the issue. Representatives of the Screen Players Union (SPU) were seeking the right to bargain with film producers for the extra players. They wanted the NLRB to establish a separate unit that included film extras who were paid $50 a day or less. Representatives of the producers and SAG were in court opposing the idea, pointing out that SAG bargained for Class B members. It was the contention of SAG that if a new bargaining unit was to be set up for lower-pay extras then in SAG, the unit should include Class A and Class A (Juniors) players who performed bits and did small parts. Leaders of the SPU objected to that, fearing that A and A Junior players in any new unit would outnumber the B members and by their votes would prevent the forming of the new unit in the first place.[51]

As that NLRB hearing continued into April, Pat Somerset (a SAG official) testified as to the various wages paid in films: "I have worked in a picture for $250 a day when others doing the same kind of work got $500 or $150. Pay is based on the individual's own bargaining power." He added that since it was formed in 1933, SAG had taken in 24,804 members. Then at a low point, the Guild had about 8,500 members. At its peak it had 13,000. Records showed, Somerset continued, that in 1943, not a "lush" year, the union collected $194,655 in revenue and spent $188,095 with salaries consuming more than $97,000. The union's lower class members, according to testimony, were more numerous. In 1943 they paid more than half of SAG's income. Dues in the Guild ranged from a low of $18 a year for a Class B extra to a high of $60 annually for stars (Class A). Initiation fees then were about $50 (a one-time fee to join). Essentially, the motion picture industry was then a closed shop with no one allowed to work (with some unique exceptions) as players in films without joining the union. Somerset considered himself to have been one of the champions and organizers of the lower class players from the start. Ryan, the NRLB trial examiner, was considering the Screen Players Union petition that sought an order from the NLRB for an election. The SPU hoped to have the extra players in the election vote their bargaining power away from SAG and over to the SPU, which then would have complete jurisdiction over the extras. Testimony reportedly disclosed that six different unions had tried over time to get into the field of exclusive control of film players with none succeeding, except SAG. Alexander Schullman, lawyer for SPU, argued that in 1943 a group of members against SAG rule "contemplated strike action" to prevent the Guild from admitting more B members as "temporary war members." SAG attorney William Berger said that although SAG had been closed since 1938 to "practically any more members at all," it had in 1943 admitted between 400 and 500 new members because of a temporary shortage of a certain kind of player. Schullman charged there was no shortage and that the new members were brought in to offset opposition among B members to the Guild regime.[52]

As the NLRB hearing continued, Pat Somerset testified people were still eager to get jobs as film extras. He said that in the fall of 1943 when there was a sudden opening for about 300 new extras, more than 2,000 people applied. Somerset added that 150 people a week came to SAG to try and join but in the past six years the Guild had accepted only about 1,100 extra players and had in more recent times lost more than that number. According to him, SAG then had about 6,000 extra players but only about 2,000 of them "make anything like a living"—earning $1,700 to $1,800 annually.[53]

As of June 1944, leaders of the recently formed SPU were making overtures to studio executives for higher wages for extra players. SAG, at that point, still had its demands for higher wages for the extras before the producers. Those film studios balked at any further dealings on the subject when the SPU appeared on the scene and began its efforts to induce the NLRB to order an election that would offer extras an opportunity to switch their affiliation from SAG to SPU. Officers of SPU were making offers to break that impasse by having the producers, SAG, and SPU sit down together and work out new wages that would go into effect at once regardless of the outcome of the SPU case before the NLRB. At the latest session of that hearing Central Casting Bureau head Howard Philbrick disclosed that in 1943 somewhat more than 12,000 extra players earned about $6,103,000. However, 4,000 to 5,000 of them did the most of the extra roles and got all of the $6.1 million except for $300,000 to $400,000. All of the remainder did only a few days of work for the most part over the entire year.[54]

On July 5, 1944, the end came to the long NLRB hearing on the SPU petition. It began back in 1943 with the filing of the SPU petition. Hearing sessions had been held intermittently since March of 1944. All of the transcripts had to go off to the NLRB's Washington office. Not only did the NLRB have to decide whether or not an election should be held but it had also to determine who could or could not vote in such an election. The SPU wanted the election confined to players who got less than $50 a day with none allowed to vote who had a rating above Class B in SAG. On the other hand SAG, while opposing an election, would have the voting confined (if a vote was ordered) to those who did atmosphere work, that is, those who did not speak lines.[55]

A vote was indeed ordered. Film extras voted on December 17, 1944, 1,451 to 456 for the newly formed, independent Screen Players Union as their collective bargaining agency over SAG, but the Guild announced on the night the results were released that it did not intend to abide by the decision. When the ballots were counted George Murphy (SAG president) issued the following statement: "In the just-completed National Labor Relations Board election, a majority of those extras who voted cast their ballots in favor of Screen Players Union. In doing so they have selected a new bargaining agent for extra players." He went on to add that SAG, a branch of the American Federation of Labor "will continue to represent all actors in the motion-picture industry and will continue to assert exclusive jurisdiction over all acting work in the industry. The producers are being notified of our position in this matter." Martin Zimrink, NRLB field representative who conducted the election, said that an official certification of the SPU as bargaining agent for the extras would be issued unless valid objections were filed within the prescribed five-day limit. The electorate was limited to certain employees of the 10 major Hollywood film studios (the MPAA cartel). Of the 3,300 eligible voters, 1,912 valid votes were cast (there were five "no union" votes). As well 213 votes—not enough to influence the result—were challenged and ruled invalid. Thus, 2,125 of the 3,300 cast a vote, 1,175 did not vote.[56]

In the aftermath of the vote SAG, acknowledging defeat, called a special meeting of the board of directors where it remained defiant; insisting it would continue to represent all players. At the same time it was hinted actors might refuse to work with SPU members if the latter attempted to claim jurisdiction over bit part work, and so forth. Top actors, however, appeared divided. Many felt extras had the right to select their own representatives and were inclined to feel the Guild should work out a deal on a friendly basis rather than continue to fight them. "Campaign leading up to the election was the longest and bitterest intra-guild battle in the history of Hollywood, involving months of contention, legal opinions, charges and counter-charges, investigations, mass meetings and underground pulling and hauling for votes," concluded a *Variety* reporter.[57]

On February 2, 1945, an estimated 2,500 to 3,000 film extras were ordered to go on strike because of a jurisdictional dispute between the independent SPU and the AFL-affiliated SAG. The strike call came, said SPU spokesman Michael Jeffers, after the MPAA rejected a proposed interim working agreement with the union. Meanwhile, SAG officials said they would consider the action a strike against SAG and that all SAG members—including stars—would be told to ignore any and all SPU picket lines. The principal dispute between the rival unions reportedly concerned jurisdiction over borderline players, such as bit players and singers. On February 3 the SPU ordered its members back to work, ending the one-day walkout of film extras. Jeffers issued the order after he received a telegram from the war labor board asking that the strike be ended and promising early investigation of the union's jurisdictional dispute with SAG.[58]

Despite losing the election to SPU, SAG and the AFL were not ready to give up the fight, or control over the extras. They simply manufactured a new union out of thin air, the Screen Extras Guild (SEG), which was independent from SAG (in theory) but affiliated with the American Federation of Labor in the same way that SAG was. Despite the NLRB decision, after the election, granting to the SPU jurisdiction as collective bargaining agent for 4,500 film extras, the Associated Actors and Artistes of America (AAAA), which had jurisdiction over all performers in the entertainment field under the American Federation of Labor, announced on May 18, 1945, its decision to give full support to the Screen Extras Guild as representative of the extras, and reject the SPU. Both SEG and SPU had applied for a charter to the AAAA. (Usually the AFL chartered a union directly but in the entertainment field a middleman — AAAA — was used. The reason for that dated back to jurisdictional battles between the White Rats, Equity and SAG in the 1920s and 1930s. In order to get around awkward jurisdictional disputes, the middleman AAAA had been invented and inserted between the AFL and the individual entertainment unions. The AAAA was largely a ghost organization with no individuals as members, waking up only rarely and then only to deal with awkward jurisdictional conflicts.)[59]

Paul Dulzell, president of the AAAA, said that his organization's decision was made "in order to insure all motion picture extras of democratic control over their own affairs." Dulzell pointed out that jurisdiction over film extras had long been in dispute and that the AAAA acted after a "thorough investigation of the extra situation" before granting the jurisdiction to SEG. Thus SEG would then become part of the AAAA and its component groups: the American Federation of Radio Artists, Actors Equity Association, SAG, American Guild of Variety Artists, American Guild of Musical Artists, Chorus Equity Association, and four foreign language groups. In his explanation of why the AAAA rejected SPU, Dulzell declared the AAAA was not willing to turn over control of the union affairs of some 4,500 extras to a group that was not "representative of the extras." He added that his group had the responsibility for union jurisdiction in the entertainment field and was determined to maintain it. The AAAA believed that a charter to the Screen Extras Guild would give all the extras the opportunity of deciding their own affairs, while the new organization could be assured of the active support of all component parts of the AAAA. An election was to be held to select officers and directors, with all extras formerly affiliated with SAG Class B and desiring to belong to SEG eligible to vote. At that time some extras were reportedly members of both SEG and SPU.[60]

In the summer of 1945 SAG and the Screen Extras Guild signed an interchangeability agreement whereby SEG members could remain in SAG and perform acting work on payment of one-half of SAG regular dues, or $9 yearly. In making the announcement of that deal, Ed Russell, president of SEG, pointed out SEG members thus would enjoy all the benefits of interchangeability that were then enjoyed by all the other members of the components of the Associated Actors and Artistes of America. It was also stated that SEG would shortly initiate an action before the NLRB to undo the certification of SPU as the exclusive bargaining agent for extras and that the AAAA would stand behind SEG in any and all efforts to get the latter declared the sole representative of the extras.[61]

Late in 1945 SPU said it would resume negotiations with major film studios and contracts were expected to be reached shortly, said Don Wayson, SPU secretary.[62]

Attempts to amalgamate the two rival unions for extras grew rancorous in the middle of December 1945 with SEG and SPU each charging the other with rejecting recommendations drawn up under the auspices of the Los Angeles Central Labor Council (AFL affiliated). Screen Actors Guild hinted that SPU sought amalgamation terms under which Herbert Sorrell could take SPU into his Conference of Studio Unions. (Sorrell was the leader of a recent Hollywood strike of the Studio Unions, which was a rival, and not part of, the AFL.) Spokesmen for the SPU, however, charged SEG with stalling tactics and alleged that SEG was a tool of SAG and the AAAA, in their concerted drive to destroy the SPU. In its statement SEG accused SPU of refusing a plan for immediate organization of one large union because the SPU wanted to negotiate and conclude a contract with producers before the amalgamation.

The SEG position, the statement explained, was that a contract covering extra work had to be negotiated by a committee representing all the extras and having the united support of all AFL organizations. To that complaint, the SPU countered that it was then the only certified collective bargaining agent for the extra players and that as such it should do the negotiating and added that it would continue to negotiate and conclude a contract with the producers. And the SPU was continuing to negotiate with the producers.[63]

Early in 1946, Stewart Meacham, regional director for the NLRB, announced that a new election for extras to determine who would be their collective bargaining agent would be held on March 3. Eligible to vote in that election were those 3,300 extras that had been eligible to vote in the earlier NLRB jurisdictional election in December 1944, whereby the SPU was selected. Choices in the March 1946 election were, of course, SEG and SPU.[64]

That election was held in the auditorium of Hollywood High School with the polls open from 9:00 AM to 9:00 PM. In this account SEG was described as "a new union that arose out of dissatisfaction with S.P.U. to challenge its right to represent extras." The SPU claimed the backing of most of the studio unions under Herbert K. Sorrell, with whom it participated in the 1945 film strike. SEG was endorsed by William Green, president of the AFL, Paul Dalzell, president of the AAAA, the AFL Los Angeles Central Labor Council, and others. Then a third group appeared. This organization claimed to have a "substantial number" of extra players as members. It had petitioned the NLRB not to certify the winner of the election as bargaining agent for the extras. This new group was called the United Actors' Association. In a petition for leave to intervene in the matter, the association charged that neither of the two contestants in the election was properly qualified to represent extras, for various reasons. Thus, the association requested the NLRB to hold a hearing on its charges before it decided whether or not to certify a winner.[65]

Film extras selected SEG as their bargaining agent over SPU in that election. Final vote in the NLRB sanctioned and supervised vote was 1,227 for SEG and 821 for SPU. According to this report there were 3,500 extras eligible to vote out of a total of 5,000 in the industry.[66]

It did not take long for the AFL and SAG to purge out the rebels after that election. All atmosphere players had to be members of SEG in order to obtain work in the major film studios after April 8, 1946; it was announced less than one week before that date. That was the gist of an agreement reached between SEG and the MPAA film cartel pending completion of negotiations for a new contract covering wage increases, improved working conditions and retroactive pay.[67]

That was not quite the end of the SEG/SPU matter. Charging that they were blacklisted by SEG and were unable to obtain employment, eight Hollywood film extras filed suit on July 6, 1946, in Superior Court against SEG, Central Casting, and nearly all of the major and minor film studios in Hollywood, asking for an injunction against their work ban. They said in their complaint that they represented 60 other film extras that had been similarly barred. They charged that SEG and its officers refused to grant them "clearance cards," which were necessary to show them as members of the union in good standing in order to obtain work. The eight extras, who alleged they had worked as extras for years, said they had offered to join SEG after the election but that its acceptance committee had refused to permit them to do so. As well, they requested monetary damages in an unspecified amount based on their estimated earnings of $60 weekly, for all the time they had been barred. Those who filed suit were: John Lind, Larry Stamps, Ivan Bell, Judy Marlow, Phil Chain, Allen Charles, Tommy LaVerne, and John Zuniga.[68]

As of December 1948, SEG and the major film studios had a new contract for the period ending July 31, 1953, that provided for a union shop and preferential hiring for the 3,800 extras then registered with Central Casting. It was the first contract for SEG, replacing one in effect since 1946. Continued under the new deal was the basic daily wage rate for an extra of $15.56 and the dress extra rate of $22.23 per day. A major stumbling block had been a disputed $9.45 daily rate for mob extras. No settlement was reached on that matter and it was put over for further discussions.[69]

SEG apparently never satisfied the needs of the extras. During negotiations for the 1992 film industry agreement between SAG and the producers, SAG won jurisdiction, again, over motion picture extras, thus bringing to an end the Screen Extras Guild, aged 46 years.[70]

6

Rags to Riches

Although Hollywood ran lots of campaigns designed to keep would-be extras out of the film capital due to the surplus of atmosphere players, there also appeared, on the other hand, lots of publicity and press accounts of the rags-to-riches stories of extras who had, supposedly, made the jump to stardom. Dorothea Love was a New York girl just approaching her 20s at the end of 1925, who had long cherished an ambition to succeed in films. But the road to film fame, said a reporter, "is a long and rocky one" (although the story suggested the reverse). She had to content herself as an extra. Love heard of the plan to start the Paramount Pictures School and tried for admission but failed the test. When the opportunity of appearing in the big cabaret scene in D. W. Griffith's Paramount film *That Royale Girl* was offered to her, she accepted. She reported for her extra role in evening clothes and was placed at tables with 175 others, all providing atmosphere. During the rehearsal of that scene Griffith noticed her and, reportedly, recruited her to do a bit — rush toward actor Harrison Ford and vamp him. Griffith was impressed and offered her the major role of Lola Neeson (still unfilled at that point). And Dorothea Love's career was born, or so it was written.[1]

A 1927 piece profiled actor Charles Farrell, who was starring in *Old Ironsides*, then premiering in Hollywood at the famed Egyptian Theater. That article told of Farrell's rise in the brief two or three years he had been in Hollywood from extra to film star. And he had been an extra. When he started out, Farrell could not act (as he readily admitted), had no experience, and his physique was not good. That article was, of course, the stuff that dreams were made of.[2]

One year later the same newspaper ran another publicity-type piece touting the idea that you too could become a star. Lady Luck was said to have smiled upon Edna May: "Not long ago she graduated from the ranks of the thousands of film extras to leading lady for Johnny Hines, the comedian." Soon thereafter she signed to be a leading lady in a series of comedies at the U. M. Dailey studios in Hollywood.[3]

Another rags-to-riches story was detailed in the *Washington Post* on February 2, 1929. It told of James Murray, then playing romantic leads in films, a real star. He was discovered by King Vidor after he had spent five years trying to escape the ranks of extras. Murray had finished work as an extra one night at the MGM studio but as he was only an extra — a man of meager means and no car — he was marooned that night as the rain poured down, so he hung around at the studio hoping someone would give him a lift. King Vidor, directing at that studio, happened along, saw Murray, gave him a lift and, as they say, the rest was history. Shortly thereafter Murray was playing the leading male role in Vidor's *The Crowd*. James Murray was born in New York City on February 9, 1901. In 1922 he began his theatrical career playing on the stage, mostly small parts. Murray went to Hollywood in 1925 playing first as an extra in the Buster Keaton film *Hospitality*.[4]

Syndicated columnist Hubbard Keavy spoke to O. P. Heggie, late in 1929, a new face to film but an old one in terms of experience on the stage. That chat was in response to Keavy's comments that every film extra — "and there are about 20,000 of them" — thought he was a potential star and blamed directors and others because he had not advanced. Said Heggie, "There is room at the top for every good actor. There always will be a need for good actresses and actors." He added, "Directors and players are always on the lookout for new faces. Any director will tell you that he never passes up an opportunity to try out extra players he thinks are capable of better things."[5]

A Star is Born was not the only Hollywood screen epic to feature extras in the plot. The 1931 release *Forgotten Women* was the story of the life of movie extras and the lure of the film capital.[6]

A 1932 press report declared that although Marlene Dietrich won almost overnight fame in the United States for her work in *Morocco* and *The Blue Angel*, she really began her career as a film extra. She disclosed that fact to an interviewer while starring in, and shooting, the Josef von Sternberg production *Blonde Venus*. Dietrich explained that the crash of the German currency was responsible for her becoming an extra player. She had just given her first recital as a violinist when the crash came and left her and her family destitute. An injury to her hand prevented her from further concert work for months, so she tried extra work at the German UFA studios in an effort to help her mother financially. "I worked at this for several months without recognition, so decided to try the stage," she explained. "It was while I was appearing in a Berlin theater that I was sent for by Mr. von Sternberg and offered the lead in *The Blue Angel*." That was her first feature part, although it was released in the Untied States after *Morocco*.[7]

A slight variation of the theme, sort of a riches to rags to riches, could be found in the story of Jessie Pringle. One day in 1933, out of a crowd of spectators, film extras in a courtroom scene in a film, Pringle, who played six years with Frank Bacon in *Lightnin,'* was rescued and brought into a film role by an old acquaintance. Her film savior was Ralph Morgan, who had also played in *Lightnin'* with Pringle. When the actor chanced to see her face among a crowd of extras employed in a film, he left the set and called James Ryan, casting director. Some 15 minutes after that Pringle left the "crowd," a contract in her hands for a part in a new motion picture. Pringle had played Bacon's wife in *Lightnin'* and for many years was featured in stock theater companies from coast to coast.[8]

Another motion picture to feature an extra as a character in the story was the 1934 release *The Countess of Monte Cristo*, featuring Fay Wray and Paul Lukas. It told of how an "impetuous" female extra was turned into a sensational front page story and stardom.[9]

And then there were the famous extras—that is, famous for something other than film work, or stars reduced to extra work. Perhaps one of the most unlikely of movie extras was the man described in the brief 1932 *Washington Post* account of the story as the "former war lord of Soviet Russia"—Leon Trotzky (as it was spelled), who was once a $7 a day extra in an American film studio. It all happened, reportedly, sometime before World War I when Trotsky was a struggling nonentity, trying his hand at writing, lecturing, and even movie acting to provide a means of livelihood. When czarism crumbled in Russia, Trotsky and his colleague Lenin quickly made their way back to Russia to set about building the new state there. The very grainy photo with the text of the story showed Clara Kimball Young front and center in the still with three men, one behind her barely visible, one on the left and Trotsky on her right. No other details of the film were given, or perhaps known.[10]

While Los Angeles was cheering new Olympic heroes in August 1932, a reporter observed, a one-time American Olympic hero, Jim Thorpe, was out at Burbank trying to earn his "moderate stipend" as a film extra. But it was a bad day for the native Indian, and he ended up in the emergency ward of a hospital. Thorpe was working in a film wherein he was to ride a horse Indian style, with no saddle. But the horse began to buck and it threw him. Thorpe's injuries were described as numerous lacerations and bruises and a wrenched shoulder.[11]

Also in 1932, journalist Dan Thomas wrote a longer piece about such people. He started out by saying; "Once their names were in headlines.... Now they are obscure movie extras and bit players." It was a statement that applied not only to former celebrities of the movie world but also to those of the great outside world. For years Hollywood had been the melting pot for former celebrities from the world at large, wrote Thomas. "They have come here hoping to capitalize upon their fame and perhaps win new laurels on the silver screen. In this practically all of them fail. Some get discouraged and go elsewhere." No matter how long they failed and labored in Hollywood obscurity they continued to hold on to the hope that tomorrow they would be discovered. "And, as a matter of fact, the traits which made them outstanding once before give them better chances than the average extra enjoys." According to Thomas, Jim Thorpe, also once one of the greatest of all football players, was discovered a couple of years earlier in Los Angeles digging ditches. As a result of that publicity he enjoyed a brief, renewed spate of public attention, with the result that studios sought his services. Then that renewed interest quickly died. Thorpe continued in films but only as an extra or bit player whose name never appeared on the screen. Grace Cunard (who earned and spent $1 million when she was a star) and Francis Ford (also a one-time screen star) both were then doing bit parts, when they could get them. Robert Louis Stevenson (nephew and namesake of the famed author) was found doing a small bit in *Dr. Jekyll and Mr. Hyde*. He had done other bit parts but nothing of enough importance to warrant screen billing. Louis van den Ecker (one of France's greatest war heroes) came to the United States as a member of Marshal Foch's staff and never returned to France. He had done small bits in films. Florence Lawrence (once a huge star) was then doing just bit parts. Art Loeb, hero of the Eastland disaster in Chicago (a tragic ship sinking that took 844 lives in 1915), which made him a big name for a time, managed to work quite regularly as an extra. Pat Somerset, one of the leading matinee idols of his time, was then taking any extra or bit work he could, whenever he could get it. Others who had been headliners in show business but were satisfied to be classed as "atmosphere" players in 1932 included, Thomas summarized, Helene Chadwick, Alice Lake, Barbara Tennant, Vola Vale, Ted Doner, Ruth Renwick, and Wilfred Lucas.[12]

Author Ring Lardner put in two days' work as an extra on *Little Lord Fauntleroy*. He turned that episode into a humorous one-page newspaper article based on his experience as an extra. Apparently, it was a one-off experience for the author.[13]

Not only did the famous become extras sometimes, but also the infamous. Northern California police officers listened in amazement on September 15, 1936, to a tale of exploits by Robert Miller Barr, wanted for murder, on his return there from Los Angeles where he had been arrested as a burglary suspect. Arriving in Yreka in the custody of Sheriff Chandler, the prisoner told officers that while evading capture in Southern California he had worked as an extra in a film. Barr said he had appeared in eight different scenes of the motion picture while it was being filmed at Lake Tahoe. Later, he said, he saw the film when it was screened at Long Beach. "That was at the time the manhunt was at its height," Chandler said, "and that bozo had the audacity to give his name to the casting director as Robert Miller, the alias we were seeking him under." Barr's partner in the crime of killing two police officers already had been lynched by a mob in Siskiyou, so Barr was placed in Folsom Prison for reasons of safety.[14]

Reporter John Miles wrote a 1937 piece that appeared in the *Washington Post* and mused on the fickleness of fame. It could be argued, he said, that players of 10 to 15 years earlier were more susceptible to success than those of today. Those old-timers improvidently considered themselves gods and they spent accordingly. That was the era of wild parties and irresponsible acts—stigmas that the motion picture colony had been unable to blot out. One person cited as an example was Theda Bara, who achieved enormous fame as a "vamp," or siren. Quickly she came to be attacked for that image, as though it was her real character rather than a screen persona. Bara came out publicly to renounce that image to declare it was not her at all, that she loved little children, the church and so on. But if she succeeded in vanquishing the vamp image she failed to succeed in establishing a homebody image and her career suddenly and quickly died. Clara Bow (the "It" girl) experienced something similar due to the very sexual nature of her screen image. Without going into detail, or giving any names, Miles said there were 69 actors and actresses who, 10 to 15 years earlier, were making in excess of $1,000 a week and "today are pathetically regimented in the army of extras."[15]

For several years after World War I, with many of the small European countries in the throes of revolution, Hollywood became a Mecca of sorts for scores of European bluebloods, Russian princes, Austrian and German barons, Bulgarian counts, Turkish sultans, and so forth, not to mention generals and admirals from countries unfamiliar to most people. They flocked to Hollywood and found it possible to earn a living in pictures, according to a news report. "With the publicity value of titles above par, many foreigners began knighting and decorating themselves until Hollywood had enough nobility to start a Burke's Peerage of its own and enough phony blue blood and generals to start a new empire in the hills of Malibu," wrote a *Variety* reporter. That sham royalty invaded the film industry with a rush, most of them becoming technical advisors on pictures with foreign locales. However, their so-called advice was so often off the mark that film studios began to get protests from real representatives of those foreign countries "that stories and native customs were all wet and that Hollywood had better get wise to itself and find out just who their technical lads were." Pretenders to foreign nobility cost the studios a lot of money and prestige before they woke up. Worst offenders were said to be the Russians. Posing as being exiled by the Bolsheviks, they received sympathy from Hollywood, "which is a pushover for anything that smacks of royalty." According to the story, those fakers remained in Hollywood "hanging on to their self-made titles, but most of them are reduced to the ranks of extras, working when foreign types are necessary."[16]

Jack Budlong, extra, who died of injuries received on a film set in August 1941, was disclosed a day or two later to be the heir to the multimillion-dollar fortune of the late Milton John Budlong, automobile pioneer, who himself had recently died (just one month before his son). The 28-year-old extra was impaled on an old-time Civil War saber when he was thrown from his horse during the filming of the Battle of Gettysburg scene for a forthcoming film, at a ranch at Calabasas. Warner Brothers was the studio producing the film. On August 8 a coroner's jury returned a verdict of accidental death in the case, after several hours of testimony. Budlong died a few days after the July 30 accident of septicemia resulting from infection of the wound.[17]

Hedda Hopper wrote a piece in 1965 about actor Grady Sutton, who starred in Hollywood as an extra in *The Mad Whirl* (1925) with May McAvoy and who went on to work his way through 40 years of films, earning as much as $1,500 weekly, up to and including Elvis Presley's *Hawaiian Paradise*. Laura LaPlante taught him to apply makeup while Thelma Todd wised him up to camera angles, back in his early years as an extra. The rest of his skills he picked up from watching. According to Hopper's account Sutton fell into motion pictures because he went to school with Bill Seiter's (film director) brother Bob in Florida. When Sutton came to Los Angeles for a visit, Bill Seiter invited him on to the set of *The Mad Whirl* and put him in as an extra in a big party scene. Everybody did their own makeup in those days, and Sutton had to buy his own. He figured if a little was good, a lot was better, so he slapped on plenty. When he saw the rushes he was not impressed with the results. Later LaPlante taught him how to use greasepaint with restraint and with better effect. Sutton took to acting, and Seiter promised to keep him working if he'd stick around. Hedda Hopper concluded Sutton was an actor who made it to featured player from the extra ranks.[18]

And then there were the film extras that had been extras so long that they became famous, at least in a minor way. On June 6, 1958, the Screen Extras Guild (SEG) honored with gold life membership cards 35 colleagues, some of whom had worked as film extras since 1911. The presentation was made by Franklyn Farnum, SEG president, at the organization's annual meeting. A proposal to permit reporters and photographers to witness the ceremony was vetoed by the extras, who lived their lives in professional anonymity. Youngest among the honored guests was 65 while the oldest was more than 80. SEG reported the 35 had worked continuously in the film industry for a total of 1,296 years (an average of 37 years each). One of the group, Silver Haar, began as an Indian rider in 1911, long before Hollywood became the center of movie production.[19]

A 1985 news story by Marilyn Zeitlin observed that Clyde McLeod had been a movie extra since 1938 and had appeared in *Gone With the Wind*, *The Hunchback of Notre Dame*, *Casablanca* and *The Great Dictator*, among others. He had been directed by the likes of Charles Chaplin, Frank Capra, and Cecil B. DeMille. McLeod had worked with Marlene Dietrich, Claude Rains and Betty Hutton and was a stand-in for Anthony Quinn, Ronald Reagan, Rock Hudson, Tex Ritter, Joseph Cotton, Raymond Massey, and Maurice Evans, among others. At the age of 68 (in 1985) McLeod was still working as an extra; becoming a principal actor had never been his goal. "I got into the business because it was what my mother wanted me to do," he recalled. As a member of SEG McLeod then earned a minimum of $91 for an eight-hour day (nonunion extras made $35) and received health and welfare benefits as well as a pension. Although his real estate investments had helped supplement his acting income, he claimed he was one of the few actors to make a living principally through work as an extra. McLeod admitted that it was difficult for outsiders to get into SEG and recalled his early union days in the 1930s—before SEG. All union actors had to belong to SAG at that time, and "it was impossible to get in. The only way you got in was to get letters from producers saying they planned to use you. I asked for my father's help. He knew Mr. Chaplin and producer Walter Wagner. I got letters from both, and I was in the guild the next day." His father, Ted McLeod, worked in vaudeville shows in the 1920s and appeared in short-subject films for Warner Brothers in the late 1920s.[20]

After getting in, McLeod did stunt riding and doubled for stars on horseback and in punching scenes in Westerns and was a stand-in for many big-name actors, helping to get the lighting just right while the star was off the set. In those days, said McLeod, union pay ranged from $5.50 to $16.50 for an eight-hour day. "We all wanted the $16.50 jobs—that was for dress extras who wore white dinner jackets and tails and looked perfect as millionaires or guests at a Du Pont party." To increase his chances of getting the best-paying jobs, McLeod began collecting clothes and accessories for all occasions. One room of his house was wall-to-wall clothes. He had tuxedos with wide and narrow lapels, 10 "period" suits (from the 1930s to the 1960s), elevator shoes, canes, hats, pocket watches, and outfits for riding, skiing, polo, duck hunting and snorkeling. He said the most difficult work call he ever had in his film work was from Carl Joy of Central Casting, who wanted to know if McLeod could appear in a 1940s white, double-breasted, wide-lapel dinner jacket with maroon boutonniere, a pair of blue pleated pants, gray suede shoes, shirt with maroon bow tie and a gray homburg hat. Clyde told him, "Right away." He showed up on the MGM set for the film *Poltergeist* the following morning dressed, as ordered, for the part. From the start he put his earnings into real estate and was then well off. Having been an extra then for 47 years, and counting, Clyde McLeod said he had no intention of retiring.[21]

If things were not hard enough for Hollywood extras trying to scratch out a living by providing atmosphere for the movies, they sometimes got harder still when they found themselves losing out to free extras and to real people as extras. Those extras were up in arms in 1928, protesting against the use by film studios of wealthy transient visitors in Southern California who wanted to play extra for a day or two, just for the thrill, for no money. "These visitors, who certainly don't need the money, pull strings, which, somehow, always seem to be hanging out, to get on the sets," wrote a journalist. "Each keeps some struggling extra out of a day's pay that means a lot." It was said there were hundreds of those visitors in Los Angeles every year, acquainted with someone who had some semblance of pull in a studio or who, through mutual acquaintances, secured the desired introduction to the studio person. Then came the pitch from the transient visitor such as, "It would be so interesting to do it just for a day or two, that's all I care about," a line that often worked. All the major studios used Central Casting and had pledged themselves to take no extras except through Central, but the outsiders, it was reported, were being slipped in continuously just the same. "The outsiders admittedly mean nothing to the picture, the experience being simply a sop to the vanity of the out-of-towner." Central had tried repeatedly, without success, to curb the practice, leaving the registered extras to stand by seeing others take jobs they felt were theirs by right.[22]

But that was a relatively minor problem for the extras compared with the source of the greatest supply of free extras to the motion picture industry—the United States military. A 1926 news report related that Hollywood's "extra army" won an important battle in August of that year when the U.S. War Department in Washington ruled against the use of United States troops in Hollywood's dramatic film productions. Some extras had been fighting for months, through the Western Protective Association, against the employment of soldiers, sailors and marines in films. Recently that group had filed a formal complaint with the Secretary of War, charging that hundreds of actors, because of the use of real military personnel in some films, had been thrown out of employment. When it was handed down, the War Department's ruling held that the government's troops were to be used only in films of historical or educational value and when their use did not deprive others of employment. Film extras, through their group, charged that the producers violated military law in making the film *Ben Hur*.

In that film, it was said, a regiment of U.S. cavalry was used, with those soldiers being dressed in Roman costumes. Military law, it was said, forbade any soldier from appearing in a costume other than the regulation uniform issued by the army. Buckingham Ross, secretary of the extras' association, told the War Department that producers Metro-Mayer and Famous Players-Lasky were then using government troops in films, depriving hundreds of civilians of employment. The War Department was also told by the extras that those troops then being used were secured "through the political powers of Will Hays," president of the Association of Motion Picture Producers (Hays was "czar" of the major film studios' film cartel lobby group). It was also alleged that the movie producers were getting the soldiers "for little or nothing." In one case it was claimed a studio in Hollywood gave the marine base at San Diego a steam shovel for a "contract" to use troops. So dire had the situation become, with respect to extras losing out on employment, that the Western Protective Association announced it would bring legal action to bear on the War Department if relief was not granted. But then relief was granted, apparently, and the extras breathed more easily.[23]

Despite that ruling little seemed to change and the issue returned in March 1927 when it was reported the U.S. War Department had recently vetoed a request from a film studio to allow 3,000 or so of its soldiers to double as Germans in *The Patent Leather Kid*. That led a reporter to check with the War Department and being told that henceforth such would be the policy of the Department — no more American soldiers would double as extras. That order was reportedly sent to each corps area commander, following a protest from the American Federation of Labor (AFL). It was argued by the AFL that with thousands of extras unemployed soldiers on the government's payroll should not be used to save the film studios money.[24]

Yet nothing seemed to change. A protest against the alleged increasing use by film studios of United States soldiers, sailors, and marines in pictures, thus depriving extras of work, was filed in October 1934 with the NRA Code Authority by Aubrey Blair, secretary of the Junior Screen Actors Guild. As well, copies of the complaint had been sent to the Secretaries of War and Labor. "There have been scores of military pictures made, with Hollywood actors walking the street out of work," said Blair. "I think it is about time the government ceases to be a competitor of these men."[25]

Then, in February 1936, it was announced that laws prohibiting the army and navy from turning equipment, military bases, and personnel over to Hollywood studios for feature films were in the offing as a result of strenuous protests to Congress about cooperation of military and naval services with the film industry. Stirred up by the Junior Screen Actors Guild, complaints by the Los Angeles Central Labor Council and American Federation of Labor were submitted to Secretaries Woodring of the War Department and Swanson of the Navy Department, complaining that soldiers and sailors working for free in Hollywood productions had deprived civilian talent of months of employment in recent years. Although hopeful the two departments would tighten up on conditions under which ships, planes, and personnel were made available to studios, unionists were placing most of their hopes on Congress, especially on the Senate, "which is predominantly pro-labor." Efforts were to be made to write into appropriations bills soon coming up amendments stipulating that none of the cash could be used to pay personnel or finance loan of equipment to the film industry.[26]

Complaints by the unionists contended that 100,000 man-days of employment — involving upwards of $1 million in wages — were lost to extras in the previous five years because of the general aid given Hollywood producers by the army and navy. Those complaints emphasized studios saved tremendous amounts by getting the government to foot bills, not only for talent but also for gasoline, sets, costumes, and equipment. Listing 18 films made with army and navy personnel, in which civilian actors could have been used, unionists focused attention on the U.S. Army's cooperation with Warner Brothers in making *Captured*, and pointed out to numerous congressmen the "scandalous" arrangement by which U.S. noncommissioned officers and enlisted men were dressed in German uniforms, while American Army planes were repainted to resemble German planes. The complaint was buttressed with a list of 80 semi-military and semi-naval films made in the same period with civilian actors taking the parts of officers and enlisted men. If those could be produced with government direct help then all such films could be, argued the unionists.

Also pointed out was that the navy especially had spent thousands of dollars of taxpayer money maneuvering ships for film purposes, noting huge sums of money were consumed each time an anchor was weighed. The other 17 films on the list were *Flirtation Walk* (WB), *Marines Have Landed* (Rep); *Devil Dogs of the Air* (WB), *Here Comes the Navy* (WB), *Fleet's In* (Par), *Miss Pacific Fleet* (WB), *Hell Divers* (Metro), *Annapolis Farewell* (Par), *Seas Beneath* (Metro), *Suicide Fleet* (RK), *Shopworn Angel* (Par), *Shipmates Forever* (WB), *Here Comes the Band* (WB), *Sons of a Sailor* (WB), *Rendezvous* (Metro), *All Quiet* (Universal), and *Cavalcade* (Fox).[27]

However, a protest against the use of coast guardsmen as extras in the Columbia film *Tars and Spars* was filed with the Navy Department in the summer of 1945 by the Screen Players Union, with the announcement that similar protests would be made against the use of army and navy personnel in all future films. Mike Jeffers, business representative for the Screen Players, declared the sailors were depriving regular extras of their means of livelihood. He added that any government agency bargaining for the use of servicemen in films was violating the National Labor Relations Act.[28]

Also cutting into the work available for registered extras was the use of real people. Usually a studio would send a request to Central Casting for, say, 10 males, under 30, Italian working-class. What they got were 10 people who "looked" Italian if that was not their real background. Sometimes, though, a studio would, instead, go to an Italian working-class neighborhood and find 10 "real" people for the film, to get a more authentic atmosphere. These real people got paid, of course, for the most part, but they did reduce the amount of work available for registered extras. In 1924, it was reported that "Several hundred negroes of the regular 'shuffle along' type found only in the old Southern states were brought to Culver City as extras to give local color to plantation scenes in the Thomas Ince production *Her Reputation*." All of the plantation scenes were filmed at the Ince ranch house in Beverly Hills. It was said one old "Carolina mammy" felt at home right away and all they had to give her was a sunny spot in one corner of the house and plenty of tobacco for her corn cob pipe "and contentment was written all over her face." And half a dozen of these imported black kids found school wasn't half bad with May McAvoy (the film's star) as their teacher, and "before the company had been on the location a week, Miss McAvoy had a staunch friend in every one of the negro youngsters." In conclusion, said the report, "the dark actors had so much fun working for Mr. Ince that they left regretfully, when the picture was finished."[29]

A piece in the *Washington Post* late in 1926 declared the policeman, football player or sailor in modern movies frequently was the real thing. The public's demand for realism is primarily responsible for actual types supplanting professional extras, or so the article argues. Fred Fleck, chief of the Paramount casting office on Long Island, was asked to furnish six Hindus for an East Indian scene. Although the filing cases were filled with names of extras, sorted according to nationality, there were no Hindus. Fleck finally thought of Columbia University, and there he found a few Hindu students. One of them was asked to bring as many countrymen as could be located, preferably with their native costumes. At the appointed time, 30 young Hindus were present with their costumes. All of this was used to illustrate the idea that the casting director, when called upon to get a cripple, an Indian, a fireman or a waiter, went out and got him, instead of having an extra dressed and made up to look the part. Soldiers were easily obtained, said the account, from the local armories. The novelty and amusement of the work, as well as the pay, ranging from $7.50 to $12 a day, were said to be inducements for the real-life recruits. A call for eight cheerleaders for a football movie came during the summer of 1926. One cheerleader from Fordham University was located in a downtown broker's office. He, in turn, found several other young men who knew the art of cheerleading. If Fleck wanted a dozen armless or legless men he went to the veterans' service bureau. Indians were available at the New York State reservation near Watertown. Blacks could be recruited in Harlem, while seafaring men were plentiful along the waterfront. Female swimmers and divers could be obtained from the Women's Swimming Association.[30]

During the summer of 1927 it was reported that an average of 2,750 disabled war veterans were being placed in extra bits at the studios every month. Placements were made by an agency called the Central Employment Bureau for Veterans, maintained by the Community Chest charity in downtown Los Angeles. Only those veterans who were assessed as unfit for anything but light work were in line for movie jobs. According to Ross Lopez, manager of the bureau, the agency had been in operation for two years. No fees were charged the former soldiers for the jobs but, stressed Lopez, "a careful check-up is made of every individual applying for a job to see that he isn't trying to put anything over." That bureau for the veterans received the full cooperation of Central Casting, with a direct line telephone maintained between the two organizations to handle calls for extra jobs.[31]

Sometimes those real people were used as extras — for free — without even knowing it. After First National paid Al G. Barnes $10,000 rental for his complete circus to make scenes for *Do It Again* featuring Lloyd Hughes and Mary Astor, the producing company invited the general public to sit in and see a genuine circus performance for free, thereby saving about $6,500 that they would have paid to extras who would have been hired to be spectators for the circus audience background. As a result of First National having saved money by depriving extras of work considered legitimately theirs, the extras were circulating petitions for presentation to the film producers asking that the practice of using the public as film extras without compensation be stopped. Producers had recently staged circuses, sports events, and so forth, for motion pictures with the public invited to see the affair for nothing and the producer getting a big crowd without paying the regular extra fees. Staged circus scenes for *Tillie's Punctured Romance* featured the general public in the stands as atmosphere; Universal periodically staged shows of various sorts for the public in order to obtain big crowds in the backgrounds of scenes, and Roger Manning staged a football game in 1926 at a good-sized stadium to watch Red Grange play for a film production before a crowd of 5,000. In each of the above instances a few professional and paid extras were used.[32]

A bleak article on the future for extras, published in March 1932, declared their future to be dismal. Not only was the use of large mobs in film scenes at its lowest point in the industry's history — due to the Depression — but the tendency of directors was to demand nonprofessionals when extras were needed. For example, director Sam Wood had real college students recruited for the crowd scenes in *Huddle* (Metro), claiming that an extra's idea of a college boy was poor. "Fact that the students are delighted with a $5 payoff, whereas the professionals would rate $7.50, might also have something to do with it," observed a journalist. Similarly, for *World and the Flesh* at Paramount, director John Cromwell refused to use the standard extra crowd and had a technical director populate his Russian village from genuine Russians in Los Angeles. Another reason said to be responsible for this move to using more realistic extras was that the talk had to be authentic. The arrival of talking pictures dealt a hard blow to the old-time mob because in the talkies, "even a background murmur has to sound right. Extras have been fairly versatile in looking like various classes and nationalities but they're not as good as the original for the soundtrack."

For *Thunder Below* at Paramount, director Richard Wallace used all-Mexican mobs, while director Cyril Gardner insisted on genuine Germans and Austrians for Universal's *Mountains in Flame*. For *Shanghai Express* at Paramount and *Hatchet Man* at Warner Brothers, the Chinese mobs came from Chinatown, and that's where the money went, not to Hollywood extras.[33]

As of the summer of 1936, Cecil B. DeMille was rounding up some

2,000 Indians for Paramount's *The Plainsman*. He had scouts on the Cheyenne reservation contacting the people there.[34]

Status existed among the extras, with two distinct classes—dress extras and everybody else. Dress extras were the chosen people among the extras, getting the highest pay and a disproportionate share of the work. They got, of course, all the extra work with exacting wardrobe requirements but also got much of the regular extra work, just because they were well known. However, to achieve that status required a huge financial outlay to maintain a vast, extensive wardrobe, to add to it each and every year to keep up with every changing style and to constantly spend even more money to repair, maintain, and clean that wardrobe. And every penny of that expense was borne by the dress extra that had to fit in at a dinner party given by a millionaire, or be in seagoing togs when on a luxury cruise, or sporting the latest golf attire when on the links with major industrialists, and so forth. It was clothing that rarely if ever they wore in their real lives and if it were all deducted from their wages, the dress extras probably netted less than the ordinary extra. But they did have status, at least among the extras in general.

An article in *Variety* in August 1928 declared, "The major requisite of a screen player is a costly wardrobe. The humble extra is expected to appear on the set as well dressed as the featured players or star." Recently a director ordered a set of costly furs to be worn by the star. The furs were rented from a furrier. When 50 well-dressed extras appeared on the set to furnish atmosphere, it was discovered that one of the extras was wearing the exact duplicate of the white fox piece worn by the star. There were so many girls wearing costly white furs that the director decided to let them wear them and changed the star's fur to a black one. That was said to be just an example of how some of the extra players maintained their wardrobe and the higher-priced players were kept on edge worrying about how they could retain the exclusive in gowns and other wearing apparel. It was necessary for the extras, continued the story, to scheme the best way they could in keeping their wardrobe up to the exacting and high standard expected by the studios that became partial to calling the well-dressed extra for work. "Without a good wardrobe the extra doesn't have a chance to survive. With it, they are just as much out of luck," said a reporter. "It costs in excess of what they can earn to dress according to the way the studio expects them to dress."

A survey made among a group of well-dressed extras revealed that while their earning capacity averaged around $1,400 a year, the cost of their wardrobe over the same period was $1,700. Concluded the article, "How they managed to pay the landlord and buy the necessities is just another Hollywood mystery, unless the one indulging in this losing game is known to have other income and is tolerating the losses for the glamour of studio life."[35]

A January 1932 article stated the obvious fact that while most Hollywood extras did not get much work, "there is one group of atmospheric players in such demand that studios sometimes rearrange picture schedules in order to acquire their services." And those were the dress extras, that favored group "totaling less than 150 men and women, the molds of form and fashion, who comprise the atmosphere in scenes where the ultimate in sartorial elegance is demanded." While they got a higher rate of pay than the ordinary extras, "they must maintain their own expensive wardrobes and have qualifications that enable them to appear at ease in a London drawing room, a fashionable Paris café, a New York millionaire's penthouse apartment or a mansion." Their age range was said to go from the 20s to the 60s with all of them described as being expert dancers and with each one thoroughly conversant with the rules of etiquette.[36]

A 1933 newspaper story remarked that a Hollywood extra had to have a complete wardrobe and keep it up to date with all the current styles. "A complete but inexpensive wardrobe represents an investment of $1,000 and it calls for constant replenishing." Profiled was June Carter, who had been a Hollywood extra for two years. Her first chance to get out of the extra army came recently when she was singled out for a small part — with screen credit — in *It's Great to Be Alive*. A partial list of Carter's wardrobe included evening gowns, dinner gowns, afternoon frocks, street dresses (for all four seasons), bathing suits, beach apparel, beach pajamas, sports clothes, riding habits, bags, hats, shoes, and lingerie. In answer to the reporter's own rhetorical question as to how the dress extras could do it, he estimated that a Class A dress-extra girl could last as such only for three years. That was to say, she could not make enough money on an average of three calls a week to pay rent, groceries, and buy new clothes. Reportedly, Carter, 19 years old, was one of the few able to beat the game. "I can sew well. That's terribly important. In the second place, I adopt a color scheme — blue," she explained. "One hat — the one I have on — has been remade four times in the last two years — looks well with any one of several outfits because there's no color clash." Carter added that the same was true of shoes. "Sometimes I get tired having everything in shades of blue, but the color flatters me and the shade I get photographs well." The hat in question had cost Carter $22 when new and each of the four alterations was made at a cost of $2.[37]

When *Variety* reported on extras in October 1934 it declared that no extra working in Hollywood films expected to make more than $1,500 that year, "although most of them in the dress class are called on to maintain wardrobes valued at from $1,500 to $2,500."[38]

When Hollywood wished to replenish its supply of dress extras it often turned to a "dress parade." One of these events was held on Tuesday, December 11, 1934, at the Cathay Circle Theatre, when over 500 men and women paraded for the final elimination. Those who gained recognition as eligible for the coveted $15 a day work calls would learn within a period of time if they were selected. The local Chamber of Commerce did the counting. Despite the parade, studio casting officials still insisted that there were less than 200 people, men and women, who could be relied upon to fill the bill when "class dress sets" needed extras having complete wardrobes. The "no request" rule had been in effect at Central Casting since Campbell MacCulloch had taken charge — meaning studios could only request a type of extra through Central, but no request could be made for a specific name — at least in theory. Studio casting officials claimed, though, they would have to request specific people in order to keep themselves off the spot in selecting people who did not have sufficient enough wardrobes to fill the bill. A tip-off to the fact that a dress parade was in the offing could be found at one clothing house that rented out men's formal attire. It rented out $400 worth of clothing on the day before the parade. According to this account 1,500 extras spent close to $80,000 outfitting themselves for the first call. A great number of those attending the dress parade admitted they had gone into debt in order to get the necessary outfits, with most claiming they charged or bought their attire in the $1 down stores. At the dress parade actor Ben Bard functioned as emcee for the final performance. An organist furnished incidental music, with the overture being Elgar's "Land of Hope and Glory."[39]

A dress parade also held in 1934 was reported in greater detail in the pages of *Variety*. In this case over 950 women of all ages answered Central Casting's call for dress extras and the possibilities of earning $15 per day instead of the usual $5 and $7.50 paid the average extra. This contest, sponsored by Central, for eligibility as a dress extra was decided upon after numerous complaints had been made charging favoritism in handing out the $15-a-day work calls. It had long been claimed by studio casting departments that less than 100 women had complete wardrobes necessary for those who answered the dress calls. Complaints from other extras asserted that there was a much larger number, with favoritism shown to that 100. The dress parade was the result of that dispute. According to the journalist the dress parade affair "was sad, at times cruel." Contestants came garbed in all sorts of costumes, supposedly to indicate class. They paraded before the judges who assessed them according to style. "They were garbed in the height of fashion, in cheap wraps that screeched bargain basements, in dresses made by mama and in borrowed and begged finery," said the news account. "Cruel was the treatment of the less fortunate, less stylish of the hopefuls by their clothes-horse sisters, who missed no opportunity to get laughs at the inexperienced, to criticize their costumes." Dress extras had to have at least a dozen complete changes from sport to formal wear. Judges for the event were Reginald Barker and Mitchell Leisen, directors; John Arnold and Victor Milnor, cameramen; Fred Fleck and Walter McGough, assistant directors; William Mayberry and Marcella Knapp, casting directors; and Dolly Tree and Peggy Hamilton, fashion experts. The dress parade started at 9:00 PM and ended the next morning at 3:00 AM. On the following evening 400 men went through the same process. The parade of the male hopefuls was described as "less exciting, had few spectators." Judges selected 250 men out of the mob, and a little fewer than 100 females.[40]

At the start of February 1935 it was announced that from Hollywood's recently staged mass dress parade (perhaps the one in December 1934) held to form a select list of dress players, 161 girls had been chosen for that list — all to be registered at the Central Casting Bureau. The distinction of being on that list carried with it a $15-a-day pay rate, noted the journalist, "and a chance for more work instead of less pay and still less work for those on the list." From that list of 161, three were nominated for "best dressed" girl extra; Irene Thompson, Alice Adair, and Kay Sutton. Each of them estimated her wardrobe was worth $2,500. Irene had 12 evening gowns, Alice nine, and Kay eight. And the average life of an evening gown was only four or five pictures. After that either it went out of style or the film director recognized it. Another had to be bought to replace it. Each of the girls had a plentiful supply of smart street costumes, formal afternoon dresses, sports outfits of every type, tailored traveling suits replete with luggage, to say nothing of the countless hats, shoes, gloves, purses, scarves, handkerchiefs, and other accessories. The two biggest items of expense to the dress extra girl, all three agreed, were cleaning bills and beauty shops. "Body makeup almost ruins any dress," said Adair, "and it must always be worn with evening clothes. Three days wearing a dress with makeup and it is ready for the cleaner." Each of the three said she had an average of five costumes cleaned a week and with many of them being fancy evening dresses, the bill ran high. As well, each of them visited a beauty shop twice a week.[41]

As of the summer of 1935 the official wardrobe demands issued by Central Casting Bureau were as follows, according to reporter Douglas Churchill. Requirements for $15-a-day male extras were full dress complete, tuxedo complete, cutaway complete, boulevard complete, and riding habit complete. Then appeared the note, "The above to include top coat, silk hat, muffler, cane, gloves, etc. For this type of work wardrobe must be an 'acceptable modern' wardrobe." For $15-a-day female extras the requirements were evening gowns complete, requiring suitable wraps, fur or otherwise but no shawls or mufflers, dinner gowns complete with suitable wraps and no shawls or mufflers, formal afternoon clothes complete, suitable street clothes requiring furs or fur coats. It had to all be modern. Requirements for $10-a-day extras were "smart clothes." In addition to good physical qualifications these people were required to maintain a wardrobe suitable for picture purposes as follows— men: light and dark business suits, light and dark coats, bathing suits including robes, slippers, and so forth, lounging pajamas with robes and slippers, Palm Beach suits, flannels. All were to be "strictly up-to-date." For the $10 women; light and dark street clothes, light and dark coats, bathing suits with robes and slippers, lounging pajamas with robes and slippers, and sports clothes. Requirements for the $7.50 a day extras (this group made up the bulk of the extras) were that girls had to have an ordinary wardrobe such as the "average girl" would have, including light and dark street clothes, sports clothes, bathing suit, and light and dark coats. Men in this group were required to have "nice-looking" street clothes and overcoats, both light and dark, bathing suits, and flannels. The studios furnished special costumes for women in this group such as for maids, nurses, peasants, and so forth. They also furnished the men in this group with all uniforms needed. No wardrobe requirements were listed for the $5 a day extras with the studio supplying all apparel or it was a come-as-you-are work call.[42]

Churchill continued by saying that recently, in an effort to correct the dress extra situation the new management at Central (MacCulloch) attempted to create a list of dress extras that would be assured enough work to make it worth their while to maintain a substantial wardrobe. That effort failed. Thus the call went out that Central Casting would conduct a dress parade and that a dozen judges would select the men and women for that list. (This was apparently the third major dress parade held within a year, although the dates were confusing or not given and perhaps only two parades were involved. However, the numbers selected for the list were different enough in the articles to suggest three separate events.) "It was as pitiful a sight as this town has ever provided," wrote Churchill. "Elderly men with dress clothes of the last century, green with age, competed with young fellows who had mortgaged their cars to buy a new wardrobe for the event." Girls borrowed every bit of finery they could lay their hands on. One girl would march across the stage in a borrowed dress worth $200 and covered with a fur cape. When she had been judged she would rush behind the scene and give the cape to a friend, who would then parade. Hollywood clothing stores were cleaned out for the occasion. That night it was impossible to buy or rent a dress suit. *Daily Variety* estimated that $50,000 had been spent or charged in boulevard shops by the extras to outfit themselves. "If the scene was pitiful, it also was ludicrous," declared Churchill. The men were judged on one night, the women on another.

Almost 1,000 women paraded across the stage on their night. *Variety* said it presented a most interesting spectacle to a wealthy society woman present. That woman said she had never seen so many gorgeous gowns at society balls and wondered just where some of the extra women had acquired mink and chinchilla wraps; she also wondered why women with such finery needed to work. This parade resulted in 258 men and 223 women being selected out of about 3,000 candidates. Following that affair Central Casting estimated that for those people to dress as they did on the evenings of the parade, women would have to spend from $1,200 to $2,000 for their wardrobes while men would need from $1,500 to $2,300. Each would need also a minimum of $500 a year to maintain and replace their clothes. Churchill believed females were more star-struck and Hollywood-oriented than males were. Central Casting had twice as many women registered as men but studios used twice as many male extras as female ones. Thus, 1,600 females fought for 100 jobs a day while 800 males competed for the available 200 work calls. When the new regime took over at Central (MacCulloch) it planned, as part of its reorganization, on allocating the work so that everyone would get at least three days of work a week. "Due to internal friction in both the studios and the extra ranks, they failed," remarked Churchill.[43]

During 1937, 12,000 of the 16,000 film extras in Hollywood earned less than $200 each; 4,000 averaged about $700. Only 96 earned $2,000 or more and only three earned more than $3,100. Top money earners were Betty Kimbrough, 28, and Herschell Graham, 34. Both were classed as "dress extras," and their vast and extensive wardrobes were responsible in each case for their heading the earnings list. Kimbrough valued her clothes at $5,000. Graham, who paid $75 for street suits and $100 for evening clothes, estimated his wardrobe as being worth $2,000. Graham, unmarried, had been an extra for 12 years. He studied at the Oklahoma Agricultural and Mechanical College for three years, worked in oil fields for a time, and then came to California with no particular objective in mind, finally drifting into motion picture work. Betty Kimbrough was a photographer's model in New York when friends helped her get into film work some four years earlier. She was divorced and had a five-year-old son who was boarded out while she lived with a female roommate who was also in pictures. Betty was five feet, five inches tall, a gray-eyed brunette with a very fair skin. She earned extra money by modeling lingerie. Frequently her hands were "doubled" in films for those of stars. Her wardrobe included 20 "working" gowns, 20 pairs of shoes and slippers and accessories to match her outfits, several fur coats and wraps, sports and street clothes. A designer styled and made the gowns for her. Evening dresses cost her from $50 to $100 and sometimes went as high as $300. She might wear a gown half a dozen times, put it away for a few months and then wear it again if it was not outmoded. If she tired of the item she sold it for a fraction of its cost, or gave it away to a friend. Kimbrough thought she was "rather lucky" to get as much work as she did in 1937 but Graham believed, in his case, that it was a matter of being known.[44]

Among the oddities was a 1926 newspaper article that wondered about the backgrounds of extras, about where they came from. George Archainbaud, who directed *Men of the Dawn,* set out to answer those questions for his own satisfaction, and to that end he did a survey of the extras playing the roles of soldiers in his film, a romance involving the French Foreign Legion. He found, among his atmosphere players three former members of the real Foreign Legion; one of those was an Italian who had once been a banker in Naples. Another of them was a German, a former overseer in a Congo rubber plantation, while the third was a British Army officer who had been cashiered in India.

Among his other extras he found a former British sergeant major, a former Russian major, who fled to America after the Bolshevik Revolution in his homeland, two Australians (one a former gold miner and the other a sheep rancher), three former cowboys, a one-time Chicago bartender, and a member of a wealthy English family who had been a remittance man in British Columbia before drifting to Hollywood seeking a better climate.[45]

A different type of survey was conducted in 1932. RKO studios had a little over 100 principals and extras working in the film *Fraternity House* that year. Director Gregory La Cava wanted to make the college atmosphere as authentic as possible so he had his staff of assistant directors distribute a questionnaire to the extras and principals. It went to 50 males and 50 females, with many of the extras being present or former college and high school students. Of the 100 queried, only 62 believed feature movie parts would eventually be available to the $7.50 a day extras, while the other 38 had little hope. Of the males, only 14 of 50 would trade their chances in film for a steady job in business. Of the females, 39 of the 50 said yes, they would marry for money. Within that group of 90 some extras, the average that each extra was able to obtain work in the movies was about one day in every five, meaning about $9.80 in salary every week.[46]

Another news report in 1932 declared that girl extras with brunette hair were rapidly becoming extinct in Hollywood. Reportedly, the latest figures showed a proportion of three to one in favor of the blondes among female extras. Reasons behind that trend were said to include the number of blondes that had recently won film contracts as stars or major players (such as Jean Harlow) and that with the new lighting for talkies (compared to silent pictures) peroxide hair stood out on the screen and enabled the blondes to steal scenes. When the talkies arrived some three years earlier, it was said, the dark-haired extras led by virtually the same three-to-one ratio that then favored the blondes. The statistics on which these averages were based were taken from a chart prepared by Busby Berkeley of Samuel Goldwyn's studio on the 50 females appearing in Eddie Cantor's most recent comedy, *Palmy Days*.[47]

An even more obscure member of the extra army was the stand-in. According to a 1933 *Variety* article, they first entered the film business when screen stars became temperamental over delays in getting scenes shot. Someone who resembled the star in body type—not necessarily in looks—was engaged to take the star's place under the hot lights while the lighting and cameras were arranged. When that was all completed the star stepped in and the stand-in stepped out. "Few stand-ins ever get far in pictures. Most of them after a while in pictures become glorified valets or maids," said *Variety*. "Stars become attached to them and want them around, giving them extra recompense to take care of personal affairs." Salary for stand-ins ran from $30 to $40 a week. According to their value to the star, they were sometimes kept on salary between pictures, but most of them worked from film to film, with work as a regular extra filling in between their stand-in jobs. "Unless things are tough, and food must be eaten, extras shy from stand-in jobs, fearing they will become typed as such and possibilities of a career are curbed," concluded the piece. "They'd rather miss a few meals than take a chance on becoming what they consider a feudal chattel."[48]

Tragically, suicide among the extras was not unknown, reportedly in despair over failure in Hollywood. Kay Miller, a 26-year-old extra, died on June 17, 1933, after she swallowed what police said were 100 poison tablets because, said a news report, "of despondency over her failure to make a rapid advance in the films."[49]

Sigrun Solvason, in her home in Iceland, dreamed of Hollywood where, it was reported, "She believed all she read in the film magazines about how stars were elevated from the ranks of extras." She saved her money, and by the time she was 16 she had enough for the fare to Hollywood. Then, in May 1934, Sigrun, estranged wife of Fred Hessert, a mining man, was found dead in her apartment in Los Angeles. Police said she died after swallowing poison. "Once an understudy of Greta Garbo, Mrs. Hessert, known on the screen as Rae Randall, had failed to reach the heights to which she aspired," remarked a journalist. She was 29 years old when she died and had been dead for several days before her body was found by neighbors.[50]

And then there was the story of the Hollywood extra who got his girlfriend to steal money for him in the hopes of advancing his career. In August 1937, Rose Marie Gennarelli, 28, confessed to stealing $6,200 from her employer, the Securities Service Corporation in Chicago, and giving the money to her boyfriend, Patrick J. Billings, film extra, to promote his movie career. She accused Billings of urging her to steal the money for him. After the woman told her story, Billings lost his reserve and wept. "I was in love with you," he told her, "and I can't deny what you say. I had planned to marry you and have a beautiful home in Hollywood." The pair had faced each other after the fact in the state attorney's office, after which both were locked up.[51]

When the trial got under way in January 1938, Gennarelli explained she had met the 29-year-old extra some four years earlier and was enthralled by his stories of being a rising film star. "I was a fool and he wasn't worth it," she declared, in the Criminal Court of Judge Rudolph Desort. Billings was then on trial on charges of conspiracy to defraud the securities firm she worked for. He had been free on bond but Gennarelli had been locked up the whole time as she could not raise her $5,000 bail. It was said her love for Billings cooled when she learned there were 48 other women listed in his diary.[52]

On the stand Rose told of her romance with the former movie extra. She met him first in a northside ballroom. As his courtship progressed he began asking for money, and she at first gave him her own funds. Later she turned over the proceeds of bond coupons intended for clients of her company, she declared. When he demanded larger sums and she refused, he threatened to tell her parents of the earlier cash advances, she said. Rose was to be tried separately.[53]

On January 18, 1938, Patrick J. Billings was found guilty of conspiring to defraud the Securities Service Corporation. The verdict carried a penalty of one to five years in the penitentiary and a fine of $1,000. Rose smiled at the verdict against Billings. Patrick, in his own testimony, said he considered the girl to be a friend only and took the money as a loan, not knowing where she obtained it. He claimed he was much surprised and deeply shocked when he learned she stole it. The outcome for Gennarelli in this case does not appear to have been published.[54]

7
Wages and Statistics

Metro-Goldwyn shot their big *Ben-Hur* Circus Maximus scene on the special set erected outside of the studio proper in the fall of 1925. Some 3,500 extras appeared in the scene, the largest number of atmosphere players ever used in a motion picture. Those people were all placed in the various stands and paid, reportedly, from $3 to $10 per day, with the total payroll being an estimated $20,000 for the day. So that there would be no disturbance or disorder from those extras in the various sections of the stands, Los Angeles policemen, garbed as extras themselves, were planted among the ordinary extras. Every policeman wore his ancient Roman attire over his regulation police uniform and was given the additional task of aiding the unit managers on the film in having their orders carried out properly.[1]

A June 1926 article in *Variety* stressed the oversupply of actors in Hollywood with the gloomy conclusion that 22,500 were idle in Hollywood. According to the report there were 800 principal actors with about 500 of them continuously at work, while of the 25,000 extra people never more than 2,500 were in demand. Not even an average of 10 extras a year were ever elevated to permanent principal roles, said the article. "Within the past 10 years the known names in filmdom today of those who entered pictures as extras will not reach 25, and those nearly all women," was one conclusion drawn by the journalist. With respect to the average earning capacity of the 2,500 extras who were looked upon as standbys, this account said the amount did not exceed $75 weekly, each, at the highest, with from $40 to $50 a closer average for the majority. And of that money, a portion had to go for the necessary wardrobe an extra in demand was required to keep at the ready. It was a wardrobe that included evening dress, uniforms, sports clothes, and so forth, with "modish shoes and hats." Despite such poor prospects it was estimated herein that extras were coming to Hollywood at the rate of 200 people per day. Many of the 22,500 idle extras, who all believed they belonged in films, felt discrimination was being used against them through the steady call for the 2,500 "standards." But, the reporter observed, of the 25,000 extras there were not 40 of a type that could play a banker or preacher for "atmosphere," and those 40 were, of course, included in the active 2,500. As well, a similarly low number was to be found to play "ladies and gentlemen," and they, naturally, were also in the active 2,500. Those idle extras were all waiting for the "big day" when they would get their chance. The last such day came when a call was sent out for 5,000 (in this account) extras for *Ben-Hur*, some eight months earlier. Those 5,000 were engaged for one day only. The following day their number was reduced to 3,000; on the third day to 2,000; on the fourth day to 1,000; and thereafter to 500 per day. Extras received $6 a day for the *Ben-Hur* work. Extra pay then was graded into three levels (for all films except specials such as *Ben-Hur*): $7.50 a day, $10, and $15, for eight hours. Any fraction of work over eight hours was overtime and paid in blocks of two hours, with one-quarter additional pay for each two-hour block. Income for the steadily employed extras was then frequently increased through an extra working for one director for eight hours during the day and for another director for eight hours at night.[2]

At the Central Casting Bureau, said this account, presided over by Dave Allen, it was said that all the names of the 2,500 extras filling requirements were known in the bureau, that they supplied every extra need, and that when more of a certain type were needed, they were secured from the neighborhood that type could be found in, as a preference to having some of the idle extras made up for the types directors demanded, to be played more naturally. Allen had been in charge of Central since it was formed in January of that year. Previously Allen conducted his own casting agency for extras that he had created years before. He gave that up with his appointment as general manager of Central Casting. Reportedly, there were then no private casting agencies in Los Angeles for extras. Those agencies had been the bane of the extras' existence. Extras were charged no commission by Central Casting. Film studios obtained all their extras—at least in theory—through the bureau and paid Central 5 percent of the amount they paid the extras. That 5 percent collected from the producers was used to fund the operation of Central Casting. So far, said Allen, Central had been "extremely satisfactory to the producers and directors but not so much to the discontented contingent of unemployed extras." Allen said that he saw that as a problem he did not believe would ever be regulated until "the mass of hopeful but useless motion picture actors stop flooding this way." According to the reporter, "Outsiders are not wanted nor needed in Hollywood picture making, said Mr. Allen. It's a long chance but the lure of the picture is terrific, he added." To further emphasize the waste of time it all was for newcomers, Allen pointed out he employed two clerks in Central Casting whose sole, full-time duties were to inform the "incoming mob why they cannot hope to land in picture making." Of late Central Casting had gone even further in its endeavor to prevent the encounter of problems by "ill-advised applicants." Central then requested to know the previous occupation of the applicant. If that occupation was something on the order of bookkeeper, barber, clerk, waitress, seamstress, manicurist, and so forth, an effort was made by the bureau to find them a position in their earlier field in the Los Angeles area. "Several aspiring extras already have been so placed and are working at their former labor," concluded the article.³

During the first six months of its operation (January through June 30, 1926), Central Casting Bureau provided employment for 113,837 people who earned a total of $983,903, of which no portion was paid to agents or agencies for placing them. The office was operated by the Motion Picture Producers Association with Fred W. Beetson as president of the organization (Beetson was also the west coast representative for the Will Hays-led MPAA, headquartered in the east) with Dave Allen, general manager, in charge of the day-to-day running of the bureau. All of the operating expenses of Central were met by the producers through the 5 percent levy. During those six months the average daily placements by Central Casting were 629 extras with the average daily wage being $8.64 per person. Of those placements, 75,875 were men who earned from $3 to $15 a day, with 24,119 getting $10 while 29,610 earned $7.50 a day. Only 812 of that number worked at the $3 scale. They were mostly "mob" people who probably worked two or three hours in one scene. In that period 34,796 women got work with 11,730 earning $10 a day and 13,975 drawing $7.50, while 1,071 got $15 "for playing small bits by wearing better class gowns and wardrobes supplied by themselves." Only 464 of the women worked at the $3 scale, while 330 females were given bits which brought them a daily wage exceeding $15. As well, there were 1,780 boys and 1,386 girls of school age employed during this period, with 517 boys and 440 girls getting $7.50 a day and 1,027 of the former and 747 of the latter getting $5. In addition to extras' pay the producers paid $49,195 (the 5 percent) to Central. Had the people worked under the old system (private, commission-charging agencies supplying the extras), said the account, of the $983,903 the extras earned, they would have had to pay $88,200 to the casting offices for these placements. Though 113,837 people were placed during this period the work was split up in such a way that only about 4,500 specific people in total actually profited. Because a few thousand of the extras were well known among the studios, officials of those producers, in placing work order calls at Central, in most cases, requested specific people by name. Most of those extras were in the $7.50 a day and up class and, on average, they could obtain work on about 200 days a year. The other 20,000 or so extras found little employment during the course of a year.[4]

Early in 1927, Fred W. Beetson released the bureau's statistics for the calendar year of 1926, the first full year of the bureau's operation. It meant that for the first time in the motion picture industry statistics that were more or less reliable were available. During 1926 a total of 259,259 placements of extras were made through Central Casting. It meant that an average of 710 extra people was employed daily. (This count used the full 365 days in a calendar year to work out the average; later statistics from Central did not always do so. In its releases Central never defined how many days made up a year. Those numbers referred only to the extras employed by the MPAA film cartel member film producers. Studios that were truly independent and outside of the cartel used a certain number of extras that they obtained by means that did not include Central. Still, estimates were that something on the order of 80 percent of all extras that were used came through Central and the Hollywood majors.) When he released his numbers, Beetson observed that with 18,000 or more people in Hollywood, all ready to take those extra positions, and to hold down the number of people desiring to come to Hollywood for the purpose of "going into pictures," Beetson issued a ruling that under no circumstance should any more people be registered for work in the Central Casting office. That closing of the books made it "impossible" for anyone coming to the film capital for picture work as an extra to secure a position, as all placements were made through Central Casting and none but the registered would be called. That was true, however, only in theory. Anyone arriving in the film capital with any connection, strong or weak, near or far, direct or indirect, to anyone with any influence in the industry could usually get registered. That was always a major problem with efforts and regulations to limit the number of extras on the books—those regulations were often ignored, and when they weren't there were always loopholes.[5]

During 1926 a total of $2,195,395 was earned from those 259,259 placements, while film cartel members paid an additional $109,769 (the 5 percent) to Central Casting in order for the latter to run its office. Another item pointed out by Beetson was that the placement total of 259,259 was the largest made by any employment bureau in the world. It secured twice as much work during its first year for film extras as did the 10 labor bureaus operated by the state of California for every field of labor and work during the same period, or so the bureau claimed. Central had one of the largest telephone exchanges of any private industry. There were 42 trunk lines feeding the switchboard with over 8,000,000 calls (almost 22,000 per day) being cleared through it during 1926. With respect to the daily placements, Beetson said the average daily placement was 710 for the six working days of the week and ranged in pay from $3 a day to $15 a day, with the average being $8.46. A total of 4,336 (1.62 percent) worked for the $3 a day wage rate: 3,415 men, 822 women, 69 boys, and 30 girls. The largest percentage of placements was in the $7.50 a day class—108,185 (36.92 percent) of the gross dollar amount and 41.18 percent of the total number of placements. Next largest pay scale was the $10 a day group, 36.40 percent of the gross, or 79,916 placements (31.02 percent of placements). The $7.50 a day group drew $811,387 while the $10 a day extras drew $799,160. In the $12.50 a day class, 7,231 people earned $90,387; the $15 a day group saw 9,407 people earn $141,105. A total of 2,899 extras were paid more than $15 a day in 1926, of which 2,268 were men, 577 women, 23 boys, and 31 girls, with that group totaling $103,922. The $5 a day group (often thought to be the most prevalent extra group) comprised 18.42 percent of all placements drawing $236,425 for 28,424 men, 14,600 women, 2,392 boys and 1,869 girls. Average daily placements, slightly less than 3 percent, went to children, 1.63 to boys and 1.24 percent to girls.[6]

Statistics for Central for the first half of the calendar year 1927 were similar to the number from 1926, that is, a high majority of the calls were for men. Usually cited as a main reason for the discrepancy was the prevalence from the film studios of outdoor-type motion pictures with the expected dominance of male characters, from stars and featured players all the way down to extras. Most of the women in the higher wage scales of $12.50 and $15 were used for fashion show scenes and beauty shop scenes. Reportedly there were some 4,000 children around Hollywood ready to answer those 20 calls per day for child extras. To be an extra, each child so employed had to have some responsible adult (parent, guardian, or other) with him while he was working in the studio. Based on 25,000 people eager for extra work, over the 18 months from January 1, 1926, to June 30, 1927, the total spent by all the studios on extras worked out (if divided equally among all 25,000) to $1.44 per day.[7]

At the beginning of 1928 *Variety* reported that the working population of the West Coast picture colony numbered 42,546 and that they produced 82 percent of the entire world's output of films. In Southern California were nine major and 45 minor studios producing motion pictures and employing technical and office workers that approximated 13,500 (part of the 42,546). Those major studios were Paramount, First National, Warner

Brothers, Pathe, Metro-Goldwyn-Mayer, Fox, Universal, United Artists, and Film Booking Office (these producers, excluding Pathe and Film Booking Office but adding in Columbia, comprised the Hollywood cartel, MPAA). According to this account there were about 27,000 extra players in Hollywood, of which 16,500 were registered at Central Casting Bureau. On the freelance side the list of featured and bit players numbered around 3,000 in addition to contract players included on the studio payrolls and extras, freelance and registered.[8]

For the calendar year 1927, according to Central Casting figures, a total of 330,397 extra placements were made, which generated $2,838,136, an average of $8.59 daily per placement. Daily wages paid ranged from $3 to $25. On the Central registration rolls were to be found three times the number of women registered for employment as there were men, while there were twice as many jobs for the men during 1927 as for the women. This account, in *Variety*, said there were some 35,000 people registered with the Central Casting Bureau, seemingly a large exaggeration. During the year Central expended an average of 32 cents a head in the placement of adults and 55 cents in placing each child, who amounted to 4 percent of total placements. For men that year a total of 220,345 jobs were found: 103,015 paid $7.50; 2,429 paid $3; 37,085 at $5; 59,793 (most wearing dress clothes) at $10; 8,353 (better dressed or playing bits) paid $12.50; 8,816 at $15; and 862 paid over $15 and under $25. Women received 97,547 jobs as follows: 53,800 (44.74 percent of the female total) at $7.50; 31,004 at $10; 865 were paid $3 a day; 16,595 at $5; 2,086 at $12.50; 2,976 were paid $15; and 221 received over $15 and under $25. For children a total of 12,148 days of work were found, 7,074 for boys and 5,074 for girls. About 54 percent of the jobs given the boys were at the $5 rate while nearly 61 percent of the placements given girls were at the $5 a day rate. A total of $46,428 was paid to boys and $31,755 went to girls. All the studios maintained schoolrooms and teachers for the children while they were on the lots (as required by California law). That expense was said to have cost the major studios better than $50,000 a year.[9]

In that year, 1927, there was an average of 905 placements each day, with 603 for men, 269 for women, and 33 for children. Only 55 women out of all the female extras registered at the Central Casting Bureau averaged 2.5 or more days of work each week (for the full 52 weeks); 12 of them had 2.5; 23 received 3.0; 13 got 3.5; 5 received 4.0; one got 4.5; and one woman averaged 5.0 days of work per week over the full year. Of those 55 women, 84 percent (46) were listed on the Central rolls as "dress" women — those who had extensive and expensive wardrobes. As for the men, a total of 135 (out of all the male extras registered at Central) averaged 3.0 days of work or more during the full year; 74 got 3.0 days; 40 received 3.5; 13 had 4.0; 4 received 4.5; and 4 men averaged 5.0 days of work a week over all 52 weeks of the year. Of this total of 135 men, 75 percent (88) were classified in the "dress" men category at Central. Also within the total placements were 23,765 that were given to veterans of World War I, with their total wage bill being $168,499. Placements for "colored" people were 3,754 for $30,036 in wages. Apparently this number for blacks was much higher than in a usual year and was explained as being due to an "unusual demand during the year for colored people." Registered extras called the Central Casting Bureau twice a day to ask if any work was available for them. If there was and they had not called Central, then the bureau phoned them. During 1927, on average, the number of daily calls made by Central informing people of jobs was 493, while 893 made calls each day during the busiest hours to inquire whether there was work for them.[10]

With the arrival of talking pictures the use of large groups of extras was cut down considerably. Work calls to Central were then for many less people in the interior scenes but the work was said to last much longer. For 1928 Central Casting reported a total of $2,469,711 spent on extras for a total of 276,155 placements, with an average daily wage of $8.94 for an extra in 1928. Only one male and one female managed to work an average of 5.0 days per week, over all 52 weeks: two of each sex got 4.5 days; 10 men and 4 women worked 4.0 days; 35 males and 11 females received 3.15 days of work; 40 men and 15 women got 3.0 days; 94 men and 36 women had 2.5 days a week; and 132 men and 87 women worked an average of 2.0 days per week, for all 52 weeks in 1928. According to this account, some 45,000 people around Hollywood were ready to jump at the call from Central Casting for extra work. Central continued to run a special department for war veterans, and in many instances they reportedly got preference over other people on work calls. Noted was that Central was still not taking new registrations of extras "unless requested by studio officials who agree to give the parties registered work through the office sufficient to average two days a week on the year."[11]

For the year 1931 jobs for extras were the scarcest in six years, from Central Casting's figures. Average daily placements that year were 606, two jobs for men for each job for a woman, with an average daily pay of $9.32. Of 17,500 registered extras at Central Casting, just 619 managed to average 1.0 days of work per week, over the full year. If $18.64 a week could be said to be a living wage in Hollywood (two days as an extra), then only 218 extras made a living. Payroll that year was $1,766,479 on 189,589 placements. The scramble for extra work was intensified by the arrival of a swarm of new applicants. Besides the 17,500 reported to be registered at

Central, "hundreds of studio letouts and unemployed from other industries joined" the horde. That was a reference to the economic difficulties encountered by people in the depths of the Depression. Although Central was maintained jointly by the major studios, individual studios did more of their own picking of extras in 1931, bypassing Central, even though that was a violation of the bureau's rules. "Many studios, where departmental help had been cut to the bone, handed the extra checks, to ex-employees when possible. This caused the appearance of electricians, carpenters, clerks, stenos, and even some directors as atmosphere." Over the previous year or two Central had changed its practices a bit. The arrival of sound started it, requiring the bureau to add a talking ability category to each individual's registration file. Then in 1929 the "musical stampede" compelled special departments for singers and dancers be set up at Central, to be scrapped the following year. In 1930 the industry went in a big way for foreign versions of its films, and special files were established on extras who spoke foreign languages. Although the Depression year of 1931 resulted in a drop of some 25 percent in total extra placements the bureau was kept busy. "Studio letouts with letters requesting registration. Needy unemployed shunted to pix from social agencies. Increased phone calls from regulars," said a reporter for *Variety*. In 1931 a total of 74 women and 144 men averaged 2.0 days of work per week for the full year and just 63 men and women managed to work over 2.0 days a week. With the 401 people who averaged one day of work each week that made 35 of each 1,000 registered "working consistently." Men got 63 percent of all jobs in 1931 and 63 percent of all the money. Children were used sparingly, with only 15 percent of those called who managed to work more than 10 days in the entire year. Figures for black and Chinese extras were only partially included in the general totals as the "majority" in those categories were recruited by native agents and paid off elsewhere.[12]

A rotating system of employment was instituted at Central Casting in 1934 in an attempt to spread the employment around. Under that system the work calls for any one extra were to be limited to three a week. It was said that limiting the calls to three a week didn't mean that any one person would get three calls a week: "Indications are that from now on an average of one call a week will be topper," said a reporter. In 1933 only four people earned more than $2,000 as extras; 23 more earned over $1,500. One woman said she had been on the list for eight years and had never received any calls; another claimed she had received only two one-day calls in six years.[13]

A February 1935 news story headlined the fact that only 12 film extras earned a living wage. That was based on the fact that in 1934 only six male extras and one female extra earned $2,500 or more; five other female extras earned less than $2,500 but more than $2,000. All 12 were dress extras, listed in Central Casting's books as "Class A dress people." The man who earned the most was Oliver Cross, paid $2,846.25 for 195 days of work. Women extras were led by Gale Ronn, who received $2,641.25 for 167 days of work. In that year 219,859 extra placements were given to about 4,000 specific extras, for which they received $1,984,697, with the average daily check being $9.03 per day.[14]

For the calendar year 1935 Central Casting figures revealed that 278,486 placements were made at a total cost of $2,571,293. An average of 889 extra jobs was provided each day with an average daily paycheck of $9.23. Male extras drew almost 60 percent of the money ($1,521,017) from 182,650 (65 percent) of the total placements. By wage rates the breakdown for men was as follows: $7.50 ($416,977 on 55,597 jobs); $10 ($530,470, 53,047); $15 ($328,860, 21,924); $3.20 ($43,016, 13,443); $5 ($187,530, 37,506); $12.50 ($14,162, 1,133). In the wage rate scale ranging from $3.20 to $7.50 per day that year, there were 24,024 "racial group" placements. Of those, 5,705 jobs went to blacks, 2,804 to Chinese, 2,499 to English, 2,232 to French, 1,873 to Hawaiian, 1,595 to Mexicans, 1,450 to Russians, 1,389 to Italians, 1,029 to Spanish, 711 to Arabs, 518 to Scots, 545 to Polynesians, 268 to Cubans, 204 to Germans, 351 to Indians, 183 to Armenians, 157 to Greeks, 108 to Yugoslavs, with the rest being in smaller lots ranging from one to 39 and being divided among Austrians, Australians, Belgians, Canadians, Eskimos, Filipinos, Hindus, Hungarians, Irish, Poles, Swedes, Swiss, and Turks.[15]

In 1935 placements for female extras totaled 86,001 and paid $724,154. Their breakdown was as follows: $7.50 ($153,292, 20,439); $10 ($203,910, 20,391); $15 ($232,020, 15,468); $12.50 ($3,437, 275); $5 ($103,680, 20,736); $3.20 ($27,814, 8,692). Those $3.20-per-day rates existed in 1935 for all extras, adults and children, but were abolished for 1936 and onward, for adults and children, as a result of conference meetings while the parties worked on the NRA Code for the motion picture industry. That same year there were 5,447 placements for boys that generated total wages of $34,491. Average daily placements in 1935 were 583 for men, 275 for women and 31 for children, for a total of 889. New applicant interviews at Central in 1935 averaged 87 per day (64 in 1934). During 1935 weather conditions and "improper placements" resulted in a daily average of 48 cancelled calls (17 per day in 1934). Reportedly, for each of the 10 years of its existence the Central Casting Bureau operated at a profit. Earnings of the top grosser in the extra field used to be kept at Central but in 1936, with the introduction of a machine-based record-keeping system, that data was no longer kept, or so it was said. A report in the *Los Angeles Times* noted those 278,486 placements in 1935 through Central, and estimated that about 40,000 (less than 13 percent) more placements were made through other sources—that is, for extra employment given by independent producers (not part of the MPAA) in the Hollywood area.[16]

Extras in Hollywood in 1936 earned $2,420,453 from 268,436 placements. In that year the average daily placement was 858, at an average daily wage of $9.02. Male extras totaled 174,759, who were paid $1,422,137; 80,962 women were paid $658,074; 7,712 boys earned $49,263; and 5,003 girls were paid $31,658. That average daily total of 858 was comprised of 558 men, 259 women, and 41 children. In the $7.50 category 82,015 (men, women and children) were paid $615,112; $10; 71,961, $719,610; $5; 62,721, $313,605; $15; 27,181, $407,715; $3.20; 18,924, $60,556; $5.83; 3,727, $21,728; $8.33; 692, $5,764; $9; 183, $1,647; $12.50; 850, $10,625. Two extras were paid $35 a day each, while four were each paid $75 for one day.[17]

It was a record year for extras in 1937, with total receipts of $2,986,372 from 294,307 placements. Receipts for the year exceeded those of 1936 by $565,919. Part of the 1937 boom was due to the producers' contract with SAG, which became effective June 1, and raised the minimum extra check from $3.20 to $5.50, among other changes.[18]

Two investigations with reference to extras and bit players were being carried on in Hollywood in October 1939 and could result in numerous reclassifications and pay increases for the atmosphere players in films. The extra situation as a whole was being inquired into by a standing committee comprising a representative of SAG, one from the producers, and a third, neutral member. That inquiry was for the purpose of deciding who and how many extras got work, pay scales, and to determine how many actually depended on the industry for a living. A second investigation was being conducted by SAG itself, which could bring about a demand for salary increases as high as 15 percent in some extra classifications.[19]

A new pay raise program for extras and atmosphere players confronted film producers at the start of December 1939, as a result of their action a week earlier in granting a 10 percent increase to 23,000 workers affiliated with the Conference of Studio Unions and a similar increase back in October to 12,000 technicians of the International Alliance of Theatrical Stage Employees (IATSE). The Council of Class B members of SAG decided to reconsider its previous action not to go into the matter of pay increases at that time on receipt of a letter from Kenneth Thomson, executive secretary of SAG. Thomson pointed out that inasmuch as the many craftsmen were then benefiting, the Guild stood ready to petition in behalf of extras for more money. Under the proposed 15 percent increase schedule as outlined by SAG, atmosphere players then receiving $5.50 would get $6.33, regular extras then being paid $8.25 would get $9.49, and dress extras then being paid $16.50 per day would be paid $19.[20]

Later that December authorization was voted by the SAG board of directors to seek a 15 percent wage increase for film extras. Negotiations between SAG and the producers were to open later that same month. However, before the question of a general pay increase was considered, the two sides were slated to look into the reclassification of various types of extra work, any of which could result in an earnings increase for an extra who was reclassified. In 1939 motion picture extras were paid a total of $3,167,896 in salaries (an increase of over $400,000 over 1938) from a total of 294,688 placements.[21]

When high salaried stars, such as Greta Garbo and Mickey Rooney, or the lowest paid extras went before the camera to act out a scene they were engaging in a creative art. They were exercising discretion and judgment, despite the presence of a director, and their "output" could not be standardized. Therefore, they were not entitled to time and a half overtime pay should they be kept on the set for more than 42 hours per week, or so Homer Mitchell, counsel for the Motion Picture Producers and Distributors of America (MPPA), told a special examiner for the National Wages and Hours Administration in Washington, D.C., in July 1940. It was one of a number of hearings held by the Wages and Hour Division as a result of numerous petitions seeking to have redefined words in the fair labor standards act used to describe employees exempt from the minimum wages and maximum hours provisions. The 10 leading Hollywood film producers, argued Mitchell, employed a total of 18,541 workers, of which 13,153 were ordinary craftsmen and "undisputedly" were covered by the act. They were the only ones then regulated as to minimum wages and overtime pay. As to Hollywood's remaining 5,338 employees, who included actors, Mitchell said there was some question whether they could be brought under the act as it then stood. "The act specifically mentions laboring conditions," Mitchell told the hearing. "The idea was to help little fellows who couldn't help themselves. No one is sweating movie actors. Their average pay is $500 per week, so there isn't any question about minimum pay."[22]

Earnings for extras during 1941 totaled $3,118,097 (up over $500,000 from the 1940 total of $2,529,766). Average daily paycheck that year was $11.50. Reportedly, if the total amount had been distributed evenly among all the extras registered at Central Casting the average yearly earnings would have been only about $500 each — meaning some 6,236 registered extras. Job placements amounted to 255,625 that year.[23]

A court case that involved 11 film extras that attempted to collect unemployment insurance benefits in California was disposed of in November 1946. As part of the proceedings it was revealed that those 11 extras had worked an average of 23 years each, earning intermittently no more than an average of $10 a week. Those 11 people did not get unemployment insurance benefits.[24]

As of April 1, 1947, film extras received an automatic cost-of-living increase of 11.17 percent, it was announced by Screen Extras Guild. Under the new rates, pay would range from $9.45 for an eight-hour day for mob scenes to $22.23 for dress extras, riders, dancers, skaters, and swimmers.[25]

8

Conclusion

Life in the Hollywood dream factory has always been held up as one of the most desirable lifestyles one could aspire to and achieve. Undoubtedly that was true for some, but only a very few. For Hollywood's film extras the reality was always far removed from the dream-factory illusion. Far too many extras and would-be extras struggled for the far too few jobs that were available. In the early years they struggled against the private agencies that ripped them off and abused them in other ways. Later, when the Hollywood film cartel—the Motion Picture Producers and Distributors Association (MPPA)—established the Central Casting Bureau the extras still struggled. The commissions charged by the private agencies may have been eliminated but Central Casting caused the atmosphere players grief in other ways. Nor did unionization prove to be a remedy for the film extras. It was a struggle before actors, of all types, in motion pictures were able to form a union, certifying the Screen Actors Guild (SAG) as their bargaining agent. However, extras had little say or voice in the running of that union and struggled for autonomy, for a union that truly represented their interests. Eventually they did form an autonomous union and certify it as their bargaining agent, only to have SAG outmaneuver the new unit and spin off another unit, the Screen Extras Guild (SEG), through the complex and intricate ways that then existed to have a bargaining unit accepted by the AFL. Thus the extras had, in the end, not the autonomous union they wanted but one that was independent in name only while in reality still a de facto part of SAG. Decades later the sham would be dropped as SEG was banished and the extras returned to the point where they started, as members of SAG.

A lack of work, too little money for the work that was done, inadequate unions, sexual harassment (of the female extras), a centralized hiring system that was prone to discrimination, favoritism, and nepotism, and far too many extras competing for the work were the main problems that plagued the Hollywood hopefuls. Despite all the problems, people flocked to Hollywood from all over America and the world in general to try and take part in the great Hollywood sweepstakes in the hope that they would be one of that tiny, minuscule number that would take the film capital by storm and rise to stardom. And so they came to Hollywood by the thousands. The obvious entry point to the film world was to start out as an extra. If you believed in the dream then you were convinced that once you landed in a film or two as an extra you would, with your looks and personality, stand out and be noticed and move on up the ladder. Ambivalence was the response on the part of the film producers. Such a dream as that of rising to the rank of star from the extra mob, while it had happened a small number of times, did not develop and maintain legs on its own. Film producers fueled and reinforced that dream with articles that appeared across America time and time again portraying the rags-to-riches rise of some of the extras. Hollywood producers did that in order to keep plenty of fresh bodies flowing into the film capital, grist for the mill. On the other hand, once the hordes arrived they could create a great nuisance, clamoring at the gates of studios, waylaying anybody who looked as if he might be a film executive and could have some influence in dispensing work. Those hordes became such a nuisance and drain on Hollywood resources that often the film producers sent out stories and news releases about the impossibility of ever becoming a star by rising from the extra ranks. Such articles and press releases pointed out the woeful life experienced by extras and the bleak future they had to look forward to. Advice given in such material was a strong request that all would-be extras abandon hope and not undertake the trek to Hollywood.

Problems for extras in the years up to the middle 1920s were largely centered on the private employment agencies that placed people in motion pictures as extras. The meager wages paid to the extras were further reduced by the commissions charged by these agencies. Other abuses were also inflicted upon the atmosphere players, and various government bodies became involved, investigating the situation. Enough noise was generated that the Hollywood film cartel was motivated to take steps by establishing a centralized registry and hiring procedure for extras seeking work with the major film studios who were members of the cartel, and they employed in the neighborhood of 80 to 85 percent of all extras employed in the industry. This supposed self-regulation (internally dealing with a problem) was a common response in all industries, when a problem got enough attention that the industry worried the government would step in to regulate. For an industry it was always preferable to "self-regulate" than take a chance on having the government impose a solution to a problem, a

8. Conclusion

solution the industry would not like. The cartel itself (MPAA) had been established in the 1920s with Will Hays as its head and "czar" precisely to give the appearance that Hollywood was seriously addressing the various situations then drawing public and governmental attention and scrutiny, such as morality on the screen, morality off the screen with respect to Hollywood lifestyles, the monopoly nature of the industry, corrupt business practices, and so on. Central Casting was created, in part, as a piece of self-regulation. Another reason for its creation was to better manage the hordes of extras in Hollywood. That is, some of the besieging of studio gates by hopefuls would be deflected with the besieging taking place at Central Casting.

Sexual harassment of female extras and hopefuls was likely very pervasive in the time period covered by this book. After all, it was from Hollywood that the term "casting couch" originated, with its clear and explicit meaning. Of course, the term "sexual harassment" was not then in use and the problem was only mentioned indirectly and even then not very often. The few mentions of the issue did imply the problem was widespread but details were mostly vague, lacking in specific details. The few cases in which details were mentioned seemed to have ended badly for the women involved, that is, badly after and in addition to the trauma of the harassment. Any woman who was an extra in Hollywood and had been harassed and had looked at the public record would have seen a powerful incentive to not come forward with a complaint. Things did not go well for the few brave women who had the courage to come forward. Things were hard for male extras in many ways; things were equally hard for female extras in those same ways, plus one. Because extra jobs were few and far between, the people struggling for the work were often in dire financial need, and that often meant the women were very vulnerable to sexual harassment. Getting extra work was hard for everybody but even harder for women because extra jobs, in the period covered, were available in a ratio of about two jobs for men to every one job for women. Also, there were a greater number of women registered with Central Casting than there were men; things were equally hard for female extras in those same ways, plus two.

Throughout this period the problem of a surplus of extras bedeviled the industry and the extras themselves. That surplus was present and huge in 1913; that surplus was present and huge in 1945. It remained a constant in all the years in between. Everyone involved in the motion picture industry took a stab at fixing the problem, as did some with no direct connection with or to the film industry. All of them failed completely. The numbers of registered extras did sometimes decrease over time but never enough to make a difference. And any change in numbers was always temporary.

The unions involved in the acting field, SAG, SEG, and others, tried numerous times and failed; Central Casting tried numerous times and failed, as did the National Recovery Administration (NRA) as part of its efforts to generate a motion picture industry code of employment. As a Depression-era governmental agency, it tried to spread the work more evenly among people and to put a floor on wages paid in order to ease the burden on all the people suffering the economic hard times. The NRA tried for years to effect a reduction in the surplus of extras, and failed. Of course, there were any number of fairly straightforward ways of eliminating the surplus extras, and when it never happened one could only conclude that the failure was due to the simple fact that the powers-that-be (the motion picture industry) did not want to see a reduction. Central Casting had "closed" registration books for many years. In theory that meant no new extras could get work in the major studios as they could not register and get their work card. However, the film studios got around the closed books by sending people to Central with a "please register" note. Central always complied and the number of extras increased. Central always allowed a wholesale noncompliance with its rules. Studios were not supposed to request extras from Central by specific name (such as John Doe) but only by type (such as Italian male, under 30). However, studios ignored the rule and requested by name whenever they wanted, and if the requested person was not registered, then Central registered the newcomer.

Given the state of Hollywood's extras the group could hardly be said to have an elite component. However, the subset in the ranks of the extra army that reached closest to the idea of an elite section was in those called the "dress extras." This relatively small number of extras got a fair amount of work, relative to the average extra, but they paid a high price. All extras had to supply their own clothes when they got a work call (not, of course, for period films) and the dress extras had to maintain a huge wardrobe. It was a wardrobe that had to cover every conceivable setting and situation. An extra needed an extensive wardrobe for indoor events and for outdoor events, for beach wear and for winter wear. A dress extra had to have the appropriate clothing to fit in as a dinner party guest in the palatial home of a banker, or for a Mediterranean cruise on a luxury yacht owned by an industrialist. Not only was such a wardrobe expensive to acquire, it was expensive to maintain as items had to be cleaned regularly, and so forth. As well, because styles changed so often, yearly additions to the wardrobe were mandatory, and also expensive. To keep the list of dress extras up to an acceptable number and to freshen the list, Hollywood held what were called "dress parades" wherein hopefuls paraded across a stage in some of their finery as judges sat by, looked on, and assigned points to each contestant. Females paraded on one night; males promenaded the next night. All did so for the chance to make $12 a day, or $16 a day in later years, of which, perhaps, half was gobbled up on the acquisition and care of a wardrobe the extra likely had little or no use for in her real life.

Whatever category an extra fell into, he or she did not likely make enough money to live on. Most of those who did it year after year had either an independent income or somebody who supported them financially. Others perhaps lasted for only a short time in the film capital, sharing a tiny apartment with another extra with enough money saved to last them a few months, hoping for their big break before the money ran out, or going back to their home state when the break did not come and the money ran out. Things were tough enough for the film extras but Hollywood sometimes made it harder by, for example, renting a circus for a day, advertising a free performance and then filming the crowd to use for a film, without telling the crowd or compensating them. Thus, the studio got a crowd of perhaps a couple of thousand people for free. Another ploy by Hollywood studios was to use members of the U.S. military as extras, for free, in some of its films. Extras and their unions complained often about the practice, and the U.S. military banned the practice, just as often. But then, as someone once said, somewhere, "Never was a place where people had it so good like Hollywood."

Statistical Appendix

The following pages contain statistics of total placements of extras and total wages paid (selected years). A placement is one extra who worked for one day. If an extra worked five days in a row on a motion picture, or five days intermittently on the same picture, it was five placements.

All numbers refer to the extras employed by member firms of the Motion Picture Producers and Distributors of America (the majors, the film cartel), and all the statistics originated from the Central Casting Bureau, the placement arm for the film cartel. Inconsistencies exist in the statistics shown, however the data is presented as it appeared in the original source. Extras placed in the motion pictures produced by independent producers are not included in the following data, and those people were placed through sources other than Central Casting. It is estimated that in this period about 85 percent of all extras employed in the industry were obtained through Central Casting and for the film cartel.

──────── **1926** ────────

Total placements 258,759
Total paid $2,193,893
Average daily placements 710; men 485, women 205, children 20
Average daily wage $8.46

Men

Daily wage ($)	Number of placements	Total wages ($)
3.00	3,415	10,245
5.00	28,424	142,120
7.50	75,289	564,667
10.00	55,568	555,680
12.50	5,156	64,450
15.00	7,106	106,590

Daily wage ($)	Number of placements	Total wages ($)
Over 15.00	2,268	81,059
Total	177,226	1,524,811

Women

Daily wage ($)	Number of placements	Total wages ($)
3.00	322	966
5.00	14,600	73,000
7.50	30,692	230,190
10.00	23,771	237,710
12.50	1,928	24,100
15.00	2,224	33,360
Over 15.00	577	20,784
Total	74,114	620,110

Boys

Daily wage ($)	Number of placements	Total wages ($)
3.00	69	207
5.00	2,392	11,960
7.50	1,242	9,315
10.00	336	3,360
12.50	73	912
15.00	53	795
Over 15.00	23	1,039
Total	4,188	27,588

Girls

Daily wage ($)	Number of placements	Total wages ($)
3.00	30	90
5.00	1,869	9,345
7.50	962	7,215
10.00	241	2,410
12.50	74	925
15.00	24	360
Over 15.00	31	1,039
Total	3,231	21,384

Source: "Central Casting Offices." *Variety*, January 19, 1927, p. 9

1928

Total placements 276,155
Total paid $2,469,711 (This includes $176,963 in overtime, an amount not included in the numbers below.)
Average daily placements 756; men 494, women 237, children 25
Average daily wage $8.94

Men

Daily wage ($)	Number of placements	Total wages ($)
3.00	4,189	12,567
5.00	30,063	150,315
7.50	67,194	503,955
10.00	62,326	623,260
12.50	7,117	88,962
15.00	9,154	137,310
Over 15.00	389	9,452
Total	180,432	1,525,822

Women

Daily wage ($)	Number of placements	Total wages ($)
3.00	609	1,827
5.00	19,529	97,645
7.50	33,129	248,467
10.00	29,533	295,330
12.50	1,592	19,900
15.00	2,364	35,460
Over 15.00	46	969
Total	86,802	699,599

Boys

Daily wage ($)	Number of placements	Total wages ($)
3.00	49	147
5.00	2,188	10,940
7.50	2,200	16,500
10.00	585	5,850
12.50	162	2,025
15.00	127	1,905
Over 15.00	161	4,635
Total	5,472	42,002

Girls

Daily wage ($)	Number of placements	Total wages ($)
3.00	1	3
5.00	1,610	8,050
7.50	1,262	9,465
10.00	287	2,870
12.50	110	1,375
15.00	122	1,830
Over 15.00	57	1,732
Total	3,449	25,325

Black

(average daily placement, 30; average daily wage $8.22)

Daily wage ($)	Number of placements	Total wages ($)
3.00	0	0
5.00	966	4,830
7.50	5,834	43,755
10.00	2,152	21,520
12.50	324	4,050
15.00	141	2,115
Over 15.00	75	1,732
Overtime	1,424	11,700
Total	10,916	89,702

Veterans

(average daily placement, 46; average daily wage $5.69)

Daily wage ($)	Number of placements	Total wages ($)
3.00	3,111	9,333
5.00	5,936	29,680
7.50	4,786	35,895
10.00	532	5,320
12.50	218	2,725
15.00	4	60
Over 15.00	2,188	12,449
Total	16,755	95,463

Source: "Central Casting Corporation." *Variety*, January 16, 1929, p. 7

Number of extras who worked a specified number of days per week, on average over the full 52 weeks

Days	Men	Women
5.0	1	1
4.5	2	2
4.0	10	4
3.5	35	11
3.0	40	15
2.5	94	36
2.0	132	87

Source: "Coast extras cut down." *Variety*, January 16, 1929, p. 7

——— 1929 ———

Total placements 226,723
Total paid $1,878,873
Average daily placements 621; men 393, women 209, children 19
Average daily wage $8.29

Appendix—1929

Men

Daily wage ($)	Number of placements	Total wages ($)
3.00	150	450
5.00	27,622	138,110
7.50	53,130	398,475
10.00	50,898	508,980
12.00	5,227	62,724
15.00	6,516	97,740
Total	143,543	1,206,479

Women

Daily wage ($)	Number of placements	Total wages ($)
3.00	146	438
5.00	15,410	77,050
7.50	28,195	211,462
10.00	28,605	286,050
12.00	1,899	22,788
15.00	2,012	30,180
Total	76,267	627,968

Boys

Daily wage ($)	Number of placements	Total wages ($)
3.00	432	1,296
5.00	1,771	8,855
7.50	1,367	10,252
10.00	405	4,050
12.00	73	876
15.00	107	1,605
Total	4,155	26,934

Girls

Daily wage ($)	Number of placements	Total wages ($)
3.00	230	690
5.00	1,278	6,390
7.50	915	6,862
10.00	285	2,850
12.00	17	204
15.00	33	495
Total	2,758	17,491

Extras registered with Central Casting:

Total number of regular extras	9,836
Total number of children	1,446
Total number of blacks	1,132
Total number of dancers	1,350
Total number of singers	1,277
Total number of musicians	2,500
GRAND TOTAL	17,541

Source: "Jobs for extras dropped in '29." *Variety*, January 29, 1930, p. 18

1931

Total placements 189,589
Total paid $1,766,479 (includes $161,695 overtime)
Average daily placements 519; men 328, women 172, children 19
Average daily wage $9.12

Men

Daily wage ($)	Number of placements	Total wages ($)
3.00	543	1,629
5.00	18,299	91,495
7.50	44,338	332,535
10.00	48,543	485,430
12.50	2,646	33,075
15.00	5,503	82,545
Over 15.00	11	253
Total	**119,883**	**1,026,962**

Women

Daily wage ($)	Number of placements	Total wages ($)
3.00	145	435
5.00	10,954	54,770
7.50	20,578	154,335
10.00	28,544	285,440
12.50	1,047	13,088
15.00	1,625	24,375
Over 15.00	4	95
Total	**62,897**	**532,538**

Boys

Daily wage ($)	Number of placements	Total wages ($)
3.00	15	45
5.00	2,665	13,325

Daily wage ($)	Number of placements	Total wages ($)
7.50	1,509	11,317
10.00	484	4,840
12.50	64	800
15.00	116	1,740
Over 15.00	14	420
Total	4,867	32,487

Girls

Daily wage ($)	Number of placements	Total wages ($)
3.00	15	45
5.00	1,070	5,350
7.50	634	4,755
10.00	179	1,790
12.50	5	62
15.00	33	495
Over 15.00	6	300
Total	1,942	12,797

Chinese placements 5,187 for $56,617
Black placements 3,525 for $28,128

Source: "Mobs' tough year." Variety, February 9, 1932, p. 21

"Regular" extras (3-year record)

Days of work per week	1929	1930	1931
One day	545	517	401
Two days	280	237	155
Three days	84	68	55
Four days	20	11	7
Five days	1	1	1

Source: "Regulars." Variety, February 9, 1932, p. 21

——— 1935 ———

Total placements 278,486
Total paid $2,571,000
Average daily placements 889; men 583, women 275, children 31
Average daily wage $9.23

Men

Daily wage ($)	Number of placements	Total wages ($)
3.20	13,443	43,017
5.00	37,506	187,530

Daily wage ($)	Number of placements	Total wages ($)
7.50	55,597	416,977
10.00	53,047	530,470
12.50	1,133	14,162
15.00	21,924	328,860
Total	182,650	1,521,017

Women

Daily wage ($)	Number of placements	Total wages ($)
3.20	8,692	27,814
5.00	20,736	103,680
7.50	20,439	153,292
10.00	20,391	203,910
12.50	275	3,437
15.00	15,468	232,020
Total	86,001	724,154

Boys

Daily wage ($)	Number of placements	Total wages ($)
3.20	98	313
5.00	2,954	14,470
7.50	1,997	14,977
10.00	302	3,020
12.50	12	150
15.00	84	1,260
Total	5,447	34,491

Girls

Daily wage ($)	Number of placements	Total wage ($)
3.20	71	227
5.00	2,076	10,380
7.50	2,018	15,135
10.00	171	1,710
12.50	9	112
15.00	43	645
Total	4,388	28,210

Source: "$9.23 average for extras." *Variety*, January 29, 1936, pp. 3, 31

1936

Total placements 268,436
Total paid $2,420,454
Average daily placements 736; men 479, women 222, children 35
Average daily wage $9.02

Appendix—1936; Summary

Men

174,759 placements for $1,422,137

Women

80,962 placements for $658,074

Boys

7,712 placements for $49,264

Girls

5,003 placements for $31,658

Summary (1926–1936)*

Year	Wages	Placements	Daily Average (Jobs)	Daily average (wages)
1926	$2,195,395	259,259	710	$8.46
1927	2,838,136	330,397	905	8.59
1928	2,469,711	276,155	756	8.94
1929	2,401,429	262,958	840	9.13
1930	2,460,012	252,466	809	9.74
1931	1,766,479	189,589	606	9.32
1932	1,855,778	214,584	684	8.65
1933	2,048,512	251,914	805	8.13
1934	1,984,697	219,857	705	9.03
1935	2,571,293	278,486	889	9.23
1936	2,420,454	268,436	858	9.02
Totals	25,011,897	2,804,461	—	—
Average	2,273,808	254,950	788	8.75

*Data for 1926–1928 is based on a 365-day year; following years are based on a 313-day year.

Source: "$9.02 average for extras." *Variety,* January 27, 1937, p. 3

Chapter Notes

Chapter 1

1. "Extras raise Ructions." *Variety*, July 6, 1917, p. 21.
2. "Film extras taken in raid." *Los Angeles Times*, August 1, 1918, sec. 2, p. 8.
3. "Motion picture extras must get other work." *Moville Mail (Iowa)*, November 7, 1918, p. 2.
4. "Punch on jaw ends attempt at strike." *Los Angeles Times*, August 30, 1919, sec. 2, p. 6.
5. "Employment for the elderly." *Manitowoc Herald News (Wisc.)*, January 12, 1921, p. 7.
6. Catherine Fleming. "Experiences of a movie extra at sixty." *Los Angeles Times*, February 13, 1921, sec. 10, p. 6.
7. *Ibid.*, pp. 6, 23.
8. "Film extras declare war." *Los Angeles Times*, February 3, 1923, sec. 2, p. 1.
9. *Ibid.*
10. *Ibid.*
11. "Film extras accuse agent." *Los Angeles Times*, February 21, 1923, sec. 2, p. 1.
12. *Ibid.*
13. "Actors shot by guard; police halt lynching." *Los Angeles Times*, March 16, 1923, sec. 2, p. 7.
14. *Ibid.*, pp. 1, 7.
15. *Ibid.*, p. 7.
16. "Witnesses are arrested." *Los Angeles Times*, March 22, 1923, sec. 2, p. 1; "California briefs." *Bakersfield Californian*, April 4, 1923, p. 3.
17. "Second suit is sequel to film extras rioting." *Los Angeles Times*, April 14, 1923, sec. 2, p. 4.
18. "Salaries due film extras held up by agent Weiss." *Variety*, August 30, 1923, p. 21.
19. "Extras steamed up against U manager." *Variety*, October 8, 1924, p. 20.
20. "New labor law planned as aid to film extra." *Los Angeles Times*, January 13, 1925, p. B5.
21. "10 per centers for extras noticed." *Variety*, January 28, 1925, p. 30.
22. "On with the dance — perhaps." *Los Angeles Times*, May 9, 1925, p. A16.
23. "Extras, caught soldiering, now daily being checked up." *Variety*, August 5, 1925, p. 23.
24. "Don't pity poor extras." *Los Angeles Times*, October 18, 1925, p. C18.
25. Copeland C. Burg. "Coast producers spend huge sums for film extras." *Olean Times (N.Y.)*, August 7, 1925, p. 2.
26. "Extra people in Hollywood." *Variety*, October 21, 1925, p. 26.
27. "Problem of film extras to be aired." *Los Angeles Times*, November 18, 1925, p. A8.

28. "Film extra wage code agreed on." *Los Angeles Times*, January 11, 1926, p. A2.
29. "Regulating extras." *Variety*, January 20, 1926, p. 29.
30. "Extra's lot not so bad." *Washington Post*, June 19, 1927, p. F3.
31. "Theatrical and picture gossip." *Waterloo Evening Courier (Iowa)*, March 24, 1928, p. 8.
32. "Coast extras burning up over studios' alleged labor violations." *Variety*, October 24, 1928, p. 15.
33. *Ibid.*
34. "Bootlegging on small scale favored sideline of oft-changing extra work." *Variety*, September 15, 1931, p. 2.
35. "Few extras rise from ranks because as class they've no ambition, says director." *Variety*, October 27, 1931, p. 3.
36. Dan Thomas. "$9 a week." *Sheboygan Press (Wisc.)*, May 9, 1932, p. 6.
37. "Extras doubling in two pix in Warner plan to save $250,000." *Variety*, January 10, 1933, p. 6.
38. "Merry Fahrney is up at 5:30 for film work." Chicago *Tribune*, March 21, 1934, p. 22.
39. Dan Thomas. "A new deal for Hollywood's extra girls." *Port Arthur News (Tex.)*, December 12, 1934, p. 8.
40. Erskine Johnson. "Pay scale high for child film extras." *Olean Times-Herald (N.Y.)*, March 14, 1935, p. 13.
41. John Scott. "Poverty confronts thousands of film extras." *Los Angeles Times*, April 14, 1935, p. A1.
42. John Scott. "New rackets practiced on film extras." *Los Angeles Times*, September 22, 1935, p. A1.
43. "A laugh for Upton Sinclair." *Coshocton Tribune (Ohio)*, February 10, 1936, p. 6.
44. "63% increase in accidents among extras causing insurance co.'s to cancel policies." *Variety*, July 8, 1936, p. 3.
45. "Lifeguards rescue 185 in swim test for movie." *Washington Post*, February 15, 1938, p. X16.
46. James E. Bassett. "Film extras mourn Burns, who fought their battles." *Los Angeles Times*, January 11, 1939, pp. A1, A3.
47. "SAG curbs gifts by extras to execs, directors; 1 got a horse and saddle." *Variety*, July 5, 1939, p. 1.

Chapter 2

1. "About Central Casting." www.centralcasting.com/about/history. April 2, 2010 (downloaded).
2. "General engaging agency." *Variety*, September 3, 1915, p. 19.
3. "Extras' agents and commish all through." *Variety*, March 25, 1925, p. 1.
4. "Hays favors central plan." *Variety*, July 15, 1925, p. 25.
5. "Extras in movies to be considered." *Fresno Bee*, December 11, 1925, p. 25.
6. "Movie vagrants to be eliminated." *Fresno Bee*, January 25, 1926, p. 4; "Hays begins clean-up of Hollywood today." *New York Times*, January 25, 1926, p. 22.
7. "Hays back." *Variety*, February 3, 1926, p. 29.
8. "Average daily earnings of Hollywood extras—$8.64." *Variety*, July 7, 1926, p. 12.
9. "Coast extras burning up over studios' alleged labor violations." *Variety*, October 24, 1928, p. 15.
10. "Brows to lose wrinkles." *Los Angeles Times*, December 9, 1928, p. B8.
11. "Sound forces new info blanks on extras." *Variety*, April 3, 1929, p. 7.
12. "Mob extra casting for talkers." *Variety*, December 25, 1929, p. 6.
13. "New casting chief named." *Los Angeles Times*, September 12, 1934, p. A2.

14. Carroll Nye. "Inside story of how film extras get work." *Los Angeles Times*, October 17, 1934, p. 10.
15. Hubbard Keavy. "Hollywood army of extras will get better deal." *Reno Evening Gazette*, October 27, 1934, p. 8.
16. Douglas Churchill. "Glamour at $8.97 a week." *Oakland Tribune*, July 7, 1935, Screen Magazine, pp. 8–9.
17. "Device picks film extras." *Los Angeles Times*, September 16, 1935, p. 3.
18. John Scott. "New rackets practiced on film extras." *Los Angeles Times*, September 22, 1935, p. A1.
19. "Studios set own extras." *Variety*, February 14, 1940, p. 5.
20. "Ex-F.B.I. agent heads Cent'l Casting." *Variety*, April 17, 1940, p. 7.
21. "Director resigns as outgrowth of dictagraph scandal." *Fairbanks Daily News-Miner (Alaska)*, April 9, 1940, p. 1.
22. "Philbrick gets fat movie job." *Oakland Tribune*, April 17, 1940, p. 6.
23. "More 'no men' than 'yes men' there." *Oelwein Daily Register (Iowa)*, April 28, 1940, p. 25.
24. "Philbrick starts film extra cleanup." *Oakland Tribune*, April 30, 1940, p. 25.
25. Louella O. Parsons. "Central Casting gets a new boss." *San Antonio Light*, May 5, 1940, p. 36.
26. Paul Harrison. "Gangsters, job selling, labor troubles add to Hollywood's headache problem." *Daily Times-News (Burlington, N.C.)*, June 6, 1940, p. 8.
27. "Move to keep CIO out." *Variety*, June 26, 1940, p. 7.
28. *Ibid.*, p. 22.
29. "SAG probes goon squads." *Variety*, September 14, 1940, pp. 7, 20.
30. "About Central Casting." Op. cit.

Chapter 3

1. "Movie extras open studio graft war." *Mansfield News (Ohio)*, March 23, 1923, p. 16.
2. Robert Donaldson. "Campaign is now under way to secure beautiful studio for movie extras." *Monessen Daily Independent* [Pennsylvania], August 18, 1923, p. 7.
3. *Ibid.*
4. "Film colony raided and guests at gay party are taken to jail." *Zanesville Signal (Ohio)*, September 4, 1924, p. 1.
5. "Girls welfare is watched." *Oshkosh Daily Northwestern (Wisc.)*, August 9, 1937, p. 8.
6. "Girl accuses D. W. Griffith." *Oakland Tribune*, February 25, 1931, p. 2.
7. "Alters Griffith charges." *New York Times*, February 16, 1931, p. 14.
8. "Quiz of girl due in Griffith case." *Washington Post*, February 27, 1931, p. 3.
9. "Cinema man hits charge." *Los Angeles Times*, May 18, 1934, p. A20; "Faces morals charge, film man denies it." *Jefferson City Post-Tribune (Mo.)*, May 18, 1934, p. 5.
10. "Movie extras forced to submit." *Mexia Weekly Herald (Tex.)*, June 22, 1934, p. 7.
11. "Hear evidence today in film extra scandal." *Chicago Tribune*, July 11, 1934, p. 9.
12. "Allen, girl to testify." *Los Angeles Times*, July 11, 1934, p. A8.
13. "Frameup heard at opening of scandal trial." *Chicago Tribune*, July 12, 1934, p. 3.
14. "Court hears scandal tale." *Ogden Standard-Examiner (Utah)*, July 12, 1934, p. 12.
15. "Frameup denied in movie extra scandal trial." *Chicago Tribune*, July 13, 1934, p. 3.
16. "Actress to tell about wild party." *Bee (Danville, Va.)*, July 13, 1934, p. 7.
17. "Extra to be court star." *Los Angeles Times*, July 13, 1934, p. A1.
18. *Ibid.*, pp. A1–A2.
19. "Girl tells of party." *Los Angeles Times*, July 14, 1934, p. 14.
20. *Ibid.*

21. "June De Long to take stand." *Los Angeles Times*, July 16, 1934, p. 5.
22. *Ibid.*
23. "Morals trial perjury bared." *Washington Post*, July 17, 1934, p. 5.
24. "Hint tampering with star witness in Hollywood case." *New Castle News (Pa.)*, July 17, 1934, pp. 1–2.
25. "Says June told of Allen's morals long before trap." *Alton Evening Telegraph (Ill.)*, July 18, 1934, p. 3.
26. "Morals trial defense opens." *Salt Lake Tribune*, July 19, 1934, p. 3.
27. "Frameup charged in morals case." *Galveston Daily News*, July 19, 1934, pp. 1, 10.
28. "Lawyers say Allen was framed." *Hammond Times (Ind.)*, July 19, 1934, p. 50.
29. "Denies taking part in immoral party at Hollywood trial." *Winnipeg Free Press*, July 21, 1934, p. 5.
30. "Allen denies ever participating in an immoral party." *Galveston Daily News*, July 21, 1934, pp. 1, 15.
31. *Ibid.*, p. 15.
32. "Allen contends charges framed." *New Castle News (Pa.)*, July 21, 1934, p. 17.
33. "Allen trial finish seen." *Los Angeles Times*, July 24, 1934, p. A7.
34. "Allen jury disagrees." *Los Angeles Times*, July 27, 1934, pp. A1, A3.
35. "Casting bureau has new chief." *Bakersfield Californian*, September 12, 1934, p. 8.
36. "Movie man, extra girl freed in morals case." *Washington Post*, December 3, 1935, p. 9.
37. "Dave Allen divorced." *Times (San Mateo, Calif.)*, October 19, 1936, p. 2.
38. "Founder of Central Casting Corp. dies." *Los Angeles Times*, January 4, 1955, p. A2.
39. "Film extra aid charted." *Los Angeles Times*, October 23, 1934, p. A5.
40. "Film-extra relief move launched by new group." *Los Angeles Times*, October 26, 1934, pp. A1–A2.
41. "Drinking-gambling Hollywood extras face booting from films." *Variety*, January 1, 1935, pp. 1, 132.
42. "100 beautiful extras entertain executives and attacks follow." *Lowell Sun (Mass.)*, June 4, 1937, p. 48.
43. "Film party inquiry sped." *Los Angeles Times*, June 5, 1937, p. A1.
44. "Girl identifies party suspect." *Los Angeles Times*, June 17, 1937, p. 3.
45. "Attack case arrest sought." *Los Angeles Times*, June 19, 1937, p. A3.
46. "Film girl sues for $500,000." *Los Angeles Times*, February 11, 1938, p. A12.
47. Douglas W. Churchill. "Extra trouble in the Hollywood paradise." *New York Times*, August 30, 1936, sec. 10, p. 3.
48. "SAG forces studio action against salary chiseling." *Billboard*, September 5, 1936, p. 3.
49. "Pay chiseling cases dropped." *Billboard*, September 12, 1936, p. 4.
50. "Gang activity investigated in Hollywood." *Bee (Danville, Va.)*, November 24, 1937, p. 10; "Film casting heads called in L.A. quiz." *Oakland Tribune*, November 24, 1937, p. 8.
51. "Investigating charges of exacting tribute from movie extras." *Chicago Tribune*, November 25, 1937, p. 13; "Film extras deny job selling knowledge." *Los Angeles Times*, November 30, 1937, p. A3.
52. "Expose extra job sales." *Variety*, December 6, 1939, pp. 5, 8.
53. "Sag probes goon squads." *Variety*, September 4, 1940, pp. 7, 20.

Chapter 4

1. "Too many extras." *Variety*, February 27, 1915, p. 22.
2. Kitty Kelly. "Flickerings from film land." *Chicago Tribune*, April 27, 1915, p. 10.
3. *Ibid.*
4. "500 answer call." *Hamilton Evening Journal (Ohio)*, March 8, 1924, p. 8.

5. "50,000 girls jobless in Hollywood." *San Antonio Light*, March 30, 1925, p. 1.
6. "Stars less scarce than competent film extras." *Charleston Daily Mail (W.Va.)*, May 11, 1925, p. 13.
7. Doris Blake. "Hollywood as it is." *Washington Post*, October 18, 1925, p. SM2.
8. *Ibid.*, pp. SM2, SM10.
9. "Many types to be found easily at movie capital." *San Mateo Times*, December 1, 1925, p. 10.
10. "2,300 out of 3,500 extras in Eastern films don't belong." *Variety*, July 7, 1926, pp. 1, 12.
11. "11,000 film extras on coast average $6,556 daily payroll." *Variety*, October 26, 1927, p. 5.
12. "Have over-supply of movie extras." *Ogden Standard-Examiner (Utah)*, January 25, 1927, p. 1.
13. "Too many picture actors." *Variety*, November 30, 1927, pp. 1–2.
14. "Number of stranded girl film extras much below last year." *Variety*, February 1, 1928, pp. 1, 58.
15. "Movie extras find that's a poor way to earn livelihood." *Cedar Rapids Tribune (Iowa)*, November 8, 1929, p. 1.
16. "Coast bums not extras." *Variety*, August 15, 1933, p. 3.
17. "Baby movie extras." *Greeley Daily Tribune (Colo.)*, July 25, 1934, p. 6.
18. "Extras and bit players appeal to Mary Pickford." *Hutchinson News (Kans.)*, August 30, 1933, p. 5; "Mary Pickford will aid extras by phone." *Ogden Standard-Examiner (Utah)*, August 30, 1933, p. 1.
19. "Sweat shop charge of penny-ante pay takes extras' plight to Code." *Variety*, September 12, 1933, p. 7.
20. "Part time pic mob gets elbow in extras edict." *Variety*, December 12, 1933, p. 4.
21. "Committee named to fix film extras' work hours." *Los Angeles Times*, January 12, 1934, p. 2.
22. "15,000 film extras may lose listing under NRA shakeup." *Oakland Tribune*, February 8, 1934, p. 11.
23. "Movie extras to get $25 to $5 daily wage." *New York Times*, March 19, 1934, p. 12.
24. "Codists axe extra list to 1,500." *Variety*, April 3, 1934, p. 3.
25. "Ranks of film extras slashed by N.R.A. action." *Los Angeles Times*, June 24, 1934, p. A1.
26. "Movies extra list face discharges." *New York Times*, July 12, 1934, p. 20.
27. "NRA on coast approves regulations for extras." *Variety*, September 18, 1934, p. 2.
28. "Top extras $1,500 a year." *Variety*, October 23, 1934, pp. 7, 23.
29. "Blue book questionnaire for Hollywood extras by coast NRA." *Variety*, September 25, 1934, p. 3.
30. "Hollywood extra list being pruned from 17,000 to 2,500." *Billboard*, September 29, 1934, p. 3.
31. "Casting offices' aides ask NRA to set aside ban on family extras." *Variety*, November 6, 1934, p. 7.
32. "Hollywood casting chiselers warned against gypping extras." *Variety*, November 6, 1934, pp. 6, 57.
33. "Guild calls on Eddie Cantor to save extras from being tossed out by C.A." *Variety*, March 6, 1935, p. 2.
34. John Scott. "N.R.A. fails to make decision on extra code." *Los Angeles Times*, March 24, 1935, pp. A1–A2.
35. "Sag demands extra redeal." *Billboard*, April 6, 1935, pp. 4, 20.
36. "Limited film extra list idea goes into discard." *Los Angeles Times*, April 22, 1935, p. A1.
37. "The extra problem." *Los Angeles Times*, April 25, 1935, p. A4.

38. *Ibid.*
39. "Glamour at $8.97 a week." *New York Times,* September 22, 1935, sec. 10, p. 4.
40. "Surplus of film extras shown in state's report." *Oakland Tribune,* December 31, 1935, p. 6.
41. "Extras seldom rise to stardom." *Centralia Chronicle Advertiser (Wash.),* May 1, 1936, p. 10.
42. Douglas W. Churchill. "New substance for the dream city." *New York Times,* September 20, 1936, sec. 10, p. 5.
43. "One in 100,000 movie extras reach stardom." *Fitchburg Sentinel (Mass.),* January 26, 1937, p. 1; "Movie Extras find studio jobs scarce." *Hayward Daily Review (Calif.),* January 29, 1937, p. 2.
44. Hedda Hopper. "Few film stars rise to stardom." *Los Angeles Times,* July 31, 1938, p. C1.
45. "Few film extras make a living, and still fewer become stars." *Hutchinson News Herald (Kans.),* June 23, 1940, p. 10.
46. Thomas F. Brady. "Communiqué from the West Coast." *New York Times,* March 1, 1942, sec. 10, p. 3.

Chapter 5

1. "Photoplay actors fail to form new organization." *Variety,* July 25, 1913, p. 8.
2. "Extras forming union for mutual protection." *Variety,* February 25, 1916, p. 20.
3. *Ibid.*
4. *Ibid.*
5. "Supers call mass meeting and arrange for a charter." *Variety,* September 1, 1916, p. 13.
6. *Ibid.*
7. *Ibid.*
8. "Row in extras' association." *Variety,* November 3, 1916, p. 23.
9. "Extras in Eastern studios may unionize." *Variety,* September 1, 1926, p. 5.
10. "Equity not asking extras to join at this time." *Variety,* July 10, 1929, p. 7.
11. "Equity mass meeting hears Academy, Casting Co, denounced." *Variety,* July 17, 1929, p. 6.
12. "Unionization of extras by AFL again." *Variety,* August 29, 1933, p. 3.
13. "Movie guild opens doors to extras." *New York Times,* October 27, 1933, p. 22.
14. "Screen Actors' Guild sets back election." *Variety,* March 27, 1934, p. 2.
15. "Equity's Guild contract." *Variety,* October 30, 1934, pp. 3, 28.
16. "New extra group for those with NRA cards." *Variety,* March 20, 1935, p. 7.
17. "Film studios in East recognize Guild pact." *New York Times,* June 18, 1937, p. 25.
18. "News of the screen." *New York Times,* August 23, 1937, p. 22.
19. "Extras to get that personal touch again." *Variety,* July 13, 1938, p. 4.
20. "Extras claim low payment; Screen Guild investigating." *Billboard,* November 13, 1937, p. 3.
21. "Guild asks a better deal for bit and extra players." *Variety,* December 8, 1937, p. 6.
22. "Guild to make demand on producers for extras' closed shop, trim mob." *Variety,* December 22, 1937, p. 7.
23. "Junior actor Guild control in balance." *Variety,* January 19, 1938, p. 6.
24. "Producer-actor parleys." *Variety,* April 6, 1938, pp. 7, 53.
25. "Producer-actor accord." *Variety,* September 28, 1938, pp. 5, 21.
26. "Extras demand own union." *Variety,* November 16, 1938, pp. 5, 21.
27. *Ibid.*
28. *Ibid.*
29. "Stars in suit against Guild, extra players." *Ogden Standard-Examiner (Utah),* May 2, 1939, p. 12.

30. "Extras stick to Guild." *Variety*, May 24, 1939, pp. 5, 16.
31. "Court rejects injunction plea." *Los Angeles Times*, November 23, 1939, p. A2.
32. "Actors probe extra casting." *Ogden Standard-Examiner (Utah)*, October 18, 1939, p. 12.
33. "Screen actors hit job-buying." *Arizona Republic (Phoenix)*, March 9, 1940, p. 46.
34. "Broad power for extras." *Variety*, January 17, 1940, pp. 5, 18.
35. "$1,000,000 up for extras." *Variety*, January 31, 1940, pp. 5, 54.
36. "600 new actors for pix." *Variety*, April 24, 1940, pp. 7, 23.
37. "Screen extras stay in the SAG, don't like any change in setup." *Variety*, May 1, 1940, p. 6.
38. "Film extras fight for vote." *Los Angeles Times*, June 11, 1940, p. A3.
39. "SAG will recognize office workers' pickets on Coast." *Variety*, July 3, 1940, pp. 7, 20.
40. *Ibid.*
41. "Casey in 24-hour cleanup." *Variety*, July 10, 1940, p. 18.
42. "SAG drops 2,000 extras." *Variety*, August 7, 1940, p. 7.
43. Thomas Brady. "Thinning out the ranks." *New York Times*, September 15, 1940, p. 135.
44. "Producers row over closed door for extras." *Variety*, October 23, 1940, p. 6.
45. "6,500 extras beef to AFL." *Variety*, October 30, 1940, pp. 7, 27.
46. *Ibid.*
47. "Extras demand a voice." *Variety*, March 5, 1941, pp. 7, 60.
48. "Move to cut 4,000 movie extras off rolls in Hollywood gains union support." *Albuquerque Journal*, October 26, 1942, p. 3.
49. "Film extras Guild planned." *Los Angeles Times*, March 31, 1943, p. A8.
50. "Wage increase demands filed for film extras." *Los Angeles Times*, October 13, 1943, p. A6.
51. "Near fist fight enlivens film extras' labor hearing." *Los Angeles Times*, March 24, 1944, p. A1.
52. "Varying wages of film extras told at hearing." *Los Angeles Times*, April 6, 1944, p. A3.
53. "Actor describes rush for jobs as film extras." *Los Angeles Times*, April 7, 1944, p. A2.
54. "Players' union asks pay parley for film extras." *Los Angeles Times*, June 22, 1944, p. A3.
55. "Hearing on film extras closed by Labor Board." *Los Angeles Times*, July 6, 1944, p. 8.
56. "Film extras vote to break from Screen Actors Guild." *Los Angeles Times*, December 18, 1944, p. A1.
57. "Bit players union wins decisively over SAG in election on Coast." *Variety*, December 20, 1944, p. 4.
58. "2,500 film extras ordered on strike." *Wisconsin State Journal (Madison)*, February 2, 1945, p. 3; "Movie extras back at work again." *Dunkirk Evening Observer (N.Y.)*, February 3, 1945, p. 4.
59. "AAAA backs film extras' Guild in row with Screen Players Union." *New York Times*, May 18, 1945, p. 14.
60. *Ibid.*
61. "SAG, extras set interchangeability." *Variety*, August 8, 1945, p. 7.
62. "Film extras will resume negotiations." *Los Angeles Times*, December 3, 1945, p. A3.
63. "Amalgamation of film extras still in tangle." *Los Angeles Times*, December 14, 1945, p. A3.
64. "Film extras to vote on bargaining agent." *Los Angeles Times*, February 2, 1946, p. 2.

65. "Film extras to vote today." *Los Angeles Times*, March 3, 1946, p. A1.
66. "Extras select bargaining unit." *Reno Evening Gazette*, March 5, 1946, p. 13.
67. "SEG wins closed shop agreement with prods." *Variety*, April 3, 1946, p. 13.
68. "Extras charge ban by union." *Los Angeles Times*, July 7, 1946, p. 8.
69. Thomas F. Brady. "Film extras agree to a new contract." *New York Times*, December 17, 1948, p. 39.
70. "Hollywood unions approve 3-year film, television contract." *Los Angeles Times*, May 14, 1992, Metro section, p. 2.

CHAPTER 6

1. "Griffith plays Santa Claus to movie extra." *Big Spring Herald (Tex.)*, December 25, 1925, p. 16.
2. Marquis Busby. "Fortune did more than smile on Charles Farrell." *Los Angeles Times*, January 30, 1927, pp. C22–C23.
3. "Lady Luck friend of blond actress." *Los Angeles Times*, February 28, 1928, p. A13.
4. "A shower gave movie extra a chance to act." *Washington Post*, February 2, 1929, p. 8.
5. Hubbard Keavy. "Hollywood gleanings." *Nevada State Journal (Reno)*, September 30, 1929, p. 4.
6. "Forgotten Women is tale of movie extras at Palace." *Times Evening Herald (Olean, N.Y.)*, January 21, 1932, p. 9.
7. "Marlene Dietrich started as extra, says in interview." *Sandusky Register (Ohio)*, October 16, 1932, p. 2.
8. "Veteran actress is rescued from film extra ranks." *Syracuse Herald (N.Y.)*, September 25, 1933, p. 20.
9. "Movies." *La Crosse Tribune and Leader-Press (Wisc.)*, July 9, 1934, p. 9.
10. "When a war lord was a movie extra." *Washington Post*, May 15, 1932, p. SM5.
11. "Jim Thorpe hurt riding cow pony as movie extra." *Chicago Tribune*, August 10, 1932, p. 16.
12. Dan Thomas. "War heroes, Jim Thorpe among throng awaiting hits in cinema world." *Lima News (Ohio)*, March 30, 1932, p. 15.
13. Ring W. Lardner Jr. "Hollywood." *Los Angeles Times*, March 22, 1936, p. H8.
14. "Yreka mob fugitive talks of hiding as a film extra." *Los Angeles Times*, September 16, 1936, p. A2.
15. John Peere Miles. "Former screen stars in army as film extras." *Washington Post*, June 11, 1937, p. 23.
16. "Titled tramps, phoney princes sneak to extras ranks as pretense exposed." *Variety*, September 19, 1933, p. 3.
17. "Film extra killed in war scene." *Los Angeles Times*, August 7, 1941, p. A1; "Budlong heir's fatal ride as film extra." *Los Angeles Times*, August 9, 1941, p. A1.
18. Hedda Hopper. "Grady Sutton — movie extra with that extra something." *Los Angeles Times*, August 24, 1965, p. D13.
19. Thomas M. Pryor. "Film extra guild cites old-times." *New York Times*, June 7, 1958, p. 11.
20. Marilyn Zeitlin. "He enjoys the extra rewards." *Los Angeles Times*, December 20, 1985, pp. H1, H3.
21. *Ibid.*
22. "Wealthy tourists, acting as extras for fun of it, angers regulars." *Variety*, October 3, 1928, p. 5.
23. "Soldiers barred from films unless historical or for educational use, ruling." *San Antonio Express*, August 16, 1926, p. 2.
24. "No more doubling by soldiers as extras." *Variety*, March 23, 1927, p. 1.

25. "Screen players protest use of Army and Navy." *New York Times*, October 14, 1934, p. 33.
26. "Actor-labor U. S. peeves." *Variety*, February 12, 1936, pp. 5, 68.
27. *Ibid.*
28. "Extra protest Coast Guard in Tars, other pix." *Variety*, August 8, 1945, p. 6.
29. "Darkies from South work as film extras." *Wakefield Advocate (Mich.)*, May 24, 1924, p. 3.
30. "Movie extra types supplied by real life." *Washington Post*, November 28, 1926, p. R6.
31. "2,750 war vets as extras monthly." *Variety*, August 10, 1927, p. 5.
32. "Coast extras hot as public sits in for film atmosphere." *Variety*, November 23, 1927, p. 5.
33. "No future for extras." *Variety*, March 15, 1932, p. 3.
34. "2,000 ughs." *Variety*, July 8, 1936, p. 3.
35. "That Hollywood front." *Variety*, August 1, 1928, pp. 1, 55.
36. "One film group in much demand." *Reno Evening Gazette*, January 12, 1932, p. 12.
37. "Wardrobe of movie extra costs $1,000." *Chicago Tribune*, August 27, 1933, p. E5.
38. "Top extras $1,500 a year." *Variety*, October 23, 1934, p. 7.
39. "Hollywood dress extras go in hock to strut at glad rags parade." *Variety*, December 18, 1934, p. 3.
40. "Only 1 out of 10 makes grade in extras' clothes-horse parade." *Variety*, December 4, 1934, p. 3.
41. "Best dressed film extras find title costs money" *Oakland Tribune*, February 4, 1935, p. 6.
42. Douglas Churchill. "Glamour at $8.97 a week." *Oakland Tribune*, July 7, 1935, Screen Magazine, pp. 8–9.
43. *Ibid.*
44. "Figures show film extras' wages meager last year." *Los Angeles Times*, February 7, 1938, pp. A1–A2.
45. "Movie extras come from all walks of life." *Davenport Democrat and Leader (Iowa)*, October 3, 1926, p. 16.
46. "Movie extras cling to hope despite want." *Chicago Tribune*, June 30, 1932, p. 16.
47. "Blondes numerous in Rialto picture." *Chronicle Telegram (Elyria, Ohio)*, January 11, 1932, p. 4.
48. "Part time pic mob gets elbows in extras edict." *Variety*, December 12, 1933, p. 4.
49. "Girl extra in movies takes suicide route." *Independent (Helene, Mont.)*, August 30, 1933, p. 5.
50. "Film extra turns to death in despondency as dreams of stardom fail to materialize." *Los Angeles Times*, May 10, 1934, p. A2.
51. "Love for movie extra gone with her boss' $6,200." *Chicago Tribune*, August 1, 1937, p. 3.
52. "Girl will tell of embezzling for film extra." *Chicago Tribune*, January 11, 1938, p. 12.
53. "Tells of movie extra's wooing—$6,200 worth." *Chicago Tribune*, January 12, 1938, p. 15.
54. "Find movie extra guilty of plot." *Chicago Tribune*, January 19, 1938, p. 3.

CHAPTER 7

1. "3,500 extra in *Ben Hur*." *Variety*, October 7, 1925, pp. 1, 34.
2. "22,500 idle at Hollywood." *Variety*, June 9, 1926, pp. 1, 18.
3. *Ibid.*
4. "Average daily earning of Hollywood extras—$8.64." *Variety*, July 7, 1926, pp. 1, 12.

5. "No more picture extras on coast." *Variety*, January 19, 1927, pp. 1, 9.
6. *Ibid.*
7. "Extra day average $8.18." *Variety*, July 13, 1927, pp. 1, 24.
8. "42,546 coast studio workers make 82 % of world's supply." *Variety*, January 11, 1928, p. 1.
9. "Extras' high daily average in '27, $8.59; 330,397 placements for 35,000." *Variety*, February 1, 1928, p. 6.
10. *Ibid.*
11. "Coast extras cut down." *Variety*, January 16, 1929, p. 7.
12. "Film mob's toughest year." *Variety*, February 9, 1932, pp. 1, 21.
13. "Top extras $1,500 a year." *Variety*, October 23, 1934, pp. 7, 23.
14. "Only 12 film extras earn living wage." *Chicago Tribune*, February 14, 1935, p. 15.
15. "$9.23 average for extras." *Variety*, January 29, 1936, pp. 3, 31.
16. *Ibid.*; "Film extras wages gain." *Los Angeles Times*, January 31, 1936, p. 9.
17. "$9.02 average for extras." *Variety*, January 27, 1937, p. 3.
18. "Year will set all-time high in extra work." *Washington Post*, February 15, 1938, p. X16.
19. "Two inquiries on film extras may result in pay scale tilt." *Los Angeles Times*, October 7, 1939, p. A3.
20. "Film extras plan pay plea." *Los Angeles Times*, December 1, 1939, p. 12.
21. "Film extras' pay rise sought." *Los Angeles Times*, December 12, 1939, p. 4; "$3,167,896 paid pix Extras in '39; bigger checks, too." *Variety*, December 27, 1939, p. 5.
22. "Movie extras create, labor examiner told." *Chicago Tribune*, July 26, 1940, p. 25.
23. "Earnings rise for film extras." *Los Angeles Times*, January 8, 1942, p. 19.
24. "Film extras lose jobless pay fight." *New York Times*, November 28, 1946, p. 36.
25. "Film extras to get cost-of-living rise." *Los Angeles Times*, February 28, 1947, p. 7.

Bibliography

"AAAA backs film extras' Guild in row with Screen Players Union." *New York Times*, May 18, 1945, p. 14.
"About Central Casting." *www.centralcasting.com/about/history*. Downloaded April 2, 2010.
"Actor describes rush for jobs as film extras." *Los Angeles Times*, April 7, 1944, p. A2.
"Actor-labor U. S. peeves." *Variety*, February 12, 1936, pp. 5, 68.
"Actors probe extra casting." *Ogden Standard-Examiner (Utah)*, October 18, 1939, p. 12.
"Actors shot by guard; police halt lynching." *Los Angeles Times*, March 16, 1923, sec. 2, pp. 1, 7.
"Actress to tell about wild party." *Bee (Danville, Va.)*, July 13, 1934, p. 7.
"Allen contends charges framed." *New Castle News (Pa.)*, July 21, 1934, p. 17.
"Allen denies ever participating in an immoral party." *Galveston Daily News*, July 21, 1934, pp. 1, 15.
"Allen, girl to testify." *Los Angeles Times*, July 11, 1934, p. A8.
"Allen jury disagrees." *Los Angeles Times*, July 27, 1934, pp. A1, A3.
"Allen trial finish seen." *Los Angeles Times*, July 24, 1934, p. A7.
"Alters Griffith charges." *New York Times*, February 26, 1931, p. 14.
"Amalgamation of film extras still in tangle." *Los Angeles Times*, December 14, 1945, p. A3.
"Attack case arrest sought." *Los Angeles Times*, June 19, 1937, p. A3.
"Average daily earnings of Hollywood extras—$8.64." *Variety*, July 7, 1926, pp. 1, 12.
"Baby movie extras." *Greeley Daily Tribune (Colo.)*, July 25, 1934, p. 6.
Bassett, James E. "Film extras mourn Burns, who fought their battles." *Los Angeles Times*, January 11, 1939, pp. A1, A3.
"Best dressed film extras find title costs money." *Oakland Tribune*, February 4, 1935, p. 6.
"Bit players union wins decisively over SAG in election on Coast." *Variety*, December 20, 1944, p. 4.
Blake, Doris. "Hollywood as it is." *Washington Post*, October 18, 1925, pp. SM2, SM10.
"Blondes numerous in Rialto picture." *Chronicle Telegram (Elyria, Ohio)*, January 11, 1932, p. 4.
"Blue book questionnaire for Hollywood extras by Coast NRA." *Variety*, September 25, 1934, p. 3.

"Bootlegging on small scale favored sideline of hungry extra mob." *Variety*, September 15, 1931, p. 2.
Brady, Thomas F. "Communiqué from the West Coast." *New York Times*, March 1, 1942, sec. 10, p. 3.
_____. "Film extras agree to a new contract." *New York Times*, December 17, 1948, p. 39.
_____. "Thinning out the ranks." *New York Times*, September 15, 1940, p. 135.
"Broad power for extras." *Variety*, January 17, 1940, pp. 5, 18.
"Brows to lose wrinkles." *Los Angeles Times*, December 9, 1928, p. B8.
"Budlong heir's fatal ride as film extra." *Los Angeles Times*, August 9, 1941, p. A1.
Burg, Copeland C. "Coast producers spend huge sums for film extras." *Olean Times (N.Y.)*, August 7, 1925, p. 2.
Busby, Marquis. "Fortune did more than smile on Charles Farrell." *Los Angeles Times*, January 30, 1927, pp. C22–C23.
"California briefs." *Bakersfield Californian*, April 4, 1923, p. 3.
"Casey in 24-hour cleanup." *Variety*, July 10, 1940, pp. 7, 18.
"Casting Bureau has new chief." *Bakersfield Californian*, September 12, 1934, p. 8.
"Casting officers' aides ask NRA to set aside ban on family extras." *Variety*, November 6, 1934, p. 7.
Churchill, Douglas W. "Extras trouble in the Hollywood paradise." *New York Times*, August 30, 1936, p. X3.
_____. "Glamour at $8.97 a week." *Oakland Tribune*, July 7, 1935, Screen Magazine, pp. 8–9.
_____. "New substance for the dream city." *New York Times*, September 20, 1936, sec 10, p. 5.
"Cinema man hits charge." *Los Angeles Times*, May 18, 1934, p. A20.
"Coast bums not extras." *Variety*, August 15, 1933, p. 3.
"Coast extras burning up over studios' alleged labor violations." *Variety*, October 24, 1928, p. 15.
"Coast extras cut down." *Variety*, January 16, 1929, p. 7.
"Coast extras hot as public sits in for film atmosphere." *Variety*, November 23, 1927, p. 5.
"Codists axe extra list to 1,500." *Variety*, April 3, 1934, p. 3.
"Committee named to fix film extras' work hours." *Los Angeles Times*, January 12, 1934, p. 2.
"Court hears scandal tale." *Ogden Standard-Examiner (Utah)*, July 12, 1934, p. 12.
"Court rejects injunction plea." *Los Angeles Times*, November 23, 1939, p. A2.
"Darkies from South work as film extras." *Wakefield Advocate (Mich.)*, May 24, 1924, p. 3.
"Dave Allen divorced." *Times (San Mateo, Calif.)*, October 19, 1936, p. 2.
"Denies taking part in immoral party at Hollywood trial." *Winnipeg Free Press*, July 21, 1934, p. 5.
"Device picks film extras." *Los Angeles Times*, September 16, 1935, p. 3.
"Director resigns as outgrowth of dictagraph scandal." *Fairbanks Daily News-Miner (Alaska)*, April 9, 1940, p. 1.
"Doesn't pity poor extras." *Los Angeles Times*, October 18, 1925, p. C18.
Donaldson, Robert. "Campaign is now under way to secure beautiful studio for movie extras." *Monessen Daily Independent (Pa.)*, August 18, 1923, p. 7.
"Drinking-gambling Hollywood extras face booting from films." *Variety*, January 1, 1935, pp. 1, 132.
"Earnings rise for film extras." *Los Angeles Times*, January 8, 1942, p. 19.

Bibliography 177

"11,000 film extras on coast average $6,556 daily payroll." *Variety*, October 26, 1927, p. 5.

"Employment for the elderly." *Manitowoc Herald News (Wisc.)*, January 12, 1921, p. 7.

"Equity mass meeting hears Academy, Casting Co., denounced." *Variety*, July 17, 1929, p. 6.

"Equity not asking extras to join at this time." *Variety*, July 10, 1929, p. 7.

"Equity's Guild contract." *Variety*, October 30, 1934, pp. 3, 28.

"Ex-FBI agent heads Cent'l Casting." *Variety*, April 17, 1940, p. 7.

"Expose extra job sales." *Variety*, December 6, 1939, pp. 5, 8.

"Extra day average $8.18." *Variety*, July 13, 1927, pp. 1, 24.

"Extra people in Hollywood." *Variety*, October 21, 1925, p. 26.

"The extra problem." *Los Angeles Times*, April 25, 1935, p. A4.

"Extra protest Coast Guard in *Tars*, other pix." *Variety*, August 8, 1945, p. 6.

"Extra to be court star." *Los Angeles Times*, July 13, 1934, pp. A1–A2.

"Extras, caught soldiering, now daily being checked up." *Variety*, August 5, 1925, p. 23.

"Extras' agents and commish all through." *Variety*, March 25, 1925, p. 1.

"Extras and bit players appeal to Mary Pickford." *Hutchinson News (Kans.)*, August 30, 1933, p. 5.

"Extras charge ban by union." *Los Angeles Times*, July 7, 1946, p. 8.

"Extras claim low payment; Screen Guild investigating." *Billboard*, November 13, 1937, p. 3.

"Extras demand a voice." *Variety*, March 5, 1941, pp. 7, 60.

"Extras demand own union." *Variety*, November 16, 1938, pp. 5, 21.

"Extras doubling in two pix in Warner plan to save $250,000." *Variety*, January 10, 1933, p. 6.

"Extras face 90% slash." *Variety*, July 24, 1934, pp. 3, 12.

"Extras forming union for mutual protection." *Variety*, February 25, 1916, p. 20.

"Extras high daily average in '27, $8.59; 330,397 placements for 35,000." *Variety*, February 1, 1928, p. 6.

"Extras in Eastern studios may unionize." *Variety*, September 1, 1926, p. 5.

"Extras in movies to be considered." *Fresno Bee*, December 11, 1925, p. 25.

"Extras raise ructions." *Variety*, July 6, 1917, p. 21.

"Extras seldom rise to stardom." *Centralia Chronicle Advertiser (Wash.)*, May 1, 1936, p. 10.

"Extras select bargaining unit." *Reno Evening Gazette*, March 5, 1946, p. 13.

"Extras steamed up against U manager." *Variety*, October 8, 1924, p. 20.

"Extras stick to Guild." *Variety*, May 24, 1939, pp. 5, 16.

"Extras to get that personal touch again." *Variety*, July 13, 1938, p. 4.

"Faces morals charge, film man denies it." *Jefferson City Post-Tribune (Mo.)*, May 18, 1934, p. 5.

"Few extras rise from ranks because as class they've no ambition, says director." *Variety*, October 27, 1931, p. 3.

"Few film extras make a living, and still fewer become stars." *Hutchinson News Herald (Kans.)*, June 23, 1940, p. 10.

"15,000 film extras may lose listing under NRA shakeup." *Oakland Tribune*, February 8, 1934, p. 11.

"50,000 girls jobless in Hollywood." *San Antonio Light*, March 30, 1925, p. 1.

"Figures show film extras' wages meager last year." *Los Angeles Times*, February 7, 1938, pp. A1–A2.

"Film casting heads called in L. A. quiz." *Oakland Tribune*, November 24, 1937, p. 8.
"Film colony raided and guests at gay party are taken to jail." *Zanesville Signal (Ohio)*, September 4, 1924, p. 1.
"Film extra aid charted." *Los Angeles Times*, October 23, 1934, p. A5.
"Film extra killed in war scene." *Los Angeles Times*, August 7, 1941, p. 1A.
"Film extra turns to death in despondency as dreams of stardom fail to materialize." *Los Angeles Times*, May 10, 1934, p. A2.
"Film extra wage code agreed on." *Los Angeles Times*, January 11, 1926, p. A2.
"Film extras accuse agent." *Los Angeles Times*, February 21, 1923, sec. 2, p. 1.
"Film extras declare war." *Los Angeles Times*, February 3, 1923, sec. 2, p. 1.
"Film extras deny job selling knowledge." *Los Angeles Times*, November 30, 1937, p. A3.
"Film extras fight for vote." *Los Angeles Times*, June 11, 1940, p. A3.
"Film extras guild planned." *Los Angeles Times*, March 31, 1943, p. A8.
"Film extras lose jobless pay fight." *New York Times*, November 28, 1946, p. 36.
"Film extras' pay rise sought." *Los Angeles Times*, December 12, 1939, p. 4.
"Film extras plan pay pleas." *Los Angeles Times*, December 1, 1939, p. 12.
"Film extras taken in raid." *Los Angeles Times*, August 1, 1918, sec. 2, p. 8.
"Film extras to get cost-of-living rise." *Los Angeles Times*, February 28, 1947, p. 7.
"Film extras to vote on bargaining agent." *Los Angeles Times*, February 2, 1946, p. 2.
"Film extras to vote today." *Los Angeles Times*, March 3, 1946, p. A1.
"Film extras vote to break from Screen Actors' Guild." *Los Angeles Times*, December 18, 1944, p. A1.
"Film extras wages gain." *Los Angeles Times*, January 31, 1936, p. 9.
"Film extras will resume negotiations." *Los Angeles Times*, December 3, 1945, p. A3.
"Film girl sues for $500,000." *Los Angeles Times*, February 11, 1938, p. A12.
"Film mob's toughest year." *Variety*, February 9, 1932, pp. 1, 21.
"Film party inquiry sped." *Los Angeles Times*, June 5, 1937, p. A1.
"Film studios in East recognize Guild pact." *New York Times*, June 18, 1937, p. 25.
"Film-extra relief move launched by new group." *Los Angeles Times*, October 26, 1934, pp. A1–A2.
"Find movie extra guilty of plot." *Chicago Tribune*, January 19, 1938, p. 3.
"500 answer call." *Hamilton Evening Journal (Ohio)*, March 8, 1924, p. 8.
Fleming, Catherine. "Experience of a movie extra at sixty." *Los Angeles Times*, February 13, 1921, sec. 10, pp. 6, 23.
"Forgotten Women is tale of movie extras at Palace." *Times Evening Gazette Olean, N.Y.)*, January 21, 1932, p. 9.
"42,546 coast studio workers make 82% of world's supply." *Variety*, January 11, 1928, p. 1.
"Founder of Central Casting Corp. dies." *Los Angeles Times*, January 4, 1955, p. A2.
"Frameup charged in morals case." *Galveston Daily News*, July 19, 1934, pp. 1, 10.
"Frameup denied in movie extra scandal trial." *Chicago Tribune*, July 13, 1934, p. 3.
"Frameup heard at opening of scandal trial." *Chicago Tribune*, July 12, 1934, p. 3.
"Gang activity investigated in Hollywood." *Bee (Danville, Va.)*, November 24, 1937, p. 10.
"General engaging agency." *Variety*, September 3, 1915, p. 19.
"Girl accuses D. W. Griffith." *Oakland Tribune*, February 25, 1931, p. 2.
"Girl extra in movies takes suicide route." *Independent (Helena, Mont.)*, June 18, 1933, p. 1.

"Girl identifies party suspect." *Los Angeles Times*, June 17, 1937, p. 3.
"Girl tells of party." *Los Angeles Times*, July 14, 1934, p. 14.
"Girl will tell of embezzling for film extras." *Chicago Tribune*, January 11, 1938, p. 12.
"Girls welfare is watched." *Oshkosh Daily Northwestern (Wisc.)*, August 9, 1927, p. 8.
"Glamour at $8.97 a week." *New York Times*, September 22, 1935, sec. 10, p. 4.
"Griffith plays Santa Claus to movie extra." *Big Spring Herald (Tex.)*, December 25, 1925, p. 16.
"Guild asks a better deal for bit and extra players." *Variety*, December 8, 1937, p. 6.
"Guild calls on Eddie Cantor to save extras from being tossed out by C. A." *Variety*, March 6, 1935, p. 2.
"Guild to make demand on producers for extras' closed shop, trim mob." *Variety*, December 22, 1937, p. 7.
Harrison, Paul. "Gangsters, job selling, labor troubles add to Hollywood's headache problem." *Daily Times-News (Burlington, N.C.)*, June 6, 1940, p. 8.
"Have over-supply of movie extras." *Ogden Standard-Examiner (Utah)*], January 25, 1927, p. 1.
"Hays back." *Variety*, February 3, 1926, p. 29.
"Hays begins clean-up of Hollywood today." *New York Times*, January 26, 1926, p. 22.
"Hays favors central plan." *Variety*, July 15, 1925, p. 25.
"Hear evidence today in film extra scandal." *Chicago Tribune*, July 11, 1934, p. 9.
"Hearing on film extras closed by Labor Board." *Los Angeles Times*, July 6, 1944, p. 8.
"Hint tampering with star witness in Hollywood case." *New Castle News (Pa.)*, July 17, 1934, pp. 1–2.
"Hollywood casting chiselers warned against gypping extras." *Variety*, November 6, 1934, pp. 6, 57.
"Hollywood dress extras go in hock to strut at glad rags parade." *Variety*, December 18, 1934, p. 3.
"Hollywood extra list being pruned from 17,000 to 2,500." *Billboard*, September 29, 1934, p. 3.
"Hollywood unions approve 3-year film, television contract." *Los Angeles Times*, May 14, 1992, Metro Section, p. 2.
Hopper, Hedda. "Few film stars rise to stardom." *Los Angeles Times*, July 31, 1938, p. C1.
_____. "Grady Sutton — movie extra with that extra something." *Los Angeles Times*, August 24, 1965, p. D13.
"H'wood's pathetic clan." *Variety*, October 10, 1933, p. 3.
"Investigating charge of exacting tribute from movie extras." *Chicago Tribune*, November 25, 1937, p. 13.
"Jim Thorpe hurt riding cow pony as movie extra." *Chicago Tribune*, August 10, 1932, p. 16.
Johnson, Erskine. "Pay scale high for child extras." *Olean Times-Herald (N.Y.)*, March 14, 1935, p. 13.
"June De Long to take stand." *Los Angeles Times*, July 16, 1934, p. 5.
"Junior actor Guild control in balance." *Variety*, January 19, 1938, p. 6.
Keavy, Hubbard. "Hollywood army of extras will get better deal." *Reno Evening Gazette*, October 27, 1934, p. 8.
_____. "Hollywood gleanings." *Nevada State Journal (Reno)*, September 30, 1929, p. 4.

Kelly, Kitty. "Flickerings form film land." *Chicago Tribune*, April 27, 1915, p. 10.
"Lady luck friend of blond actress." *Los Angeles Times*, February 28, 1928, p. A13.
Lardner, Ring W., Jr. "Hollywood." *Los Angeles Times*, March 22, 1936, p. H8.
"A laugh for Upton Sinclair." *Coshocton Tribune (Ohio)*], February 10, 1936, p. 6.
"Lawyers say Allen was framed." *Hammond Times (Ind.)*, July 19, 1934, p. 50.
"Limited film extra list idea goes into discard." *Los Angeles Times*, April 22, 1935, p. A1.
"Love for movie extra gone with her boss' $6,200." *Chicago Tribune*, August 1, 1937, p. 3.
"Many types to be found easily at movie capital." *San Mateo Times (Calif.)*, December 1, 1925, p. 10.
"Marlene Dietrich started as extra, says in interview." *Sandusky Register (Ohio)*, October 16, 1932, p. 2.
"Mary Pickford will aid extras by phone." *Ogden Standard-Examiner (Utah)*, August 30, 1933, p. 1.
"Merry Fahrney is up at 5:30 for film work." *Chicago Tribune*, March 21, 1934, p. 22.
Miles, John Peere. "Former screen stars in army as film extras." *Washington Post*, June 11, 1937, p. 23.
"Mob extra casting for talkers." *Variety*, December 25, 1929, p. 6.
"Morals trial defense opens." *Salt Lake Tribune*, July 19, 1934, p. 3.
"Morals trial perjury bared." *Washington Post*, July 17, 1934, p. 5.
"More 'no men' than 'yes men' there." *Oelwein Daily Register (Iowa)*, April 28, 1940, p. 1.
"Motion picture extras must get other work." *Moville Mail (Iowa)*, November 7, 1918, p. 2.
"Move to cut 4,000 movie extras off rolls in Hollywood gains union support." *Albuquerque Journal*, October 26, 1942, p. 3.
"Move to keep CIO out." *Variety*, June 26, 1940, pp. 7, 22.
"Movie extra types supplied by real life." *Washington Post*, November 28, 1926, p. R6.
"Movie extras back at work again." *Dunkirk Evening Observer (N.Y.)*, February 3, 1945, p. 4.
"Movie extras come from all walks of life." *Davenport Democrat and Leader (Iowa)*, October 3, 1926, p. 16.
"Movie extras create, labor examiner told." *Chicago Tribune*, July 26, 1940, p. 25.
"Movie extras find studio jobs scarce." *Hayward Daily Review (Calif.)*, January 29, 1937, p. 2.
"Movie extras find that's a poor way to earn livelihood." *Cedar Rapids Tribune (Iowa)*, November 8, 1929, p. 1.
"Movie extras forced to submit." *Mexia Weekly Herald (Tex.)*, June 22, 1934, p. 7.
"Movie extras open studio grafts war." *Mansfield News (Ohio)*, March 23, 1923, p. 16.
"Movie extras to get $25 to $5 daily wage." *New York Times*, March 19, 1934, p. 12.
"Movie guild opens door to extras." *New York Times*, October 27, 1933, p. 22.
"Movie man, extra girl freed in morals case." *Washington Post*, December 3, 1935, p. 9.
"Movie stars cling to hope despite want." *Chicago Tribune*, June 30, 1932, p. 16.
"Movie vagrants to be eliminated." *Fresno Bee*, January 25, 1926, p. 4.
"Movies." *La Crosse Tribune and Leader-Post (Wisc.)*, July 9, 1934, p. 9.
"Movies extra list face discharges." *New York Times*, July 12, 1934, p. 20.

"Near fist fight enlivens film extras' labor hearing." *Los Angeles Times*, March 24, 1944, p. A1.
"New casting chief named." *Los Angeles Times*, September 12, 1934, p. A2.
"New extras group for those with NRA cards." *Variety*, March 20, 1935, p. 7.
"New labor law planned as aid to film extra." *Los Angeles Times*, January 13, 1925, p. B5.
"News of the screen." *New York Times*, August 23, 1934, p. 22.
"$9.23 average for extras." *Variety*, January 29, 1936, pp. 3, 31.
"$9.02 average for extras." *Variety*, January 27, 1937, p. 3.
"No future for extras." *Variety*, March 15, 1932, p. 3.
"No more doubling by soldiers as extras." *Variety*, March 23, 1927, p. 1.
"No more picture extras on coast." *Variety*, January 19, 1927, pp. 1, 9.
"NRA on coast approves regulations for extras." *Variety*, September 18, 1934, p. 2.
"Number of stranded girl film extras much below last year." *Variety*, February 1, 1928, pp. 1, 58.
Nye, Carroll. "Inside story of how film extras get work." *Los Angeles Times*, October 17, 1934, p. 10.
"On with the dance — perhaps." *Los Angeles Times*, May 9, 1925, p. A16.
"One film group in much demand." *Reno Evening Gazette*, January 12, 1932, p. 12.
"100 beautiful extras entertain executives and attacks follow." *Lowell Sun (Mass.)*, June 4, 1937, p. 48.
"One in 100,000 movie extras reach stardom." *Fitchburg Sentinel (Mass.)*, January 26, 1937, p. 1.
"$1,000,000 up for extras." *Variety*, January 31, 1940, pp. 5, 54.
"Only 1 out of 10 makes grade in extras' clothes-horse parade." *Variety*, December 4, 1934, p. 3.
"Only 12 film extras earn living wage." *Chicago Tribune*, February 14, 1935, p. 15.
Parsons, Louella O. "Central Casting gets a new boss." *San Antonio Light*, May 5, 1940, p. 36.
"Part time pic mob gets elbow in extra edict." *Variety*, December 12, 1933, p. 4.
"Pay chiseling case dropped." *Billboard*, September 12, 1936, p. 4.
"Philbrick fat movie job." *Oakland Tribune*, April 17, 1940, p. 6.
"Philbrick starts film extra cleanup." *Oakland Tribune*, April 30, 1940, p. 25.
"Photoplay actors fail to form new organization." *Variety*, July 25, 1913, p. 8.
"Players' union asks pay parley for film extras." *Los Angeles Times*, June 22, 1944, p. A3.
"Poverty confronts thousands of film extras." *Los Angeles Times*, April 14, 1935, p. A1.
"Problems of film extra to be aired." *Los Angeles Times*, November 18, 1925, p. A8.
"Producer-actor accord." *Variety*, September 28, 1938, pp. 5, 21.
"Producer-actor parleys." *Variety*, April 6, 1938, pp. 7, 53.
"Producers row over closed door for extras." *Variety*, October 23, 1940, p. 6.
Pryor, Thomas M. "Film extra guild cites old-timers." *New York Times*, June 7, 1958, p. 11.
"Punch on jaw ends attempt at strike." *Los Angeles Times*, August 30, 1919, sec. 2, p. 6.
"Quiz of girl due in Griffith case." *Washington Post*, February 27, 1931, p. 3.
"Ranks of film extras slashed by N.R.A. action." *Los Angeles Times*, June 24, 1934, pp. A1–A2.
"Regulating extras." *Variety*, January 20, 1926, p. 29.

"Row in extras' association." *Variety*, November 3, 1916, p. 23.
"SAG curbs gifts of extras to execs, directors; 1 got a horse and saddle." *Variety*, July 5, 1939, pp. 1, 21.
"SAG demands extra redeal." *Billboard*, April 6, 1935, pp. 4, 20.
"SAG drops 2,000 extras." *Variety*, August 7, 1940, pp. 7, 19.
"SAG, extras set interchangeability." *Variety*, August 8, 1945, p. 7.
"SAG forces studio action against salary chiseling." *Billboard*, September 5, 1936, pp. 3, 15.
"SAG probes goon squads." *Variety*, September 14, 1940, pp. 7, 20.
"SAG will recognize office workers' pickets on Coast." *Variety*, July 3, 1940, pp. 7, 20.
"Salaries due film extras held up by agent Weiss." *Variety*, August 30, 1923, p. 21.
"Says June told of Allen's morals long before trap." *Alton Evening Telegraph (Ill.)*, July 18, 1934, p. 3.
Scott, John. "New rackets practices on film extras." *Los Angeles Times*, September 22, 1935, p. A1.
_____. "N.R.A. fails to make decision on extra code." *Los Angeles Times*, March 24, 1935, pp. A1–A2.
"Screen Actors' Guild sets back election." *Variety*, March 27, 1934, p. 2.
"Screen actors hit job-buying." *Arizona Republic (Phoenix)*, March 9, 1940, p. 46.
"Screen extras stay in the SAG, don't like any change in setup." *Variety*, May 1, 1940, p. 6.
"Screen players protest use of Army and Navy." *New York Times*, October 14, 1934, p. 33.
"Second suit is sequel to film extras rioting." *Los Angeles Times*, April 14, 1923, sec. 2, p. 4.
"SEG wins closed shop agreement with prods." *Variety*, April 3, 1946, p. 13.
"A shower gave movie extra a chance to act." *Washington Post*, February 2, 1929, p. 8.
"600 new actors for pix." *Variety*, April 24, 1940, pp. 7, 23.
"6,500 extras beef to AFL." *Variety*, October 30, 1940, pp. 7, 27.
"63% increase in accidents among extras causing insurance co.'s to cancel policies." *Variety*, July 8, 1936, p. 3.
"Soldiers barred from film unless historical or for educational use, ruling." *San Antonio Express*, August 16, 1926, p. 2.
"Sound forces new info blanks on extras." *Variety*, April 3, 1929, p. 7.
"Stars in suit against Guild, extra players." *Ogden Standard-Examiner (Utah)*, May 2, 1939, p. 12.
"Stars less scarce than competent film extras." *Charleston Daily Mail (W.Va.)*, May 11, 1925, p. 13.
"Studios set own extras." *Variety*, February 14, 1940, pp. 5, 25.
"Supers call mass meeting and arrange for a charter." *Variety*, September 1, 1916, p. 13.
"Surplus of film extras shown in state's report." *Oakland Tribune*, December 31, 1935, p. 6.
"Sweat shop charge of penny-ante pay takes extras' plight to Code." *Variety*, September 12, 1933, p. 7.
"Tells of movie extra's wooing—$6,200 worth." *Chicago Tribune*, January 12, 1938, p. 15.
"10 per centers for extras notices." *Variety*, January 28, 1915, p. 30.
"That Hollywood front." *Variety*, August 1, 1928, pp. 1, 55.

"Theatrical and picture gossip." *Waterloo Evening Courier (Iowa)*, March 24, 1928, p. 8.
Thomas, Dan. "A new deal for Hollywood's extra girls." *Port Arthur News (Tex.)*, December 12, 1934, p. 8.
____. "$9 a week." *Sheboygan Press (Wisc.)*, May 9, 1932, p. 6.
____. "War heroes, Jim Thorpe among those awaiting bits in cinema world." *Lima News (Ohio)*, March 30, 1932, p. 15.
"$3,167,896 paid pix extras in '39; bigger checks, too." *Variety*, December 27, 1939, p. 5.
"3,500 extras in *Ben Hur*." *Variety*, October 27, 1925, pp. 1, 34.
"Titled tramps, phony princes sneak to extra ranks as pretense exposed." *Variety*, September 19, 1933, p. 3.
"Too many extras." *Variety*, February 27, 1915, p. 22.
"Too many picture actors." *Variety*, November 30, 1927, pp. 1–2.
"Top extras $1,500 a year." *Variety*, October 23, 1934, pp. 7, 23.
"22,500 idle at Hollywood." *Variety*, June 9, 1926, pp. 1, 18.
"Two inquiries on film extras may result in pay scale tilt." *Los Angeles Times*, October 7, 1939, p. A3.
"2,500 film extras ordered on strike." *Wisconsin State Journal (Madison)*, February 2, 1945, p. 3.
"2,750 war vets as extras monthly." *Variety*, August 10, 1927, p. 5.
"2,300 out of 3,500 extras in Eastern films don't belong." *Variety*, July 7, 1926, pp. 1, 12.
"2,000 ughs." *Variety*, July 8, 1936, p. 3.
"Unionization of extras by AFL again." *Variety*, August 29, 1933, p. 3.
"Varying wages of film extras told at hearing." *Los Angeles Times*, April 6, 1944, p. A3.
"Veteran actress is rescued from film extra rank." *Syracuse Herald (N.Y.)*, September 25, 1933, p. 20.
"Wage increase demands filed for film extras." *Los Angeles Times*, October 13, 1943, p. A6.
"Wardrobe of movie extra costs $1,000." *Chicago Tribune*, August 27, 1933, p. E5.
"Wealthy tourists, acting as extras for fun of it, angers regulars." *Variety*, October 3, 1928, p. 5.
"When a war lord was a movie extra." *Washington Post*, May 15, 1932, p. SM2
"Witnesses are arrested." *Los Angeles Times*, March 22, 1923, sec. 2, p. 1.
"Year will set all-time high in extra work." *Washington Post*, February 15, 1938, p. X16.
"Yreka mob fugitive tells of hiding as film extra." *Los Angeles Times*, September 16, 1936, p. A2.
Zeitlin, Marilyn. "He enjoys the extra rewards." *Los Angeles Times*, December 20, 1985, pp. H1, H3.

Index

Abraham Lincoln 46
Academy of Motion Picture Arts and Sciences 90
accidents and injuries 29
Actors Equity 68–69, 89–90
Adair, Alice 26, 130
Adams, Harry 56
agents 5–6, 9–12, 14–16, 28–29, 84–85; cheating 11–12, 14, 33
Alexander, Rex 62
Allen, Dave 11, 34, 71, 138; career and death of 58; morals charge 47–58
Allen, Mae Evelyn 57
Alpine Movie Club 16
ambivalence, by Hollywood 7
American Federation of Labor (AFL) 84–85, 94, 109, 122
Archainbaud, George 133
Arlen, Richard 23
Associated Actors and Artists of America (AAAA) 109–110
automation 37–38

babies 27, 70–71
backgrounds, of extras 133
Ballerino, M. F. 13
Bara, Theda 118
Barker, Thomas 9–10
Barr, Robert Miller 117–118
beauty contest 67
Beetson, Fred 16, 19, 33, 62, 66
Bell, George H. 87
Ben-Hur 137–138
Berger, William 107
Berkeley, Busby 134
Bernheim, Julius 14
Billboard 76
Billings, Patrick J. 135–136

blacklists 10–11, 21, 42, 84, 105
blacks 27, 124
Blackton, J. S. 87
Blair, Aubrey 92, 99
Blake, Doris 66
Bloch, Louis 80–81
Booth, Edwin 81
Boushey, H. A. 13
Bow, Clara 23
Braden, Amy Steinhart 66
Brady, Thomas 82, 102–103
Brady, William A. 87
Brown, William J. F. 61
Budlong, Jack 119
Burg, Copeland 18
Burns, Harvey 29–30

Cagney, James 105–106
California Industrial Accident Commission 29
California Industrial Welfare Commission 19
California Labor Department 9–10, 15, 19, 44
California Motor Vehicle Department 40
California State Board of Charities and Corrections 66
Callis, Ethel 81–82
calls, for extras 39
Captured 123
carfare 19, 91
Carter, June 128
Casey, Joseph M. 89–90
categories, of extras 73
Central Casting Bureau 23, 27, 31–43, 59, 92–93, 97; advisory council 58–59; first data 68; formal opening 33–34;

front door 40; present day 43; statistics 137–147; wage data 137–147
Central Employment Bureau for Veterans 125
Charge of the Light Brigade 29
charity assistance 69
Chevret, Lita 23
child extras 26–27
Churchill, Douglas 36–37, 130–131
Cinema Players 94
circus 15, 125–126
civil suits 14
closed shop 92
clothing 8
commissions 9–13, 33
complaint bureau 36, 40
Compton, Betty 18
conditions 23–26, 29–30, 37; for women 44–62
Conference of Studio Unions 111
Congress of Industrial Organizations (CIO) 94
Coniff, Vincent 60
Conville, Robert 46
Cook, Paul 83
Cooper, Gary 81
costume fittings 19
The Countess of Monte Cristo 116
Cullison, Webster 6–7
Cunard, Grace 117
Cunningham, Charles 73

Dahlen, Edward 94
Dahlen, J. C. 51
dancing abilities 35
Datig, F. A. 46
Davis, E. L. 13
De Camp, Victor 62
Dee, Francis 81
De Long, June 47–57
DeMille, Cecil B. 24, 126–127
depression-era reductions 23
destitution 66
Dietrich, Marlene 115–116
disabled 125
discounting, of pay 9
discouragement 81–82
Do It Again 126
Donaldson, Robert 44
Douglas, Patricia 59–61
dress extras 18, 127–133
dress parade 129–132
drinking 59
Dueck, Ben 13

Dulzell, Paul 110
Dvorak, Ann 81
Dyer, William 89

earnings 27–28, 38 137–138
economic data 137–138
economic position 69, 80
Eilers, Sally 81
elderly 7
employment agencies 14–16; early 31–32
employment, of unregistered extras 34
enticement articles 7–8
extortion from extras 30

Fairchild, Marjorie 47
Farrell, Charles 23, 114
Faulkner, Carl 54
favoritism 72, 76, 97
females, reputation 45–46
Ferguson, Perry 13
film advisors, foreign 118–119
film colony numbers 69
Filmograph 30
films, about extras 115–116
Fineman, B. P. 66
fingerprinting 41
Fleck, Fred 125
Fleming, Catherine 7–8
Flynn, Emmet 17–18
Flynn, W. J. 14
The Fool 65–66
Ford, Francis 117
foreign émigrés 118–119
foreign players 69
Forgotten Women 115
Fort Lee, New Jersey 5
Fox studio 87
Frayne, Hugh 86
French, Will J. 69
Frohman Film Corporation 87

Gable, Clark 81
gambling 59
Garcia, Allen 49
Garden of Allah 29
Garland, Gordon 40
Gaynor, Janet 23, 81
Geisler, Jerry 47
Gennarelli, Rose Marie 135–136
Gentry, H. M. 11
Gibson, John 54
gifts from extras, forced 30
Gill, Charles 5

Index

Gillmore, Frank 89–90
glamour, supposed 17–18, 20–21, 67–68
Grable, Betty 23
graft 44
Graham, Herschell 132–133
Grange, Red 126
Green, Ursula 54
Griffen, Robert L. 54
Griffin, William 11
Griffith, Al 16
Griffith, David Wark 46–47, 114

Haar, Silver 120
hair color 65, 134
Harlow, Jean 81
Harmon, Pat 49
Harrison, Paul 41
Haver, Phyllis 18
Hays, Will 15, 32–34, 45, 122
hearings, governmental 10–11, 19–20
Heggie, O. P. 115
Heim, Ed 96
Hoffman, Charles 13
Hollywood Picture Players' Association 78, 91
hoodlums 41
Hopper, Hedda 82, 119
Huddle 126
Hughes, Lloyd 18
humanizing, of system 40
The Hunchback of Notre Dame 11

ill-treatment 85–86
image of extras 69–70
Ince, Thomas 18
Industrial Workers of the World (IWW) 12
insurance 29
International Alliance of Stage Employees 84
International Business Machines 38
investigations 33

Jeffers, Mike 124
job ratio, gender 18
Johnson, Erskine 26

Keavy, Hubbard 36, 115
Kegley, Carl 51
Kelly, Kitty 64–65
kickbacks 31, 37, 97
Kimbrough, Betty 132–133
Kinney, Mabel E. 72, 74–75
Koenig, Bill 24

La Cava, Gregory 133
Lane, Bernard 12–13
languages 35
Lardner, Ring 117
Lawrence, Florence 117
Lebaron, Jules 46
Lehman, Rose 13
Lewis, Walter 14
life of extras 18, 24
Lloyd, Jack 54
location shoots 68
Loeb, Art 117
Loeb, Edwin 62
Lombard, Carole 81
Los Angeles Central Labor Council 123
Los Angeles Police Department 6, 12–13
Love, Bessie 18
Love, Dorothea 114
Lyon, Ben 21

MacCulloch, Campbell 28, 35, 37–38, 46, 57, 62, 81, 97
MacDonald, Allen 36
makeup 8
management of extras 65
Mannix, Edward J. 61
Marcell, Tex 11
Marsh, Gloria 47–55
Matthews, Blayney 54
May, Edna 114–115
McCarthy, J. M. 54
McCrae, Joel 23
McKinney, Myra 53
McKinnon, Muriel 25
McLeod, Clyde 120–121
McNee, Emery 13
Meacham, Stewart 111
Mel, Marion 19
Merry Go Round 11
military, use of extras 121–124
Miller, Charles 90
Miller, Hymie 62
Miller, Kay 134
minimum wage 27
Mitchell, Homer 147
mob scenes 15, 35
Montgomery, Robert 93
morality 37, 44–63
morality, advisory council 58–59
Morgan, Ralph 97, 116
Motion Picture Alliance 51
Motion Picture Code (NRA) 25, 71–77
Motion Picture Extra People's Association of Greater New York 86

Motion Picture Producers' Association (MPAA) 10, 31–33, 62, 97, 141–142
Motion Picture Supporting and Extra Players' Association 53
Mountford, Harry 86
Movie Extras Ball 16
Murphy, George 108
Murphy, Helen 25
Murray, James 115
musical abilities 35

National Labor Relations Board 94, 106–107
National Recovery Administration (NRA) 70–71
nepotism 40, 76
New York License Bureau 14
New York State Labor Department 14
newsreels 29
night work 19
no request rule 39
Nolan, Edward 80–81
number of extras 14, 23, 31, 36–37, 68, 74; in New York 68

O'Brien, George 23
Olson, Culbert 39
Ostrom, Charles 48, 56
overtime 5, 19–20, 89
Owings, Pearl 47–55

parades, dress 129–132
Parker, Edwin G. 54
Parson, Louella 41
The Patent Leather Kid 122
pay rates 8, 18, 65, 71, 92, 93, 137–148; for individuals 37, 80
payroll, annual 15, 18, 33
Perlas, H. 13
Philbrick, Howard 39–40, 42–43, 63, 82, 99, 105
physical attractiveness 65
Pickford, Mary 71
picnic scenes 24
Picture Players' Alliance 78
police activity 11–12
police raids 6
political use of extras 28–29
Polly at the Circus 5
preparation time 19
Prevost, Marie 18
Pringle, Jessie 116
Producer SAG Standing Committee 101–102

producers, independent 28
propaganda, studio 7–8, 17–18, 22; on radio 36, 81
punch-card machines 37–38
purging, of undesirables 33, 39, 112

questionnaires 75–76

racketeering 41, 62–63
rags-to-riches stories 114–116
Ray, Charles 18
real people, as extras 24, 124–127
reductions of extras 25, 70
Reed, Colin 65
registrations 23; closed 34, 68; special 72
regulations, official 19–20
Reynolds, W. R. 10
Rhythm on the Range 29
riding abilities 103–104
rioting 11–12, 21
Roach, Hal 61
Rolfe Picture Corporation 88
Rosenblatt, Sol 74, 77–78
Ross, Buckingham 122
Ross, David 60–61
Rowe, Paul 40
Rowland, Serena 53
royalty, sham 118–119
rules for extras, proposed 74–75
Russell, Ed 110
Russell, J. Buckley 91
Russians 21, 35

SAG *see* Screen Actors Guild
St. Alwyns, Harry 9–11
salary cheating 61–62
Saunders, Bernice 26–27
scams 16, 87
Schullman, Alexander 107
Scott, John 27, 38, 77
Scott, Randolph 81
Screen Actors Guild (SAG) 30, 40, 41–42, 61–62, 63, 77, 84, 90–113
Screen Extras Guild (SEG) 109–113, 120, 148
Screen Players Union 107–108, 124
Screen Talent 11
self-regulation 16, 31
Selznick, Lewis J. 86, 87
Service Bureau 9–13, 44
Setril, Fern 46–47
sexual harassment 37, 45–46
sexual scandal: Allen 47–58; Douglas 59–61; Griffith 46–47

Index

Shaw, Robert 14
Shearer, Norma 23
Sheer, George 85
Sheer, William A. 85
Sherrill, W. L. 87
Sinclair, Upton 28–29
Skiff, Charles 13
Smith, Jessie B. 48
Smith, Kate 36
Snyder, Ann 51
Social Buccaneers 11
soldiering on the job 16–17
Solvason, Sigrun 134–135
Somerset, Pat 107–108, 117
Sorrell, Herbert 111
speaking a line 77
stand-ins 134
A Star Is Born 81
stardom, illusion of 18
statistics 68, 137–148; amount of work per week 68
Stern, Isador 88
Stevenson, Robert Louis 117
strikes, labor 6
students, college 126
Studio Club 44–45
success stories 64, 114–116
suicide 134–135
surplus 64, 68–82; 1915 64–65
survey 133–134
Sutton, Grady 119
Sutton, Kay 130
Swanson, Gloria 18, 23
swimming trials 29

talent-picking committee 70
talkies 23, 34
Tars and Spars 124
Taylor, Art 94
Taylor, Earl W. 47
telephone calls, incoming 43
The Tender Hour 20
That Royale Girl 114
Thomas, Dan 22–23, 25, 116–117
Thompson, Irene 130
Thomson, Kenneth 42, 63, 90, 91, 99–100
Thorpe, Jim 116–117
Tillie's Punctured Romance 126
top money earners 42
Torres, Raquel 81
tourists 121
Triangle Film Corporation 57

Trotsky, Leon 116
Troupers, Inc. 78
types, of extras 65–66, 68

unionization 84–112
unions: company; 90; dual cards 96; dues and income 107; geographic scope 91; infighting 88–89, 91, 94–96, 99–101, 109–111; jurisdiction 86–87, 104, 110–111; legitimate stage 89–90; voting rights 90, 96, 97–98, 105
United Actors' Association 112
United States Department of Justice 105–106
United States military 121–124

value of extras, in wartime 6
Vandergrift, Monte 54
Variety 5, 14, 15, 34, 63, 75–76, 85
Veitch, Arthur 48, 52, 57
Vidor, Florence 18
Vidor, King 115
Von Eiszner, Merry Fahrney Pickering 24–25
Voshell, R. E. 40

wages 137–148
waivers, nonunion 83
wardrobe 127–133; costs 37, 67, 127–128; demands, official 131
wardrobe return 21
warnings, to hopefuls 66, 68–69, 80, 81–82
weather permitting calls 20, 91
Weiss, Ben 14
welfare functions 36
White Rats union 86, 89
Whittier, Grace 48
Willis, Henry M. 57
Wilson, Emmet H. 96
wiretap scandal 40
Women's Christian Temperance Union 48
work amount 137–148
working conditions, of women and children 19–20
World War I 6, 118–119
Wyatt, Ginger 60–61
Wyman, C. C. 33

YMCA 44–45

Zimrick, Martin 108

www.ingramcontent.com/pod-product-compliance
Lightning Source LLC
Chambersburg PA
CBHW032102300426
44116CB00007B/859